AMERICAN IMMIGRATION

American

THE CHICAGO HISTORY OF AMERICAN CIVILIZATION

Daniel J. Boorstin, EDITOR

mmigration

By Maldwyn Allen Jones

 THE UNIVERSITY OF CHICAGO PRESS
CHICAGO AND LONDON

Library of Congress Catalog Number: 60-8301

THE UNIVERSITY OF CHICAGO PRESS, CHICAGO & LONDON
The University of Toronto Press, Toronto 5, Canada

© *1960 by The University of Chicago. Published 1960*
Fourth Impression 1965. Printed in the U.S.A.

Editor's Preface

The growing study of American immigration has brought a new cosmopolitanism into the writing of our social history. For the history of immigration to the United States is always the history of emigration from somewhere else. Unless we understand why they left we cannot understand what they wanted to make of America. Mr. Jones's book helps us see American immigration as a two-sided phenomenon, for he sees the newcomer both as emigrant and as immigrant. He shows us how deeply our own history has been affected by the coincidences of life elsewhere: by the European industrial and agricultural revolutions, by famines, by political uprisings, and by wars for national independence. He also suggests how the surge of immigrant waves, the lingering loyalties to distant places, and the problems both of living in an American ghetto and of assimilating into the American mainstream—how all these have affected presidential elections, the declaration (or non-declaration) of wars, and the character of American labor movements. He reminds us that the immigrant, by providing a scapegoat for recurrent nativist movements, has deflected the issues of domestic politics. Immigrants have been attracted here by the improvements in transatlantic shipping, by the building of American railroads, and by the growth of American industry. They have also helped make all these possible.

American history is the story of how this gathering of immigrants from many nations became unified into a new nation. Yet, ~~until~~ recently, our historians have done little with the subject. We have had numerous popular and readable sagas of individual immigrant adventure—the life of a Thomas Cooper, a Carl Schurz, an Andrew Carnegie, an Edward Bok, or an Enrico Fermi. In some parts of the country there has been a fervent personal interest in genealogy. From time to time we have heard bitter debate over whether the newcomer from this or that country was an "undesirable" citizen. But only within the last generation have some of our ablest historians begun to describe immigration as an American institution.

Our many different kinds of immigration, as Mr. Jones explains, have given a spice, an unpredictableness, and a motleyness to American life which have been missing from nations with more homogeneous or more stable populations. As a Briton, he writes from the vantage point of the emigrant continent, and he reminds us that the newcomer to America (excepting those who were transported as punishment for crime or who were brought as slaves) was making a choice. During much of American history, great numbers of Europeans were moving also from one to another European country, or to other parts of the world. Knowing intimately the American documents and American life, Mr. Jones is especially well situated to see our immigration in its world perspective and

Editor's Preface

so to give us a less provincial definition of what has been peculiarly American about it.

The "Chicago History of American Civilization" aims to make each aspect of our culture a window to all our history. The series contains two kinds of books: a *chronological* group, which provides a coherent narrative of American history from its beginning to the present day, and a *topical* group, which deals with the history of varied and significant aspects of American life. This book is one of the topical group.

DANIEL J. BOORSTIN

Table of Contents

Introduction / 1

I. American Foundations / 6

II. Ethnic Discord and the Growth of
American Nationality / 39

III. The New Nation and Its Immigrants / 64

IV. The Rise of Mass Immigration / 92

V. Patterns of Distribution and of Adjustment / 117

VI. Nativism, Sectional Controversy, and Civil War / 147

VII. New Sources of Immigration / 177

VIII. Immigrants in Industrial America / 207

IX. The Demand for Restriction / 247

X. The Consequences of Restriction / 278

Conclusion / 308

Important Dates / 320

Suggested Reading / 325

Index / 343

Illustrations

	Facing Page
An advertising poster of Enoch Train's White Diamond Line of Boston and Liverpool Emigrant Packets, 1854	106
Irish and German immigrants being recruited for the Union army at Castle Garden, 1864	107
Naturalization of immigrants at election time, 1868	142
Steerage passengers to America, 1870	143
Embarkation for America, Liverpool, 1870	210
The American River Ganges. Anti-Catholic cartoon by Thomas Nast, 1871	211
Entering a new world, 1892. Jewish refugees from Russia passing the Statue of Liberty	266
Sicilian immigrants at Ellis Island, 1909	267

Introduction

Immigration, which was America's historic *raison d'être*, has been the most persistent and the most pervasive influence in her development. The whole history of the United States during the past three and a half centuries has been molded by successive waves of immigrants who responded to the lure of the New World and whose labors, together with those of their descendants, have transformed an almost empty continent into the world's most powerful nation. The population of the United States today, except for the Indians, consists entirely of immigrants and of the descendants of immigrants. American society, economic life, politics, religion, and thought all bear witness to the fact that the United States has been the principal beneficiary of the greatest folk-migration in human history.

It is, of course, true that other new countries, like Australia and Argentina, are also the product of immigration. But no other land has had for immigrants the attraction of the United States. Of the seventy million or so people who have migrated from Europe since 1600 about two-thirds have gone to America. Nor has any other country been settled by such a variety of peoples. Four-fifths of the immigration to Australia, for instance, has been British; more than three-quarters of Argentina's immigrant population has come from Italy and Spain; and nearly all of South Africa's immigrants have been either Dutch or British. America, however, has drawn heavily for her population upon many parts of the world. Even in the colonial period Americans were a conglomerate breed. Though much of the colonial population was English it contained substantial groups of Germans, Scotch-Irishmen, and African Negroes as well as Dutch, Swedish, French, Swiss, and Irish elements. Still more cosmopolitan were the great migrations of the nineteenth and early twentieth centuries, during which the United States received great blocs of Germans, Britons, Irishmen, Slavs, Italians, Russians, Scandinavians, Canadians, and Mexicans. In the same period came smaller but still significant numbers of Greeks, Syrians, Armenians, Portuguese, Chinese, Japanese, Filipinos, and Puerto Ricans, besides a host of other groups. In short, the size and the diversity of her foreign-born population have made America the classic country of immigration.

American culture is thus a blend of the cultures of millions of immigrants of different languages, religions, and mores. But inherited ways were subtly modified in the New World environment. How inheritance and environment interacted is the theme of this book, which attempts to tell briefly the story of American immigration from the planting of Virginia to the present.

It may be objected that the time is not yet ripe for a comprehensive account of this vast subject. It is true that there are still great gaps in our knowledge, that much work remains to be done before the picture can be painted in all its detail.

Introduction

Yet the historical and sociological investigations of the past thirty years into various aspects of the subject have meant that the study of immigration is no longer monopolized, as it once was, by enthusiastic ancestor-worshipers and by social scientists concerned with contemporary immigration "problems." Indeed, progress has been such as to justify a fresh attempt at synthesis.

In the pages that follow we shall consider why men chose to move to America; how they influenced and were influenced by the society they entered; why and in what form distinctive immigrant communities developed; what reaction the arrival of immigrants provoked from earlier comers; what happened when groups of different background were brought together; and what were the forms in which ancestral ways and loyalties persisted. In seeking the answers to these questions we shall dwell at some length upon the European background, an appreciation of which is essential to an understanding of the immigrant in America. We shall touch upon the actual process of immigration, particularly the Atlantic crossing, of which there has been a good deal of graphic, and sometimes exaggerated, description. We shall be concerned with the ways in which the immigrant responded to the various national crises which tested his adjustment to America. And we shall endeavor to explore, within the limits of the space available, the interconnection between immigration and the other major themes of American history. The immigrant will appear as a significant factor in a whole range of matters—economic growth, social development, political alignments, sectional conflict, the westward movement, and foreign policy.

It has long been customary for historians to distinguish between "colonists" (implying all who reached America before

1776), "old" immigrants (northwest Europeans who came chiefly between 1820 and 1880), and "new" immigrants (southeast Europeans who came mainly after 1880). Such distinctions seem, however, to be both unhistorical and misleading. Of those who came to America before 1776 only a tiny fraction were "colonists" in the sense of being either first settlers or of being members of organized colonization projects; the remainder, whether they came voluntarily or not, were just as much immigrants as those who came after the colonies had become independent. There seem likewise to be no valid grounds for the distinction, invented by late nineteenth-century nativists and adopted by subsequent historians, between "old" and "new" immigrants. The "new" immigrants came later than the "old" and there were more of them; but that is hardly reason to differentiate sharply between groups which, however much they differed culturally, were very much alike in their reasons for coming, in the resources and skills they brought with them, and in their ability to adapt to American conditions.

Widespread use of the traditional classification of immigrant groups has served to obscure an essential truth about immigration, namely, that as a social process it has shown little variation throughout American history. The motives for immigration, for instance, have been very similar from first to last; they have been always a mixture of yearnings—for riches, for land, for change, for tranquillity, for freedom, and for something not definable in words. The lure of American plenty bulked large for Englishmen, Scotch-Irishmen, and Germans in the colonial period, for Irish, German, Italian, and Slavic peasants in the nineteenth century, and for Mexicans and Puerto Ricans in the twentieth. But the economic motive

Introduction

has at no time been either universal or exclusive. Almost every decade since 1607 has given America a fresh quota of political and religious refugees, and even those who came primarily to improve their material lot have not been unmindful of America's other attractions. The experiences of different immigrant groups, too, reveal a fundamental uniformity. Whenever they came, the fact that they had been uprooted from their old surroundings meant that they faced the necessity of coming to terms with an unfamiliar environment and a new status. The precise nature of the adjustment could and did vary; but its essence remained the same. What did vary, and vary enormously, was the character of the immigrant impact. In assessing this we must constantly bear in mind not only the immigrant's Old World antecedents but the time of his arrival. The America to which he came was a constantly evolving, rapidly changing society, and his impact upon her was never the same for more than a decade or two.

The story of American immigration is one of millions of enterprising, courageous folk, most of them humble, nearly all of them unknown by name to history. Coming from a great variety of backgrounds they nonetheless resembled one another in their willingness to look beyond the horizon and in their readiness to pull up stakes in order to seek a new life.

I

American Foundations, 1607-1776

The concern with fundamental causes which characterized Tocqueville's *Democracy in America* is nowhere more evident than in the thesis which the author himself described as the key to almost the whole of that celebrated work. "If we carefully examine the social and political state of America, after having studied its history," he wrote, "we shall remain perfectly convinced that not an opinion, not a custom, not a law, I may even say not an event, is upon record which the origin of that people does not explain. . . . Methinks I see the destiny of America embodied in the first Puritan who landed on those shores."

Expressed in these terms the thesis is clearly an oversimplification. In particular it fails to take account of those environmental influences which subtly but decisively altered the outlook and aspirations of the Europeans who settled the American wilderness. Yet Tocqueville was undoubtedly right in emphasizing that in any society the primary factor is the human one, and in asserting that American development can hardly be understood without giving full weight to the character of those who peopled the colonies and to the circumstances of their coming to the New World. Not merely the firstcomers, however, as Tocqueville seemed to believe, but all the motley groups who crossed the Atlantic in the colonial period contributed significantly to the early development of the United States. The growth and expansion of the colonies, their underlying unity no less than their diversity, their distinctive social and political characteristics, and their swelling desire for independence are all traceable in some measure to the course of immigration during the century and three-quarters before 1776.

By the time of the Revolution popular tradition in New England had developed a clearly defined view of the purposes for which the original settlers of the region had come to the New World. To this tradition John Adams gave eloquent expression in an essay written during the Stamp Act controversy in 1765. To Adams the settlement of America was an event to be contemplated with reverence and wonder, for it represented "the opening of a grand design and scene in Providence for the illumination of the ignorant, and the emancipation of the slavish part of mankind all over the earth." According to Adams, the firstcomers had been fully conscious of the special destiny Providence had marked out for them. Oppressed and persecuted in their native land, they had fled to a distant wilderness with the intention of establishing there a plan of ecclesiastical and civil government "in direct opposition to the canon and feudal systems."

Adams' interpretation of colonial origins drew its inspiration from what he, and New Englanders generally, conceived to have been the motives of their Puritan ancestors in coming to Massachusetts Bay. But during the Revolution this interpretation came to have a wider application. Revolutionary leaders increasingly sought historical sanction for their defense of colonial rights in the circumstances of their forefathers' migration. They asserted that in resisting British tyranny Americans were merely upholding the ideals the first settlers had planted in the New World. Thus in 1775 the Second Continental Congress, in justifying its decision to take up arms, could imply that Americans generally, Virginians no less than New Englanders, were the descendants of men who had left Europe in order "to seek on these shores a residence for civil and religious freedom." And by the time independence had been won, this concept—because of the support it afforded to the ideals of the new nation—had become part of the American faith.

Though popular traditions owe much of their vitality to the aspirations of those who accept them, they can rarely develop unless suggested by the facts. And the "legend of the Founding Fathers" was by no means entirely without historical basis. It was, nevertheless, an idealized version of the past and provided only a partial and in many ways misleading picture of America's founding. Modern scholarship does not share John Adams' view of the role of Providence and is much less confident than he of the devotion of the first Americans to the principles of universal liberty. Still less does it agree with the opinion Adams expressed later in life, that the idea of independence had been in the minds of Americans "from the first settlement of the country." Perhaps the only part of the traditional interpretation which squared with historical fact was that which emphasized that the founders came not as colonists sent out at the expense of the mother country, but as free men who had paid their own way to America and had conquered a wilderness largely by their own unaided efforts.

The motives of those who betook themselves or were transported to the colonies in the seventeenth century were too complex to be inclosed within a simple formula. There were some who came chiefly for reasons of piety; others were motivated by restlessness, a desire for novelty, or a love of adventure; and still others came in the hope that the New World would afford them a better competence than had been their portion in the Old. But whatever their motive for migration, the vast majority appear to have had no quarrel with the greater part of their heritage. They thought of America in the same way that John Donne in 1622 thought of England, namely, as "the suburbs of the Old World." And this was broadly true, both of the Jamestown settlers, and of the men who founded colonies elsewhere along the Atlantic seaboard.

It was no less true of those who came to the colonies later. Between them and the first arrivals there seems to have been no great difference in motive. Throughout the colonial period, as at the beginning, there were groups who came principally for religious reasons. Nevertheless, most of those who followed the founders were inspired chiefly by a desire for economic betterment. This was particularly true of the many thousands who came as indentured servants, a group which accounted for somewhere between one-half and two-thirds of all the white people who emigrated to colonial America. Large numbers of these white servants were carried to America involuntarily, so that for them the question of motive does not arise. Nor does it apply to the vastly greater number of Negroes brought to the colonies from Africa and the West Indies.

If then, by the time of the Revolution, Americans had developed ideas of freedom, equality, and independence, the explanation is not to be sought in the motives that led their ancestors to leave the Old World. Part of the explanation lies in the economics of colonial promotion. In order to attract settlers, colonial proprietors found it expedient to promise political and religious freedom. And even where these privileges were not promised beforehand, they became in many places a practical necessity. Moreover, in communities confronted with the task of subduing a wilderness, new forms of social organization became essential. Where European concepts of social stratification were both impracticable and irrelevant, the equality of men was a self-evident truth even before the Declaration of Independence proclaimed it to be so. Important, too, was the English heritage of the majority of the colonists. The Stamp Act controversy was to show that Americans retained a well-developed sense of their rights and liberties as free-born Englishmen. It was surely significant, too, that representative institutions failed to develop in the American colonies of either Spain or Portugal, and that the philosophy of the great Declaration struck no chord in what had been until recently French Canada. But perhaps most important of all in fostering the idea of independence was the nature of the colonists' New World experience. As Crèvecœur pointed out, the American environment made of the European a new man, with different interests and opinions from those he had left behind. Of this the idea of independence was a necessary corollary. For, as Stephen Vincent Benét says in *Western Star:*

American Foundations, 1607–1776

. . . the country is where the life is, not elsewhere.
The country is where the heart and the blood are given.

It is not surprising that in the traditional account of colonial origins little emphasis should have been placed on the early history of Virginia. To the Revolutionary leaders it was as apparent as it is to us that in an enterprise that began as a trading post and developed into a commercial colony, the paramount motive was economic. Nonetheless, one should guard against dismissing the planting of Virginia (1607) as a mere money-making transaction. The venture did, after all, have a specific religious purpose in its frequently announced intention of converting the Indians. Moreover, in the cosmology of the seventeenth century, with its emphasis on the doctrine of divine Providence, economic conceptions were always closely allied with the religious; and the early settlers of Virginia could conceive of the society they were erecting in the wilderness only within a religious framework. Even so, the Jamestown settlers were, first and foremost, seekers after wealth, and only secondarily militant Protestants eager for the advancement of religion.

At first they had no intention of making America their permanent abode. As one of Virginia's earliest historians, Robert Beverley, was to remark in 1705, "the chief Design of all parties concern'd was to fetch away the Treasure from thence, aiming more at sudden Gain, than to form any regular Colony." More specifically, they went in the hope of finding precious metals, discovering a Northwest Passage, and developing trade with the Indians in a great variety of exotic products. Only when these hopes were seen to be ill-founded was the notion of permanent settlement accepted. Once tobacco cultivation became established, the character of the enterprise changed rapidly. Nothing better illustrates the transition from trading post to colony than the Virginia Company's decision in 1619 to transport shiploads of maidens, "whereby the Planters' minds may be faster tyed to Virginia by the bonds of Wyves and children."

But even when emigrants began crossing the ocean with the intention of living and dying in Virginia, they went resolved "still to be Englishmen," with no thought of adopting any but traditional principles for their new society. Believing as they did that inequality of rank and birth were divinely ordained, they considered democracy—if they thought about it at all—to be both unworkable and against the law of God. They could, in fact, be given no better reassurance than that provided by the Virginia Company in 1620 when it promised prospective emigrants that in the New World they would enjoy "the religious and happy gouernment of their native Countrey."

The men who planted Virginia were drawn from a variety of social classes. Hardly any of them, however, were of noble birth, and the tradition that seventeenth-century Cavaliers were the ancestors of the Virginia planter aristocracy of the ante-bellum period has long been discredited. Most of the early planters came, in fact, from the English squirearchy or from yeoman stock, or were the sons of substantial merchants. They were attracted chiefly by the prospect of obtaining land, and those who came possessed of enough capital to buy extensive landed estates formed the nucleus of the first ruling class. Yet it was "the disinherited, the dispossessed," to use Benét's apt phrase, who made up the bulk of Virginia's first settlers. After about 1620 the majority were people who, unable to pay their passage across the Atlantic, received free transportation by binding themselves as indentured servants for periods of from four to seven years. This system had obvious advantages for the planter who, by paying for a servant's transportation, became entitled not only to his labor but to the fifty acres of land allotted to every immigrant under the headright system. Whether the servants benefited equally may be doubted, for although they were assisted to reach the New World and assured of employment on arrival there, their lot, as we shall see, was often a hard one.

Virginia's indentured servants were a motley group. Besides those who came voluntarily, there were transported convicts, vagrants, and paupers shipped by the English poor law authorities, and military and political prisoners sent from Scotland and Ireland by Cromwell. Virginia's population was also augmented by another group of involuntary immigrants whose status was at first very similar to that of white servants. The twenty Negroes brought to Jamestown by a Dutch man-of-war in 1619 were the first of many such cargoes, but as late as 1660 they still formed a small proportion of Virginia's population and their status was still undetermined.

The early immigration history of Maryland closely paralleled that of Virginia. Lord Baltimore had conceived of Maryland not only as a source of profit but as a refuge for English Catholics. But Catholics were only a minority of those who founded Maryland in 1634. And in them it is difficult to distinguish religious from economic motives for, as even their Jesuit leaders remarked, "while we sow spiritual seed, we shall reap carnal things in abundance." Moreover, the Protestant passengers on the "Ark" and the "Dove," consisting chiefly of servants, craftsmen, and yeomen, seem to have had no religious motive in emigrating, while those who followed them did not share the proprietor's faith in religious toleration. Indeed, it was Lord Baltimore's generous land policy rather than his religious liberalism that attracted most settlers and, as in Virginia, the headright system became the standard method of immigration.

It is easy to exaggerate the contrast between the Chesapeake colonies and New England. However much they eventually differed in their social and economic arrangements and in their ecclesiastical polities, the two communities at first had much in common. Piety and profit, though in somewhat different proportions, were the compelling motives for emigration in each case, while both societies drew the bulk of their original populations from the same type of middle-class English Puritan. Nevertheless, one cannot deny the existence of real differences between the two communities, not only in their leaders but in the purposes they hoped to fulfil in the New World.

The little band of religious Separatists who came to New England in 1620 on the "Mayflower" were simply fugitives from apprehended danger, and little thought to serve a larger purpose by migrating. Though they had found toleration and hospitality in Holland when persecution drove them out of England, the Pilgrims were anxious for a more secluded refuge where potential backsliders would be less exposed to the taint of the world. After a decade in exile at Leyden, economic pressure and the imminence of war with Spain obliged them to "dislodge betimes to some place of better advantage and less danger." And although they welcomed the opportunity that removal to America would give them of "advancing the gospel of . . . Christ in those remote parts of the world," they did not come inspired with any particular sense of mission.

It was otherwise with the Puritans who came to Massachusetts Bay in 1630. To the leaders of the Great Migration the mission upon which they were engaged both explained their presence in the New World and set them apart from the Englishmen living elsewhere in America. Writing in 1646, John Winthrop declared that while the inhabitants of other plantations had "come chiefly for matter of profit," the people he had led to Massachusetts Bay "came to abide here, and to plant the gospel and people the country." In drawing so broad a distinction, Winthrop had apparently forgotten the emphasis he had laid upon the economic motive when endeavoring in 1629 to persuade his colleagues to commit themselves to the enterprise. Nor should one forget, even if Winthrop was inclined to do so, that the Great Migration originated partly in such events as a depression in the cloth trade and a succession of bad harvests in East Anglia. Again, while a majority of Winthrop's followers were Puritans, this was not the case with all; they included many yeomen, artisans, and servants whose motive was simply wider economic opportunity. Nevertheless, there is ample evidence that religion was the mainspring of the movement, and the Reverend John White was probably not far from the truth when he wrote in *The Planter's Plea* (1630):

Necessitie may press some; Noveltie draw on others; hopes of Gaine in time to come may prevaile on a third Sorte; but that the most, and most sincere and godly part, have the advancement of the Gospel for their main Scope I am confident.

One should not imagine, however, either that religious persecution forced the Puritans to flee from England or that they went to America to establish civil and religious liberty. That they suffered persecution is true enough, though it was far less intense than some of their descendants have liked to think. But far from being driven from England, they left it voluntarily with the full knowledge and consent of the authorities. Unwilling to go on living under an ecclesiastical system they detested, they went to America to establish a form of government in church and state that would allow them to worship in the manner they desired. And, convinced as they were that theirs was the only true religion, they were determined to tolerate no other form of worship.

Yet in going to America the Puritans were not turning their backs on the "depravations of Europe." They believed the essential purpose of their "errand in the wilderness" to be the redemption of Europe; the polity they went to perfect would not only insure their own salvation but would serve as a model for imitation by those they had left behind. In this conception, more than in any other, may be seen the germ of the idea to which Jefferson and John Adams were to give eloquent expression, namely, that America was designed by Providence as a beacon and an example to the rest of mankind.

The migration of the Puritans involved much larger numbers than had gone to plant Virginia; none of the English colonies were in fact to be founded by so large an influx. Two thousand people came to Massachusetts Bay in the year 1630 alone, and by the end of the decade the number had risen to almost twenty thousand. But in 1640 the movement came abruptly to an end, for, as Winthrop remarked, the imminence of civil war between king and Parliament "caused all men to stay in England in expectation of a new world."

Between the English settlers of Massachusetts Bay and those of Chesapeake Bay lay colonies of Dutchmen on the Hudson and of Swedes on the Delaware. New Netherland and New

Sweden were both founded as trading posts, and in neither case was there a sustained or vigorous effort to plant permanent settlements. In the absence of any strong religious or economic compulsion to emigrate from either Holland or Sweden, both enterprises had such difficulty in obtaining colonists that they were obliged to recruit foreigners. Only five hundred or so Swedes and Finns established themselves on the Delaware and, lacking reinforcement from Europe, New Sweden was absorbed by the Dutch after a bare quarter of a century's existence. But shortly afterward, in 1664, New Netherland itself passed to the English. The population of the colony, and especially of the town which was now to be called New York, had already acquired the cosmopolitan character it has ever since retained. Dutchmen, Walloons, and French Huguenots had been among those brought over by the Dutch West India Company; considerable numbers of English settlers had filtered in from Massachusetts and Connecticut; there was a substantial Negro element, both slave and free; and the first sizable group of Jews to reach America had sailed into New Amsterdam in 1654, seeking refuge from Portuguese persecution in Brazil. Even so, the Dutch were the dominant strain in the colony's population of seven thousand, and New Netherland's forty-year existence was sufficiently long for the Hudson Valley to acquire an indelible Dutch stamp.

The ethnic variety of which New York was the earliest example was, in varying degree, to be a feature of all the English colonies founded after 1660. The doctrine of mercantilism, now everywhere in the ascendant in European official circles, taught that the wealth of a country was dependent upon the number of its inhabitants. Accordingly, the government of

American Immigration

Charles II took steps to discourage emigration, and fewer Englishmen than before were able to find their way to America. Later English colonial enterprises had thus to rely mainly for their population upon continental Europe, Africa, and the older English colonies on the American mainland and in the West Indies.

Carolina, founded in 1670 by a group of English courtiers anxious to promote national self-sufficiency and their own fortunes, drew its early settlers from each of these diverse sources. Only a hundred or so Englishmen sailed from London in 1669 with the expedition which was to found Charleston, and the bulk of those who settled between the Ashley and the Cooper rivers were small planters from Barbados who left their overcrowded island to seek better fortune in Carolina's fertile acres. In 1680 they were joined by a group of French Huguenots sent over by the proprietors in an abortive effort to produce silk and wine. Thanks, moreover, to the familiarity of the Barbadians with Negro slavery and to the encouragement of the headright system, Negroes were brought to South Carolina from the first, and by 1700 they accounted for one-half of the colony's population of seven thousand.

If the founding of Carolina was a purely materialistic enterprise, Pennsylvania was, by contrast, conceived in a spirit of universal philanthropy and brotherhood. In fact as in intention, William Penn's "holy experiment" was a refuge for the persecuted of every race and sect. It is going too far, perhaps, to claim that colonial Pennsylvania was, in its multiplicity of ethnic groups, "a portent of America to be." Because of the tendency of each group to settle in a distinct and separate region, and because of the jealousies that developed between them, the colony seemed at first more likely to resemble another Europe. Yet Pennsylvania did present the spectacle of men of different nationalities and faiths living together in freedom, if not always in amity.

Penn's utopian vision grew originally out of sympathy for his persecuted fellow Quakers, some of whom had already settled in America, especially in West New Jersey. And the great majority of Pennsylvania's first settlers were English, Irish, and Welsh Friends who settled in Philadelphia and its vicinity, with the Welsh concentrated in a supposedly autonomous region of their own, known as the Welsh Tract. But Penn's invitation to the New World found ready acceptance among other discontented sectarians, notably German pietists, some of them similar in belief to the Quakers, whom Penn had met during a visit to the Continent in 1677. A group of Mennonites from the Rhineland, led by a learned Frankfurt lawyer, Francis Daniel Pastorius, founded Germantown in 1683. Before the end of the century they had been followed to Pennsylvania by hundreds of Dunkers, Schwenckfelders, and other German sectarians who had in common a desire to withdraw from the world and live peaceably according to the tenets of their respective faiths. Certainly, neither they nor the Quakers were blind to material considerations, and the numbers flocking to Pennsylvania were in part a consequence of the proprietor's shrewd advertising and his exceptionally generous land policy. But the promise of civil and religious liberty was at least as great an inducement to people who in Europe had been unable to find either.

The growth of religious intolerance in France, which resulted in the Revocation of the Edict of Nantes in 1685, led to the arrival in the colonies of a group which, though relatively small in numbers, was to exert a considerable cultural influence. The largest number of Huguenots made their way to South Carolina, but sizable groups could be found in nearly every colony, especially in Pennsylvania, Virginia, and New York. Owing to the unusually high proportion of merchants, professional men and craftsmen among the refugees, considerable numbers settled in towns like Charleston, Philadelphia, New York, and Boston where, by the time of the Revolution, they had achieved an extraordinary degree of political and commercial prominence. There were also a number of separate Huguenot settlements, like Manakin Town in Virginia, New Rochelle in New York, and Oxford in Massachusetts. But for a variety of reasons, not the least important of which was the hostility of their neighbors, most of these settlements were short-lived.

Apart from a few hundred Huguenot families, scarcely any immigrants came to New England in the latter half of the seventeenth century. This was not surprising, for the New England attitude toward immigration was still that of Edward Johnson, who, in his *Wonder-Working Providence* (1654), had warned against admitting strangers to Massachusetts lest they endanger the success of the Puritan experiment. In 1680 it was reported that hardly any settlers had arrived in Boston for some years past, and in 1701 immigrants were still so few that the town authorities urged the General Court to encourage the importation of white servants to relieve a chronic labor shortage. The Chesapeake colonies, on the other hand, continued to receive a steady trickle of new arrivals, most of them indentured servants from England and Ireland. By the end of the century Virginia and Maryland had abandoned the headright system because of its numerous abuses. But planters now valued servants more for their labor than as a means of acquiring land, and masters of vessels going to the Chesapeake for tobacco found it as profitable as ever to recruit cargoes of servants for sale in the plantations. As before, the people brought over in this way were of diverse origin; they included vagabonds and convicts, paupers and abducted children, and, of course, great numbers who went voluntarily.

The practice of using the American colonies as a dumping-ground for undesirables continued into the eighteenth century, and was brought to an end only by the Revolution. The number of convicted felons who came seems to have increased considerably after 1717, when an act of Parliament created the new legal punishment of transportation, and contractors began to take out regular shipments from the jails. A recent student has estimated that Britain sent at least thirty thousand felons to America and the West Indies in the course of the eighteenth century, most of them to Virginia and Maryland. Some of these unfortunates had been convicted only of minor offenses, but there seems little doubt that many had been guilty of serious crimes.

Malefactors apart, emigration from England continued to be officially frowned upon. But it was not actually prohibited, and throughout the colonial period there was a small but steady flow to America of merchants, professional men, artisans, and laborers. Neither Georgia nor Nova Scotia, the only colonies founded after 1700, drew substantial numbers. Both were established largely as buffers against Spanish and French attack, though Georgia was also intended to be a producer of raw silk and a haven for imprisoned debtors. But the silk scheme failed and, as recent research has shown, "only a handful of debtors ever came to Georgia—a dozen would be a fair estimate."

American Immigration

Despite the comparative scarcity of new blood from England, the eighteenth century was a period of unprecedentedly heavy emigration to the colonies. Non-English peoples migrated in such numbers as to alter markedly the ethnic composition of nearly every colony. Their arrival contributed largely to the fourfold increase in colonial population that occurred in the half-century following the Peace of Utrecht in 1713. Though fresh outbreaks of war in Europe periodically interrupted the flow, it always recommenced with renewed vigor when peace returned and was still in full flood when the Revolution began.

Probably the largest single group of eighteenth-century newcomers were the Scotch-Irish. These people, originally from the Scottish Lowlands but transplanted to Ulster at various times during the seventeenth century, formed the great majority of those who crossed the Atlantic from Ireland during the colonial period. True, a certain number of Celtic Irishmen found their way to the colonies. Most of them were to be found in Maryland and Pennsylvania, where a few of the more prosperous established themselves as landowners and merchants. But, largely because of colonial obstacles against Roman Catholic immigration, there was no mass movement from southern Ireland such as occurred from Ulster.

Accurate statistics of Scotch-Irish immigration are lacking, but it has been estimated that in the half-century or so before the Revolution it amounted to as much as 250,000. The exodus began on a large scale in the second decade of the eighteenth century. Though planned and directed by Presbyterian ministers, religious discontent was not its main cause. Such disabilities as those imposed by the Test Act of 1704, which excluded non-Anglicans from public office, merely added to the sense of grievance and insecurity felt by the Scotch-Irish. Nor, though the contrary is commonly asserted, was Scotch-Irish emigration appreciably increased by the Woolen Act of 1699; Ulster, as a linen-producing region, was not in fact greatly affected by the exclusion of Irish woolens from the British market. The real source of the movement was discontent with the land system, with its absentee landlords, high rents, short leases, and consequent insecurity of tenure. What sparked large-scale departures in 1717–18 was the termination of the leases which had been granted on easy terms thirty years earlier in an attempt to attract Protestant settlers. Landlords now took the opportunity to demand much higher rents, and, as tithes rose proportionately to rents, the added burden was considerable. Feeling that they could not compete with Catholic Irishmen who were prepared to accept a lower standard of living in order to pay the higher rents, many Presbyterians preferred to emigrate.

Ten years later an even heavier wave of emigration set in, and although reports to the British government attributed it primarily to the evils of the land system and a succession of bad harvests, a variety of other causes was mentioned. The letters sent home by previous emigrants were said to have had a great effect, as were the activities of shipmasters trading to the colonies. In 1729 it was reported from Ulster that, because of the profits to be derived from the emigrant trade, ship captains "send agents to markets and fairs . . . to assemble the people together, where they assure them that in America they may get good land without either paying tithes or taxes, and amuse them with such accounts of these countries as they know will be most agreeable to them." By such methods, great numbers of Scotch-Irishmen were induced to go to the colonies, most of them as indentured servants. The estimate made in 1727 by Hugh Boulter, Archbishop of Armagh and Lord Primate of All Ireland, that fewer than one in ten of the emigrants had money enough to pay their passage was not necessarily accurate, but it reflected the general position well enough. Despite the alarmed protests of the landlords, who saw in these departures a threat to their own position and to the Protestant ascendancy in Ireland, emigration continued steadily for the next half-century. The annual departures were not usually more than about two thousand, but in the early 1770's, in consequence of a depression in the linen trade and the development of an acute agrarian crisis, the movement reached its peak with perhaps as many as ten thousand people leaving each year.

In its earliest phase the Scotch-Irish exodus flowed chiefly toward New England, where, about 1720, Scotch-Irish frontier settlements were established at Worcester, Massachusetts, and Londonderry, New Hampshire. Within a few years, however, the tide had been almost wholly diverted to Pennsylvania. This was due partly to the unfriendliness the immigrants had encountered in New England and partly to the economic opportunities and religious freedom offered by Pennsylvania. But important, too, was the character of Ulster's colonial connections. European emigration to America has always tended to follow the paths of transatlantic commerce, and in the colonial period most of the vessels leaving Belfast and Londonderry for America were engaged in the flaxseed trade, of which Philadelphia was the leading colonial center.

Although, after about 1725, the bulk of the Scotch-Irish headed for Pennsylvania, not all of them stayed there. When Penn's successors abandoned his liberal land policy, and more favorable terms were offered by landowners in the southern colonies, Pennsylvania Scotch-Irishmen moved in considerable numbers into the Valley of Virginia and the back-country of the Carolinas. There was also a certain amount of direct emigration from Ulster to South Carolina in response to the encouragement of immigration by the provincial authorities. Between 1732 and 1736 several shiploads of immigrants from Belfast settled Williamsburg township on the Santee, and during the next forty years Charleston was second only to Philadelphia as a port of disembarkation for the Scotch-Irish.

Throughout the colonies, but especially in Pennsylvania and the Carolinas, the Scotch-Irish were to be found on the frontier. For this role they were in some respects fitted by their experiences in Ulster, where they had encountered conditions not unlike those prevailing at the edge of the American wilderness. This fact was not lost upon colonial authorities anxious to create barriers against French and Indian attack. For example, James Logan, the provincial secretary of Pennsylvania, was only too glad in 1718 to settle the frontier township of Donegal with men who "had so bravely defended Derry and Enniskillen" a generation earlier. But the qualities that made the Scotch-Irish such formidable Indian fighters were not calculated to endear them to their neighbors. Travelers in the back-country frequently expressed relief when they had passed safely through the settlements of these turbulent, contentious, fiercely intolerant people.

Immigration from Scotland has sometimes been treated simply as a part of the much larger Scotch-Irish exodus. But the two movements, though similar in some respects, were largely unrelated. In the seventeenth century Scotland, as a foreign country, was debarred from British colonial trade, and

American Immigration

Scots had therefore little opportunity to reach America. Several hundred Scots were brought to settle Perth Amboy in the 1680's by the Scottish proprietors of East New Jersey, a smaller group founded Stuart's Town in southern Carolina in 1684, and some Royalist and Covenanter prisoners were transported to Virginia after the battles of Dunbar (1652) and Bothwell Brig (1679). But the Act of Union of 1707 began a new era in Scottish immigration. Taking full advantage of their newly acquired opportunities, numerous Scots settled as merchants and factors in colonial seaports, and a steady stream of Lowland artisans and laborers left Glasgow to become indentured servants in the tobacco colonies and New York. Lowland immigration reached its peak in the early 1770's when a trade depression and a substantial rise in rents induced many weavers and farmers to seek better opportunities in the colonies.

While Lowlanders generally came to America individually, most immigrants from the Scottish Highlands arrived as members of organized groups. Highland communities began to appear in the colonies in the 1730's. Having received a large grant of land from Governor Cosby of New York, Lachlan Campbell of Islay brought hundreds of his tenants to settle near Lake George; and in 1735 another Highland group from Inverness established a frontier settlement on the Altamaha River in Georgia. But even counting those transported for their part in the Jacobite rebellions of 1715 and 1745, there was still only an insignificant number of Highlanders in the colonies up to the end of the French and Indian War. In the decade after 1763, however, the movement gained momentum rapidly. Poverty had long been endemic in the Highlands, but owing to a succession of crop failures and cattle blights, this was a period of exceptional dearth and suffering, and the situation was further aggravated by rising rents and the eviction of crofters from their holdings to make way for sheep runs.

Led by their tacksmen, or intermediate landlords—who hoped to recover their lost wealth and power by transplanting the decaying clan system in America—Highlanders flocked to the colonies in the decade before the Revolution. Many went to the Mohawk and upper Hudson valleys, largely because of the favorable reports sent home by the Highland soldiers who had settled there after their regiments had been disbanded in 1763. And while great numbers went from the Isles of the Hebrides to Prince Edward Island and Cape Breton, many thousands from the Scottish mainland, encouraged by the liberal inducements offered by the North Carolina legislature, settled in the Cape Fear region. Differing as they did from the rest of the colonial population in language, dress, and social customs, the Highlanders were to find adjustment much more difficult than did their Lowland countrymen, especially as their practice of emigrating in groups could not fail to heighten their natural clannishness.

Greatly outnumbering Scottish immigrants were the Germans, who came from a bewildering variety of German states as well as from the German cantons of Switzerland. As before, they included pietist and pacifist sectarians seeking refuge from persecution. Best known of these were the Moravians, the first group of whom settled in Georgia in 1736, subsequently moving to Pennsylvania, where they founded the towns of Bethlehem, Nazareth, and Lititz. Both in Pennsylvania and in North Carolina, where in 1753 they bought a huge tract of land which they named "Wachovia," the Moravians established prosperous communitarian societies. By their educational activities and their missionary work among the Indians, they exercised an extraordinary cultural influence. But even at the time of the Revolution there were only twenty-five hundred Moravians in America, and they and their fellow sectarians accounted for only a tiny proportion of the total German immigration.

The great majority of Germans were either Lutherans or members of the German Reformed Church and were called "church people" to distinguish them from the sectarians. They came to America not primarily for religious reasons but because of economic pressure which predisposed them to seek wider opportunities. The three thousand or so Palatines who settled in the Hudson Valley in 1710 left their homeland because of the devastation caused by the wars of Louis XIV. Fleeing first to England, they were then transported to New York at the expense of the British government, which hoped thereby to promote the production of naval stores. But the scheme failed and the Palatines dispersed, some to the Mohawk Valley, others to the predominantly Dutch region on the lower Hudson, some down the Susquehanna to Pennsylvania and even farther afield.

Partly in consequence of this unhappy experience, but more because of Pennsylvania's attractiveness to immigrants, most of the later German arrivals settled in the Quaker colony. In the year 1719 alone, there arrived at Philadelphia between six and seven thousand Germans who, though popularly referred to as Palatines, were by no means all from the Palatinate. And during the next half-century, an average of perhaps two thousand Germans disembarked annually at ports on the Delaware. Many paid their own way but most were compelled by their poverty to come as redemptioners. Unlike servants from Great Britain and Ireland, redemptioners brought no formal indentures but were bound by written agreements to pay fixed sums on arrival in the colonies. Being usually unable to do this, they were obliged to become servants in order to discharge the debt.

By about 1720 the redemptioner trade had become highly systematized. Each spring Dutch merchants and shipowners sent out agents, popularly known as "newlanders"—as well as by less flattering names—to recruit cargoes of immigrants in German towns and villages and to transport them down the Rhine to Rotterdam and Amsterdam for embarkation. The trade was full of abuses, for many were induced to leave under false pretenses, and hardship and suffering on the voyage were common. But the element of exploitation has sometimes been exaggerated. The margin of profit was not great, and the system helped thousands to reach America who could otherwise never have left Europe.

Benjamin Franklin was probably right when he told the House of Commons in 1766 that one-third of the population of Pennsylvania was German, and the proportion was probably much the same a decade later, when the Pennsylvania Germans numbered between 110,000 and 150,000. Though some had remained in the Philadelphia area, the majority had settled farther west in what became known in consequence as the Pennsylvania Dutch country. By thrift, diligence, and careful agricultural methods—characteristics which contrasted sharply with those of their Scotch-Irish neighbors—the Germans made this area one of prosperous, well-kept farms which were as successful as any in America. From Lancaster County, which was their main stronghold, the Germans spilled over the Susquehanna, down the Cumberland Valley, and then fanned out into western Maryland, the Shenandoah Valley and beyond. Shrewdly settling in fertile limestone areas, with the Scotch-Irish often between them and the frontier, the Germans had by 1750 established an almost continuous string of back-country settlements that ran all the way from Pennsylvania to Georgia.

As in the case of the Scotch-Irish only a proportion of the Germans in the southern colonies came from Pennsylvania. Considerable numbers, encouraged or assisted in a variety of ways, emigrated directly from Europe. The heavy concentration of Germans in Frederick County, Maryland, for instance, owed much to the promotion of immigration by great landowners like Daniel Dulany anxious to people their vast holdings. In Virginia, the first German settlement resulted from Governor Spotswood's unsuccessful attempts to establish an ironworks at Germanna between 1714 and 1720. South Carolina's efforts to attract foreign Protestants in the 1730's brought to Charleston groups of Germans and Swiss who were sent to found new townships in the back-country. Still others were brought to America by entrepreneurs who had secured large grants of land from the crown on condition of settling them with Protestant immigrants. Among these were a Swiss nobleman, Christoph de Graffenried, who settled New Bern in North Carolina in 1710 with Palatine Germans and Swiss, and Jean Peter Pury, who founded a Swiss colony in 1732 at Purysburg, South Carolina, in yet another abortive attempt to raise silk and cultivate vineyards.

Most of the French Huguenots who came to the colonies arrived during the last fifteen years of the seventeenth century. But small groups continued to come until the end of the colonial period. As late as 1764 several hundred sailed from France to South Carolina to found the town of New Bordeaux. But the Huguenots were not the only Frenchmen to reach the colonies. In 1755, because of their suspected disloyalty, more than six thousand Acadians were removed from Nova Scotia by the British authorities and sent to the colonies to the south. Many of the wretched deportees died during the voyage or soon afterward, and only a few of the survivors settled permanently in the colonies. A large number eventually found their way to Louisiana, where their descendants have preserved their cultural distinctiveness to the present day.

In the century following the arrival of the first group of Jewish immigrants at New Amsterdam in 1654, Jewish communities developed elsewhere, notably in seaport towns like Newport, Philadelphia, and Charleston. By the time of the Revolution there were between two and three thousand Jews in the colonies. Though they could be found in a variety of occupations, most of them were merchants and traders. Nearly all were Sephardim, that is, descendants of Spanish and Portuguese Jews, and most of them came to America by way of Holland, the Dutch colonies, and England. In the hope of encouraging Jewish immigration an act of Parliament in 1740 had permitted the naturalization of Jews, and in the colonies they enjoyed a greater degree of political and religious freedom than anywhere in the world.

One of the most significant contributions to the peopling of the colonies was made by the African slave trade, which brought to the American mainland countless thousands of Negroes from the Guinea coast and the West Indies. Whether or not the Negroes were immigrants in the strict sense, they were a substantial and in places a vital element in the colonial population; their coming had momentous consequences for America, both then and later.

Within a generation or so of the arrival of the first shipload in Virginia in 1619, Negroes were to be found in all the continental colonies. Yet for a time there was a general preference for white labor, and until the end of the seventeenth century Negroes were neither particularly numerous nor were they concentrated in any one group of colonies. At first their status did not differ basically from that of white servants. Only after 1660 or so did social needs and attitudes crystallize into laws which fixed the status of the Negro as that of a chattel slave. Then, after 1697, when the monopoly of the Royal African Company was ended, the slave trade expanded rapidly. Liverpool merchants for a while dominated the trade, but before long it was attracting Americans too. New Englanders, especially, found it extremely profitable to employ their vessels in the well-known triangle which linked the northern mainland colonies, the West Indian sugar islands, and the Guinea coast.

In the course of the eighteenth century perhaps as many as 200,000 Negroes were brought to America, nine-tenths of them to the southern colonies. To southern planters they appeared to offer many advantages over white labor. They could not easily escape, they were bound to labor in perpetuity instead of for a fixed period, they were self-reproducing, they were believed to be better able than whites to endure harsh climatic conditions, and when employed in gangs were a more efficient and economical labor force. By the end of the seventeenth century, therefore, Negro slavery was well established in the southern colonies and shortly became the chief source of labor on the larger plantations.

As Negroes replaced whites, first as field workers and then as craftsmen, servant importations into the southern colonies declined sharply. Only in the back-country and on marginal plantations, where the initial cost of Negro slaves was a deterrent to their use, were indentured servants still employed to any extent. The middle colonies, therefore, and Pennsylvania especially, became henceforth the chief reception center for bound labor. Here, the growth of industry and the opening-up of new lands created a steady demand for all types of white labor, both skilled and otherwise. In New England, on the other hand, intensive agriculture and the predominance of small holdings requiring few servants made indentured labor a comparative rarity.

It is difficult to speak with certainty of the treatment and ultimate fate of indentured servants, for very few of them left records of their experiences. As we remarked earlier, the evils of servant recruitment and of the transatlantic voyage, though by no means negligible, have perhaps been exaggerated. But in the colonies themselves the evidence suggests that the servant's lot was generally a hard one. Contemporaries frequently likened the condition of white servants to that of Negro slaves, and a recent student, after a minute examination of court records, has concluded that oppression and maltreatment of servants were widespread, especially in the tobacco colonies. Even so, the white servant was unquestionably better off than the Negro slave. He retained, for example, all his political and legal rights—such as that of recourse to the courts— save those specifically denied him by contract. The limitations upon his freedom were merely for a fixed term of years; when they had passed, he enjoyed complete mobility and freedom of occupational choice. Also, at the end of his period of servitude, the servant was entitled by custom or statute to certain "freedom dues," which always included clothing, and often tools, seeds, arms, and provisions. Whether, as is generally stated, the freedom dues also embraced a grant of land is open to question. At all events, the proportion of freed servants taking up land seems not to have been large; in seventeenth-century Maryland, for instance, only about 8 per cent managed to do so successfully. It would seem that the great majority either became wage-laborers, drifted to the towns or the frontier, or even returned to Europe.

The course and character of colonial immigration did much, it is clear, to give each group of colonies a distinctive ethnic flavor. To be sure, the influences which originally made it possible to distinguish between the New England, middle, and southern colonies were those of terrain, climate, and natural resources. But as time passed, ethnic factors tended to accentuate sectional distinctiveness. Thus New England stood out, from the point of view of population, as a peculiarly homogeneous region. Even at the time of the Revolution the population of the New England colonies was still preponderantly of English origin. Among the whites the only non-English elements were handfuls of Scotch-Irishmen, Scots, Huguenots, and Jews; Negroes, too, were less numerous here than anywhere else in British America. In the middle colonies on the other hand, the population was extremely mixed. Though in the region as a whole the English were the largest element, comprising about 50 per cent of the total, there were large German, Dutch, and Scotch-Irish concentrations and appreciable numbers of Negroes, Scots, Frenchmen, and Swedes. In Pennsylvania, the English amounted to only one-third of the white population, and were scarcely more numerous than the Germans.

In the southern colonies, too, there were large German, Scotch-Irish, and Scottish minorities to modify the predominantly English character of the white population. But what gave southern civilization much of its distinctiveness was the presence of great numbers of Negroes. In 1775, nine-tenths of the half-million Negroes in British America were to be found south of Mason and Dixon's line. They formed two-fifths of Virginia's population, one-third of North Carolina's and Maryland's, nearly two-thirds of South Carolina's, and more than one-third of Georgia's. And despite their servile status, the Negroes exerted a powerful influence upon every aspect of southern life, from language to social customs.

While ethnic factors thus helped to differentiate the various groups of colonies, they were also important in determining sectional alignments within particular colonies. Thus the political cleavage between tidewater and back-country, which developed in every colony from Pennsylvania to Georgia, owed much of its intensity to ethnic and religious antipathies resulting from the peculiarities of settlement. In all these colonies, except perhaps South Carolina, the tidewater population was almost as English as in New England; the back-country, however, thanks largely to the southward thrust of population from Pennsylvania in the decades after 1730, was much more heterogeneous. Throughout the whole of the huge, irregularly shaped strip of territory running southwestward from the Cumberland Valley to the southern banks of the Savannah River, the German and Scotch-Irish streams mingled with westward-moving Virginians and Carolinians of English descent to give the region a unique ethnic pattern.

It is all too easy, however, in discussing the internal divisions of the colonists, to lose sight of the influences tending to draw them together. Despite a variety of political forms, all the thirteen colonies possessed representative legislative assemblies and identical legal systems; though split up into numerous sects, nearly all the colonists shared a common Protestant background, with all that that implied in terms of individualism and resistance to authority; and notwithstanding the babel of tongues in many areas, the English language was by 1775 paramount in every colony. These elements of unity were not, it is true, the only ones; the New World environment, as we shall see, acted as a powerful cement. Yet it was the manner in which the colonies were peopled that accounted largely for the comparative ease with which Americans united to assert their independence. Particularly important had been the overwhelming predominance of Englishmen during the first two generations of settlement. This circumstance had enabled a single set of social and political institutions to be established, which later additions to the colonial population had been unable to alter basically. It went far also to explain why it was that on the eve of the Revolution the cultural pattern from Massachusetts to Georgia was so remarkably uniform.

Even so, American development began at an early date to diverge from the English model. From the late seventeenth century onward the special problems of a wilderness existence and the fact of relative isolation from Europe began to give colonial thought a distinctive coloring. Under the influence of the New World environment the colonists, in comparison with their European contemporaries, were becoming more self-reliant, adaptable, and enterprising, more conscious of their personal rights, less inclined to accept traditional moral and social values.

American Foundations, 1607–1776

By the middle of the eighteenth century, American social life, politics, and religion all reflected the extent to which European models had been abandoned. Though the colonial social structure corresponded in broad outline to that of Europe, with social stratification everywhere in evidence, the widespread ownership of property made class lines a good deal less rigid than in Europe. Since land was also the basis of political power, the ease with which it could be obtained insured that a measure of democracy was to be found everywhere. Admittedly there was considerable variation between New England, where democratic tendencies were strongly encouraged by the Congregational form of church polity, and Virginia, where the great planters dominated political life. But even Virginia had no hereditary ruling class, and in comparison with Europe political power in all the colonies was widely diffused.

Finally, in the matter of relations between church and state, American conditions compelled a significant departure from European practice. Originally, an established church was created by law in all the colonies, and dissent was discriminated against if not prohibited. But thanks to the multiplicity of sects in the colonial population, this system had to be abandoned in fact if not in name. Though Congregationalists predominated in New England and Anglicans were in the majority in Virginia, these groups were in the minority everywhere else. In most colonies, moreover, no one religious group outnumbered the rest. Accordingly, religious liberty became a practical necessity no matter what the letter of the law proclaimed.

It was thus apparent that, by the time of the Revolution, a distinctive civilization had come into existence in the New

World. What was not yet clear was whether each of the different ethnic elements in the colonial population had been equally affected by its New World experiences. To this question the events of the Revolution itself would supply the answer.

II

Ethnic Discord and the Growth of American Nationality, 1685-1790

During the Revolutionary era the need to stress national unity sometimes induced Americans to become forgetful of their diverse ethnic origins and to overlook the persistence of cultural differences. Particularly was this so among men who were anxious that the young republic should not be fatally weakened by a denial of adequate powers to the federal government. Thus it was that, in the *Federalist* Papers, John Jay was moved to congratulate his countrymen on the fact that "Providence [had] been pleased to give this one connected country to one united people—a people descended from the same ancestors, speaking the same language, professing the same religion, attached to the same principles of government, very similar in their manners and customs. . . ."

It was, of course, true that the events of the Revolution had demonstrated the basic homogeneity of the American people.

Though deeply divided over the issue of independence, their political divisions bore no relation to their differences of origin. And once independence was won, there was substantial agreement upon essentials. Despite a prolonged debate over the apportionment of powers between state and federal governments, most Americans took for granted that independence would result in the birth of a single nation and that that nation should be a representative republic.

Yet Jay was hardly justified in assuming that political unity had developed out of a common cultural background. Even at the time of the Revolution, the various ethnic elements in the American population could generally be distinguished on the basis of differences in speech, religion, and mores. During the preceding century these differences had been so productive of ethnic discord as apparently to rule out the possibility of united action. Not until the Revolution itself, in fact, did it become apparent that cultural uniformity was not essential to the growth of a common loyalty. Throughout the colonial period, however, Americans had tended to assume the contrary.

The colonial attitude to immigration can be summed up as one of welcome tinged with misgiving. Though it was generally acknowledged that a constant influx of newcomers was an essential condition of colonial expansion, the social problems that immigration introduced or intensified led, if not to organized nativism, at least to widespread popular hostility toward certain classes of newcomers. This ambivalent attitude was reflected in colonial immigration legislation. Side by side with laws designed to promote and encourage immigration, there existed others whose purpose was to exclude or restrict it.

To the colonies, immigrants represented the solution of a chronic labor shortage, the means of promoting land settlement and of developing resources, not to speak of the increased revenue that colonial governments could count on from a growing population. But the benefits of immigration were not purely economic. Newcomers could also make important contributions to frontier defense and internal security. Nearly every colony showed itself conscious of the value of those immigrants who, by settling in compact groups on the frontier, acted as a buffer against French, Spanish, or Indian attack. It was to fulfil this role that thirty Huguenot families were granted 2,500 acres at Oxford, Massachusetts, in 1687; and in the eighteenth century, as we have seen, the Scotch-Irish were encouraged to settle on the frontier in both New England and Pennsylvania. In South Carolina the favor shown to immigrants after 1715 stemmed from something more than the need to strengthen the frontier after the near-disasters of the recent Yamasee War. White settlers were doubly welcome in a province that not only was exposed but lived in constant fear of an insurrection by its rapidly growing Negro slave population. Thus the Scotch-Irish, German, and Swiss settlements established as a result of Governor Johnson's township scheme of 1729 were designed alike to guard the frontier and to help put down slave uprisings.

Because of their practical needs as new and insecurely established societies, the colonies offered numerous inducements to immigrants or to those who transported them to America. The earliest official method of encouragement was that of granting land to individuals in proportion to the number of settlers whose fares they paid. As we have seen, this practice, known as the headright system, originated in Virginia about 1620; and in that colony and in Maryland it flourished for most of the seventeenth century. Not very different was the practice of making substantial land grants to entrepreneurs who undertook to bring immigrants from Europe to hitherto unsettled regions. Some colonies passed laws exempting immigrants for specified periods from taxation and actions for debt, and others offered bounties to defray the cost of ocean passage and provided new arrivals with free land, tools, and provisions. Colonial naturalization laws, too, were generally passed with the encouragement of immigration as their principal object. As the Virginia Assembly pointed out in 1671, the best way to promote "the advancement of a new plantation" was to invite foreigners to come by offering them equal privileges.

Throughout the period the most active encouragement to immigration came from the southern colonies. This was a measure not of the South's philanthropy but of her need for new blood and of the difficulties of attracting it. In the sparsely populated planting colonies, especially in South Carolina and Georgia, immigrants were essential both for expansion and for security. But in view of the reluctance of most Europeans to settle in a region possessing an unfamiliar climate and a large Negro population, liberal inducements had to be offered. The more densely peopled colonies to the north did not need to be so generous. In Pennsylvania the advertising campaign that Penn had conducted so successfully was not continued beyond the colony's early days. As Pennsylvania's reputation for hospitality spread and Philadelphia rose to become the center of the indentured servant trade, official encouragement to immigrants became superfluous. The New England colonies, having little unsettled land and no persistent frontier problem, saw little need to modify their traditional antipathy to newcomers, and their generally exclusive attitude was less calculated to stimulate immigration than to divert it elsewhere. But there were occasional exceptions. In 1709 Massachusetts met a temporary labor shortage by granting a bounty on imported male servants and between 1749 and 1753 made fitful attempts to promote the settlement of Maine by employing an immigration agent in Germany.

Even in colonies where immigrants were most needed, the authorities stopped short of an open-gates policy. Certain classes of newcomers were universally unwelcome, and popular prejudice against them found widespread legislative expression. Roman Catholics, for instance, though nowhere actually excluded, were commonly discouraged from coming. Most of the colonies levied discriminatory head taxes upon ship captains landing Roman Catholics, and even the colonies which attempted to promote immigration were careful to specify that only Protestants could qualify for the bounties or other inducements offered. Similar barriers were erected against those lacking visible means of support. In the seaports such persons intensified an already serious problem of poor relief, and in an effort to discourage their importation the main ports of arrival required masters of immigrant ships to give bonds that their passengers would not become public charges. Most undesirable of all, from the colonial point of view, were transported felons. Franklin's oft-quoted criticism of Britain's practice of emptying her prisons into the colonies perhaps exaggerated the unanimity of colonial opposition, for in some quarters convicts were welcomed as a source of cheap labor. But there was widespread concern at the amount of violence committed by convict servants, and colonial assemblies frequently tried to prohibit their importation, only for the prohibitive laws to be disallowed by the Privy Council upon the intervention of British merchants engaged in convict transportation.

Colonial immigration restrictions, it will be noticed, took no account of the nationality of newcomers. Instead, religious affiliation, economic status, and moral standing were the yardsticks by which the desirability of immigrants was measured. Yet it would be wrong to conclude that the colonists were indifferent to the question of national origins. At one time or another, immigrants of practically every non-English stock incurred the open hostility of earlier comers. Among the first sufferers were the French Huguenots who came at the end of the seventeenth century. Marcus Lee Hansen has pointed out that "in the popular colonial mind the fact that the Huguenot was a Protestant was overshadowed by the more evident fact that he was a Frenchman." And at a time when the colonies were entering upon a period of prolonged and savage warfare with France and her Indian allies, it was hardly surprising that refugee Frenchmen should have encountered suspicion and hostility. Because of doubts regarding their loyalty, Huguenots in New York were compelled to move farther away from the frontier, and in Pennsylvania a popular demand for stricter surveillance over French residents led to the imprisonment of a number of innocent Huguenots. Virginia treated the refugees no better and petitioned the British government to send them no more. And in 1691 a small Huguenot settlement at Frenchtown in Rhode Island was attacked and dispersed by a mob.

Ethnic Discord, 1685–1790

Similar ill-treatment was meted out to the Acadians deported from Nova Scotia at the time of the French and Indian War. But it was the Scotch-Irish and the Germans who in the eighteenth century succeeded the Huguenots as the principal objects of nativist dislike. Opposition to the Scotch-Irish was strongest in New England and, as we have seen, was an important factor in diverting them elsewhere. As early as 1718, owing to the scarcity and the high price of provisions, fears were expressed in Boston that "these confounded Irish will eat us all up." During the following decade antipathy toward the newcomers so increased in Boston that with the arrival of a number of immigrant ships from Belfast and Londonderry in July, 1729, "a mob arose to prevent the landing of [the] Irish." Five years later at Worcester another Yankee mob pulled down the newly built Scotch-Irish Presbyterian church.

Such incidents have led historians to point to religious bigotry as the sole cause of Yankee hostility. That the early Puritans were extremely suspicious of strangers of different creeds is evident enough. Yet by the time the Scotch-Irish began to come, in the second decade of the eighteenth century, toleration had so far developed that they were at first welcomed by the New England clergy. Cotton Mather, for example, had by now abandoned an earlier view that immigration from Ireland was the work of Satan and felt that from the arrival of these staunch Calvinists "much [could] be done for the kingdom of God in these parts of the world." But, as Mather discovered when Scotch-Irish ministers began to denounce the New England churches for theological error, the newcomers were no less narrow and intolerant than the most bigoted Puritan. The friction which culminated in the Worcester incident was not entirely the fault of the natives.

45

In any case religious strife was only part of the story. It was the poverty of the newcomers, rather than their religion, which in the 1720's and 1730's inspired the restrictive measures of the Boston municipal authorities, alarmed at the rising costs of poor relief. Elsewhere in New England, differences in manners were probably as important as religious sectarianism in producing nativist outbursts. The staid New Englanders could not fail to be shocked by the drinking habits, blasphemous language, and propensity toward violence of many of the immigrants. Scotch-Irish servants had a bad reputation for crime and turbulence and, as a Boston newspaper remarked in 1725, "this gives us an ill opinion of Foreigners, especially those coming from Ireland."

In Pennsylvania, which received the great bulk of the Scotch-Irish, feeling toward them was much more favorable. But even in Penn's colony their arrival occasionally produced uneasiness. In the summer of 1729 the number of immigrant ships reaching the Delaware was so great that to James Logan it looked "as if Ireland or the inhabitants of it were to be transplanted" to Pennsylvania. The influx convinced him that there were "some grounds for the common apprehensions of the people that if some speedy method [were] not taken," the Scotch-Irish would "soon make themselves Proprietors of the Province." What worried the provincial secretary particularly, and what underlay his wish for an act of Parliament to check the movement was the readiness with which the newcomers squatted on "any spot of vacant land" they fancied, without thought of payment to the proprietors. There were also repeated complaints of Scotch-Irish encroachments upon Indian territory west of the Susquehanna, a practice the offenders justified with the remark that "it was against the law of God and nature that so much land should lie idle while so many Christians wanted it to labor on and raise their bread." Finally, the mutual antagonism of the Scotch-Irish and the Germans produced so many disturbances, especially at election times, that in 1743 the Penns instructed their agents to sell no more land to Scotch-Irishmen in the predominantly German counties of Lancaster and York and to offer those who were already there generous terms to move to the Cumberland Valley.

Many of the complaints of the Pennsylvania authorities about the Scotch-Irish were levied also against the colony's large German element. In 1717 the Assembly expressed concern lest newcomers from Germany should settle "promiscuously among the Indians," and a little later James Logan complained that the Germans were as bad as the Scotch-Irish for squatting upon proprietary lands. But as well as incurring official disapproval, the Pennsylvania Germans became objects of popular suspicion in a way that was never true of their Scotch-Irish neighbors. This was particularly evident from the nativist outburst provoked in 1727 by the recent large increase in German immigration. To some extent the agitation was a consequence—as in Boston a decade earlier—of concern at the number of paupers among recent arrivals. To be sure, the statute of 1729 levying increased head taxes on alien passengers was not directed against the Germans as such, but against "lewd, idle and ill-affected persons" of all nationalities who threatened to become public charges. Yet there was also considerable misgiving at an influx of people who differed in language and customs from the rest of the province's population and whose practice of settling together in groups threatened to result in a separate German colony. The Pennsylvania Assembly, sharing popular concern at the effect this might have on provincial security, decided in 1727 to require incoming Germans to take an oath of allegiance to the king and of fidelity to the proprietors and the provincial constitution.

Twenty-five years later, Benjamin Franklin's alarmed outbursts at the growing numbers and influence of those he contemptuously dismissed as "Palatine Boors" showed that fears of Germanization had by no means diminished in Pennsylvania. At a time when hostilities with France seemed imminent in the Ohio Valley, Franklin was not alone in his suspicions, unfounded though they were, that the Pennsylvania Germans cherished pro-French sympathies. Doubts about German loyalty in the event of war with France prompted the Reverend William Smith, later to be provost of the University of Pennsylvania, to establish with English assistance a system of charity schools whose purpose was to Anglicize the Germans. Owing to the strength of German opposition, however, it was never fully implemented, and by 1763 the last of Smith's charity schools had closed its doors.

The suspicion and antagonism persisting between different ethnic elements of the colonial population serve as a warning against too literal an acceptance of Crèvecœur's frequently quoted description of the American of the Revolutionary era as the product of "that strange mixture of blood which you will find in no other country." Though Crèvecœur could cite a family whose four sons were married to women of four different nations, he was surely exaggerating the degree of intermixture—though not the effect of environment—when he wrote in 1782 that "here individuals of all nations are melted into a new race of men." The evidence seems rather to suggest that while the population of the colonies was cosmopolitan, it was very far from being an amalgam of different stocks.

Ethnic Discord, 1685–1790

As Professor Carl Bridenbaugh has remarked, "marriage within the national, and therefore religious, fold was the rule, not the exception." It could hardly be otherwise, for each ethnic group tended to congregate not only in certain colonies but in distinct and separate areas within those colonies. Not without reason has the population map of colonial America been likened to a mosaic.

The tendency to form ethnic enclaves, which was the natural consequence of group migration and of the economic and geographic forces that determined routes of settlement, was especially marked among the Germans and the Scotch-Irish. Compelled by their poverty and by their comparatively late arrival in the colonies to move west in search of land, these two groups became concentrated in such numbers as to establish exclusive control over certain areas. The most striking instance of this was in Pennsylvania where German and Scotch-Irish settlers lived in communities as completely isolated from each other as they were from English-settled communities. Alike in the Pennsylvania German country which straddled the Susquehanna, and in the Scotch-Irish communities farther west in the Cumberland Valley, the inhabitants clung tenaciously to traditional ways. As a result there were such contrasts in language, religion, customs, architecture, and agricultural methods between the two regions that they could plausibly be compared with neighboring states in central Europe. Throughout the southern back-country, too, though more particularly in Virginia, the Germans and Scotch-Irish occupied separate regions where they were able to preserve more or less intact their respective cultural inheritances.

Yet national identity could be safeguarded only through concentration and isolation. Where these were absent, assimilation proceeded much more quickly. Wherever an immigrant group was scattered or in a minority, it was soon absorbed by the dominant stock. Thus the Palatines who settled in the predominantly Dutch counties of the Hudson Valley gave up the use of German in a generation or two and spoke Dutch instead. Likewise, in the more cosmopolitan atmosphere of the seaports, both the Germans and the Scotch-Irish shed their national characteristics much sooner than their compatriots in the back-country. It is true that, like other immigrants, the urban Germans and Scotch-Irish formed distinctive charitable and other organizations, and in Philadelphia a separate German residential quarter had developed by the end of the colonial period. Nevertheless, in Philadelphia, New York, and Boston there was considerable intermingling of stocks. In these towns national identity was rarely preserved beyond a single generation, and they have rightly been described as the "first American melting-pots."

Additional light is shed on the question of assimilation by the experience of some of the less numerous stocks in the population of colonial America. Despite the fact that there was virtually no immigration to the colonies from either Holland or Sweden in the eighteenth century, the descendants of Dutchmen and Swedes who had come earlier remained imperfectly assimilated throughout the colonial period. More than a century after the dissolution of New Netherland, Dutch influence was still paramount in the religion, social customs, and architecture of the Hudson Valley. And though Dutch had given way to English in New York City by about 1760, it remained the dominant language in the rural regions for a further half-century.

A similar tale could be told of what had once been New

Sweden. Though the Swedish botanist, Peter Kalm, saw as early as 1750 that the Swedish language was doomed to extinction in America, it had not entirely died out by the time of the Revolution, when there were still Swedish churches along the Delaware. The persistence of distinctive national traits in the two areas long after ties with the European homeland had been cut was due to the comparative immobility of the Dutch and Swedes, and to the fact that other stocks made few efforts to join them. Concentrated to an extraordinary degree in the regions their ancestors had first settled, and lying outside the main paths of colonial expansion, their compact communities proved remarkably successful in preserving their traditions and individuality.

The French Huguenots were, by contrast, so well assimilated by the time of the Revolution that little remained to distinguish them from the rest of the colonial population except, perhaps, their surnames—and in many cases even these had become Americanized. Paul Revere, for instance, was descended from a Huguenot family named Rivoire; James Bowdoin, one of the revolutionary leaders in Massachusetts, was the son of an immigrant called Pierre Baudoin; and John Greenleaf Whittier's mother came from a family of Huguenots who had changed their name from Feuillevert to Greenleaf.

The speed with which the Huguenots lost their national characteristics was due partly to the fact that, between leaving France and going to America, many of them had spent a generation or more in England, Germany, or Holland. In them the "process of denationalization" was already far advanced before they even crossed the ocean. It may be, too, that the refugees made a deliberate attempt to throw off the characteristics of a country from which they felt they had been unjustly driven, and the hostility and suspicion that greeted them in America could well have contributed to the same end. It was significant also that the bulk of the Huguenots came to the colonies within a comparatively short period. Once the initial movement was over, there was no steady stream of newcomers to breathe fresh life into traditional ways.

The severance of ties with France cast a particular blight over the distinctive religious practices of the refugees. Finding it increasingly difficult to obtain French-speaking ministers, the Huguenot churches rapidly lost their identity and were absorbed by the Church of England. Yet the most influential factor in accelerating Huguenot assimilation was the extent of their dispersal. Scattering in the first place to different European countries and then finding their way to a variety of American destinations, the Huguenots were further dispersed by the accident that many of their original settlements in America lay in regions through which flowed the main streams of colonial expansion. The Huguenot experience made it clear, in short, that the rate of assimilation depended less upon the degree of cultural difference than upon the circumstances of departure from Europe and even more upon the location of American settlement.

The Huguenots were, of course, a unique case. Among other immigrant groups the process of assimilation was, as we have seen, more protracted and still incomplete at the time of the Revolution. Yet even those groups that had preserved their cohesion and cultural distinctiveness almost intact had undergone a sea-change. In a more subtle way than the Huguenots, colonists of Irish, German, Dutch, Swedish, and even of English origin had also become Americanized. Of this the Revolution itself was to provide the clearest proof. It showed that what now molded the attitudes and opinions of immigrants was not previous background but present environment.

The role of the immigrant in the American Revolution still awaits scholarly investigation. The subject has, however, attracted considerable attention from writers anxious to prove that a particular ethnic group was unanimous in supporting the patriot side. If this were true it would mean that the group in question was more united than the colonial population as a whole; as is well-known, Americans were sharply divided in their allegiance. But in fact such broad ethnic distinctions cannot be validly drawn. Each immigrant group contained both patriots and loyalists, not to mention a proportion who wished to side with neither.

This fact deserves particular emphasis for the Scotch-Irish, whose response to the Revolution was far less uniform than their apologists would have us believe. Nor, when they took the patriot side, were they motivated chiefly, as William E. H. Lecky, James A. Froude, and other historians have claimed, by a desire to avenge the injuries they had suffered in Ireland. While memories of ancient wrongs certainly persisted among the Scotch-Irish, it was American conditions that generally determined their reaction to the Revolution.

In Pennsylvania nearly all the Scotch-Irish supported the Revolution, many of them becoming ardent and aggressive patriots. To the Pennsylvania Radical Whig party they supplied a large proportion of the rank-and-file and such leaders as George Bryan, Thomas McKean, and Joseph Reed. They also contributed the majority of the officers and men of the

Pennsylvania Line, which in consequence General "Light-Horse Harry" Lee called "the Line of Ireland." True, the record of the Pennsylvania Line is somewhat tarnished by its mutiny at Morristown, New Jersey, in January, 1781, an event that Lafayette was prepared to attribute to the disloyalty of the foreigners in its ranks. But there is little doubt that the mutiny was caused simply by the ill-treatment of the Line by the Pennsylvania Assembly. And the fundamental devotion of the mutineers to the patriot cause is shown by the unanimity with which they rejected the inducements to desert offered them by the British.

Yet even in Pennsylvania the Scotch-Irish were not a solid bloc. In 1778, Sir Henry Clinton succeeded in forming in Philadelphia a loyalist regiment known as the Volunteers of Ireland, a unit which fought with great distinction in Cornwallis' southern campaigns, especially at Camden and Hobkirk's Hill. In part the regiment was composed of southern Irishmen of whom there were considerable numbers in Philadelphia and who, as Catholics, may well have sympathized more with the authors of the Quebec Act than with its intolerant American critics. But it also contained a considerable number of Scotch-Irishmen, most of them deserters from the Continental Army.

Elsewhere a uniform Scotch-Irish reaction becomes still more difficult to discern. In New England the Scotch-Irish of the frontier were among those who opposed Burgoyne's southward march in the summer of 1777; but their compatriots in Boston had two years earlier formed a body called the Loyal Irish Volunteers. An even more striking indication of the group's disunity was the fact that while the New Hampshire Scotch-Irishman John Stark rose to become a Revolutionary general and the victor of Bennington, his brother William fell at Long Island while serving as a colonel in the royal army.

But it was in the back-country of the Carolinas that the Scotch-Irish were most sharply divided. Those in North Carolina, if not outright loyalists, were at least extremely hostile to the Revolutionary cause. In western South Carolina, too, there were many loyal Scotch-Irishmen, especially in the isolated frontier settlement known as Ninety Six. In this region, however, there were some Ulstermen, like Alexander Chesney, who fought for both sides in turn. On the other hand, in the Waxhaws—the back-country borderland between North and South Carolina—the British found that the population was "universally Irish and universally disaffected." When the Volunteers of Ireland were stationed there, their commander, Lord Rawdon, complained that the Waxhaw people used "every artifice to debauch the minds of my Soldiers," and persuaded many of them to desert. To add further to the confusion, religious sectarianism had generated a good deal of internal strife among the Scotch-Irish of the southern back-country. This factor both complicated and embittered the struggle between groups split on the issue of independence, and it went far to account for the internecine character of the war in the Carolinas.

The contrast in attitude between the Scotch-Irish of Pennsylvania and those of the southern colonies was due basically to the different political conditions they faced on the eve of the Revolution. In Pennsylvania the Scotch-Irish frontiersmen had long been opposed to the Quaker oligarchy, which denied them the vote as well as adequate representation in the Assembly. A particular grievance was the Quaker failure to protect the frontier against Indian attacks. And since the Scotch-

Irish were the chief sufferers from this neglect, their discontent overflowed in 1764 in the march of the Paxton Boys on Philadelphia. Frontier grievances remained unredressed throughout the following decade, so that as friction with Britain developed, the Scotch-Irish espoused the Radical cause not merely to bring Pennsylvania into line with the continental Revolutionary movement but to overthrow the proprietary government as well.

Enthusiastic as were the Pennsylvania Scotch-Irish for American independence, the liberal and humanitarian movements that were such a feature of the Revolution seem to have evoked from them little response. Intolerant themselves in religious matters, they had scant sympathy with the ideal of religious freedom that flowered so finely in tidewater Virginia. Though the Philadelphia Scotch-Irishman George Bryan was the author of the Pennsylvania statute of 1780 abolishing slavery in the state, the measure was vehemently opposed by the back-country Scotch-Irish who had so loudly demanded freedom for themselves.

In North Carolina, too, the Scotch-Irish had been prominent in back-country struggles against eastern political dominance, and had been especially active in the Regulator movement, which erupted in the late 1760's as a result of the oppressions and extortions of tidewater officials. After a period of rioting and bloodshed the movement was crushed, but the animosities it produced persisted into the Revolutionary period and exercised a real though undefinable influence upon the attitude of the North Carolina Scotch-Irish. The precise number of Regulators who became Tories is still a matter of dispute, but it is certain that the counties which had been centers of the Regulation sent numerous addresses of loyalty to the royal governor early in 1775. Efforts to win them over by their old tidewater enemies, who now led the North Carolina patriots, produced a meager response, and even when the Continental Congress sent two Presbyterian ministers to persuade the Scotch-Irish of the "rectitude of those who advocate the American side of the question," they remained recalcitrant. The Regulator movement left its legacy of sectional hatreds in South Carolina, too. But here the Scotch-Irish who remained loyal had an additional motive for doing so. Most of them were recent immigrants who had received grants of land from the British government and feared to lose them if they joined the rebellion.

The Germans also tended to respond to the pressure of environment to the exclusion of ties of common origin. In Pennsylvania it was antagonism toward eastern political leaders that led the Germans of the central and western counties to support the Revolution. With them, even more than with the Scotch-Irish, the controversy with Britain took second place to local issues, and many Germans deserted from the army as soon as Quaker rule in the state was overthrown. To the Germans of the Mohawk Valley the Revolution offered a welcome opportunity to settle accounts with the Tory proprietors, whose exclusive land policy had hampered the settlement of the region. In Georgia, on the other hand, most of the Germans became loyalists largely because, living in an exposed frontier region, they were anxious not to lose British support against Indian raids.

There were other factors beside geography that were responsible for the split in the German ranks. More important, sometimes, was the influence of religion. The colonial Germans, it must be remembered, were not a united people but merely a variety of religious groups sharing a common language. Each of the German churches and sects tended to respond to the Revolution in its own distinctive way. It was noticeable, for instance, that while many ministers of the German Reformed Church openly supported the Revolution, the German Lutheran clergy—with the notable exception of the Reverend Peter Muhlenberg, who became a Revolutionary general—were inclined to support the British. This was probably because nearly all the Lutheran clergy were originally from the consistories of Halle or Hanover and were thus doubly bound to George III, who was Elector of Hanover as well as King of England. The German sect people, too, were out of sympathy with the Revolution largely because of their conscientious scruples about the use of force. The Moravians had additional reasons for remaining loyal. They felt nothing but gratitude to Britain, which had given them a refuge from religious persecution and had, by an act of Parliament of 1749, exempted them from the obligation to bear arms. The Moravians, in common with other sectarians, also objected to taking oaths, and the reluctance of those in Pennsylvania and North Carolina to swear allegiance to the new state governments led to their being heavily fined or deprived of their lands.

The division in German opinion was reflected in the contrasting positions adopted by the leading German-language newspapers. As the Revolutionary crisis developed, the *Germantauner Zeitung*, which had been published continuously, though under different titles, since 1739, expressed the loyalist and pacifist sentiments of its proprietor, Christopher Saur II. Then, during the British occupation of Philadelphia in 1777–78, two of Saur's sons published the virulently anti-patriot journal, the *Pennsylvanische Staats Courier*. Heinrich Miller's *Philadelphische Staatsbote*, on the other hand, was a violently radical sheet from the time of the Stamp Act onward, and, except when the British seized his type and press, Miller kept up a spirited newspaper war on the Saur family.

It would, however, be wrong to imagine that the Germans were enthusiastically and irrevocably committed to one side or the other. The great mass seems to have been little stirred by the issues of the Revolution and to have been indifferent to its outcome. Partly because of the language barrier, partly because of conservatism and a desire to go on living their lives in peaceful seclusion, the Germans had shown little interest in politics except where their immediate interests were threatened. Feeling that the controversy with Britain was none of their concern, many clung to neutrality as long as possible.

Typical of this group was the patriarch of German Lutheranism in America, the Reverend Henry Melchior Muhlenberg. "Unwilling," as he wrote, "to change my oath of allegiance nor yet to be a sacrifice to *Anarchie* at the hands of the angry mob," Muhlenberg retired from Philadelphia to the country at the outbreak of the Revolution in an effort to avoid taking sides. Though he later swore allegiance to the United States, expediency rather than conviction seems to have been his motive. When the British occupied Philadelphia in 1777 and there were rumors of a Hessian plot to hang him, Muhlenberg was quick to inform General Howe that he had remained loyal to the king as long as circumstances had allowed.

Muhlenberg's equivocal conduct was a measure of his failure to reconcile his family loyalties with his personal predilections. While his sons Peter and Frederick both abandoned the ministry to serve the Revolutionary cause, the father could not follow them because many ties still bound him to England. As a native of Hanover he was a subject of George III by virtue of birth as well as of naturalization; he had been educated at the Royal University of Göttingen; and he had received his call to Pennsylvania at the hands of the court chaplain, Ziegenhagen, in London. He recalled, too, that the religious toleration permitted by "the inestimable Constitution of the British Empire" had encouraged "many frugal and industrious Germans" to make their homes in the New World. In addition, Muhlenberg was influenced by that fact that Lutheranism taught that Christ's kingdom is not of this world and that the clergy should therefore not concern themselves with worldly affairs. Yet in his efforts to pursue an impartial course he incurred the usual fate of a neutral, being suspected as an enemy by both sides.

The nearest approach to unanimity was provided by the Scots. True, a number of individuals of Scottish birth, like John Witherspoon, James Wilson, Arthur St. Clair, and John Paul Jones, served the Revolutionary cause. Nevertheless, the Scots were almost solidly loyalist. North Carolina and New York were particularly active centers of Scottish Toryism. In Cumberland County, North Carolina, a formidable force of Highland loyalists was raised early in 1776, only to be crushed at Moore's Creek Bridge on its way to Cape Fear to link up with British regulars. This setback, however, did not shake the loyalty of the North Carolina Highlanders, some of whom fought on the British side in the battle of King's Mountain in 1780. Very similar was the record of the Highlanders of the Mohawk Valley. Many of them served under Sir John Johnson in Butler's Rangers, some participating in the Cherry Valley massacre; and after the war they formed the vanguard of the loyalist migration to Canada.

The ubiquitous Scottish merchants, too, were almost without exception on the side of the crown. This is not difficult to explain. By the time of the Revolution Scottish merchants and factors had become extremely unpopular in the colonies, largely because of the dubious business methods by which they were alleged to have achieved success. They were especially disliked in Virginia, where they virtually monopolized the tobacco trade and where they were the principal creditors of the planters. Hostility toward them reached a climax when, by their numerous violations of the non-importation agreement, the Scots lent color to the charge that they were more interested in preserving their selfish interests than in defending the rights of the colonies. Most of the Scottish merchants would probably have preferred to remain neutral in the political dispute; but, smarting under Radical attacks, they warmly welcomed Lord Dunmore's arrival in Norfolk in November, 1776, and hastened to join the "Queen's Own Loyal Virginians."

The strength of Highland loyalism is more surprising, for Highlanders had been the most conspicuous opponents of the house of Hanover in the Jacobite rebellion of 1745. But that rebellion had arisen out of clan warfare rather than out of hostility toward England, and in joining the insurgents the Highlander had simply followed the lead of his immediate landlord, to whom he owed absolute obedience. In America he followed a similar course, fighting for the crown under the leadership of the tacksmen who had planned and led his immigration from Scotland. Moreover, a large proportion of the

American Immigration

Highland settlers in both North Carolina and New York were very recent immigrants, most of them having arrived in America only in the decade after 1763. Effective though the American environment could be in most cases in transforming Europeans into new men, it was evidently incapable, in so short a time, of eradicating deeply ingrained habits of feudal subservience.

The virtual unanimity of the Scots, due as it was to their peculiar antecedents and their comparatively recent arrival, found no parallel elsewhere. Other ethnic groups tended rather to share that diversity of attitude of which the Scotch-Irish and Germans were the most striking examples. There were thus not only Huguenot patriots like John Jay, Henry Laurens, and Elias Boudinot, each of whom was at different times president of the Continental Congress; but Huguenot loyalists like the De Lanceys who fled to Canada at the end of the war, their vast New York estates confiscated because of their loyalism. There were New York Dutchmen, too, in the loyalist exodus of 1783, but others of similar origin had fought valiantly for the patriot cause.

The tiny Jewish communities of the Atlantic seaports were no less divided. Some Jews like Haym Solomon helped finance the American war effort, while others like Benjamin Nones distinguished themselves in the Continental Army. But an equally typical Jewish reaction was that of David Franks, who remained throughout the struggle an ardent Tory. The way in which the Revolution cut across ties of origin and of interest was best demonstrated, however, by the divisions it provoked among the Jewish community of Newport, Rhode Island. Some Jewish merchants, such as Aaron Lopez, withdrew from the town with the patriot forces in 1776, but others, such as the Harts and the Pollocks, remained to work for the British cause. As with the American population generally, so with its component parts, the Revolution cut through families and communities in such a way as to make it almost impossible to draw any clear line between those who supported the Revolution and those who remained loyal.

The American Revolution was essentially a triumph of environment over heredity. When men of common origin could take opposing sides, it was evident that Old World influences no longer molded their attitudes. That they differed in their response to the Revolution was largely a consequence of the variety of their New World experiences. And from these differences one should deduce not American disunity but its opposite. For they proved the essential truth of Crèvecœur's statement that, in crossing the Atlantic, the immigrant had put behind him his former prejudices and manners and, imbibing fresh ones from his new environment, had become "a new man, an American." Given the continuance of this process of spiritual transformation, the unity of the new nation was assured.

III

The New Nation and Its Immigrants, 1783-1815

The limited volume of immigration during the first generation of American independence owed nothing to reluctance on the part of Europeans to throw in their lot with the young republic. On the contrary, great numbers would have liked, in George Washington's words, "to retire from the noise and bustle of the Old World to enjoy tranquillity and security" in the New. But the restrictions imposed by European governments made it extremely difficult to leave, and the war conditions prevailing after 1793 added greatly to the normal hazards of the Atlantic crossing.

Exactly how many newcomers arrived in the United States during these years is impossible to say in the absence of official records. Not until 1820 did the federal government require masters of arriving immigrant ships to hand in lists of passengers to the Customs. But if contemporary estimates can be relied upon, the total immigration between 1783 and 1815 came to about 250,000. For about a decade after the Peace of Versailles the annual arrivals seem to have averaged about 6,000; during the 1790's the figure often exceeded 10,000; but during the Napoleonic Wars it gradually declined to only 3,000 or so, and, with the outbreak of the War of 1812, the stream dried up altogether.

Despite the small numbers involved, the period was a significant one in the history of American immigration. The mere fact that there was a comparative lull in the flow of new-comers was in itself important. By accelerating the Americanization of groups which had not yet lost their separate identity, the decline of immigration contributed to the growth of American nationality. There were, however, more direct and positive consequences than this. An unusually large proportion of those who came were men of outstanding gifts, men like William Cobbett, Albert Gallatin, Mathew Carey, and John Jacob Astor, whose influence upon American political and economic life was out of all proportion to their numbers. Moreover, immigration was itself one of the leading political issues of the period. Though there was at first a general welcome for immigrants, the whole question of immigration soon became the subject of party and sectional dispute, with especially bitter divisions developing over the political role of the foreign-born.

When immigration revived at the close of the War for Independence, it followed for some years the pattern established in the latter part of the colonial period. The most numerous group of newcomers was still the Scotch-Irish. Immigrant ships from the north of Ireland reached the Delaware even before the treaty of peace was signed, and within a year or two the movement, though never quite so large as in the early 1770's, had regained all its former regularity. In 1789, in response to an alarmed inquiry from London, the British consul at Philadelphia, Phineas Bond, estimated that well over twenty thousand immigrants had come to Pennsylvania from the north of Ireland since the peace, and the influx showed no signs of slackening.

At the same time, Consul Bond reported that "an almost total stop has lately been put to the migration hither from the Palatinate and other parts of Germany so that the few who now came hither from that country get into Holland by stealth." This, however, must have been a very recent development, for as late as 1786 Germans were still arriving in Pennsylvania in considerable numbers. In addition, five thousand Hessian soldiers settled in the United States at the close of hostilities. Some Hessians deserted from the British early in the war, seduced by offers of free land made by the Continental Congress; others managed to escape, or were allowed to do so, after becoming prisoners of war. Most of them found their way to the German counties of Pennsylvania, New York, and Virginia, where they were quickly absorbed.

As had been the case before the Revolution, most of the immigrants of the 1780's were probably indentured servants or redemptioners. Apart from the halting of the servant trade during the war and the commandeering of servants for military service the Revolution had surprisingly little effect upon the institution of indentured servitude. In the earliest years of independence dissenting voices were occasionally raised against the resumption of the servant trade. Thus in 1784 the arrival at New York of a shipload of servants led to a protest meeting of "respectable citizens" who declared that "the traffick of white people . . . is contrary to . . . the idea of liberty this country has so happily established." But in Philadelphia, which remained the center of the servant trade, there seem to have been no such protests; the outcry of the Philadelphia Irish in 1783 against the purchase of two Irish servants by a free Negro was due rather to race prejudice than to humanitarianism. The state of public opinion generally may be gauged from the fact that George Washington not only continued, with no apparent embarrassment, to purchase indentured servants for his own use at Mount Vernon but as late as 1792 presented to the Commissioners of the District of Columbia a detailed plan for the importation of German indentured labor for construction work in the new federal city on the Potomac. Far from prohibiting white servitude, Pennsylvania and New York both passed laws in the 1780's to encourage the growth of the institution. In fact, the only branch of the servant trade which was brought to an end by American action was convict transportation. In 1788, after receiving reports that convicts were being secretly transported from the West Indies, the Continental Congress urged remedial action upon the states, at least five of which responded by banning the importation of convicted malefactors.

Nevertheless, the decline of the servant trade proper was not long delayed. The first blow was the British statute of 1788 which extended to Ireland for the first time a longstanding ban upon the emigration of skilled artisans. By making it illegal for shipmasters to recruit as servants the very group most in demand in the American labor market, this law at once greatly reduced the proportion of servants on immigrant vessels from Ireland. But what finally killed the Irish servant trade was the British Passenger Act of 1803, which drastically reduced the numbers that immigrant ships could carry. With the virtual disappearance of the profit margin, captains no longer found it worth their while to recruit a cargo of servants; indeed, the effort became unnecessary, since there were always enough fare-paying passengers available to fill the reduced number of berths.

The German redemptioner trade was, of course, unaffected by this legislation. Though it declined almost to vanishing point during the Napoleonic Wars, efforts were made to revive it when peace returned in 1815. But after an epidemic had broken out in 1818 on an overcrowded redemptioner ship from Rotterdam, Congress recognized the necessity of regulation, and the Passenger Act it adopted in March, 1819, gave the *coup de grâce* to the importation of indentured labor.

Effective though the British restrictions were in crippling the Irish servant trade, they proved incapable of preventing the departure of individual artisans either from Ireland or from Great Britain. Making use of a variety of ruses in order to evade the law, skilled workers left for the United States in a steady stream in the generation after 1783. Some of them went in response to American inducements. There was widespread agreement in the United States with men like Tench Coxe and Mathew Carey, the leaders of the movement to establish American manufactures, who argued that European superiority in manufacturing technique could be overcome only by borrowing it. Accordingly, several attempts were made to import artisans, especially from Great Britain. In one such attempt George Washington was concerned for a time, but by 1791 he had decided to withdraw from the affair on the ground that "it certainly would not carry an aspect very favorable to the dignity of the United States for the President in clandestine manner to entice the subjects of another nation to violate its laws." But Washington's Secretary of the Treasury did not share these scruples. In his *Report on Manufactures* Hamilton had recommended that efforts should be made to attract skilled foreign artisans; but correctly anticipating that Congress would do nothing, he decided to act on his own. In his capacity of leading promoter of the Society for Useful Manufactures, Hamilton sent agents to Scotland in 1791 to engage framesmiths, stocking weavers, and other artisans for work at the society's National Manufactory at Paterson, New Jersey. But these and similar efforts had meager results. Some of those engaged turned out to be less skilled than they had claimed, while others displayed an annoying readiness to break contracts and quit their employment as soon as they had saved enough money to buy land.

More satisfactory were the much larger numbers of artisans who came on their own initiative. The most famous of these was the Englishman Samuel Slater, who, carrying in his head the plans of a spinning jenny, arrived in the United States in 1789 to establish the first American cotton factory at Pawtucket, Rhode Island. But Slater was only one of a great number of British artisans whose skills were a vital element in the initial phase of American industrialization. Visitors to the textile mills of New England and the middle states in the 1790's and early 1800's constantly remarked upon the prominence of Englishmen and Scots, whose function was to superintend and instruct native Americans in the new manufacturing techniques.

If some Americans looked to immigration to provide the means of developing industry, others regarded it, at least for a time, as a promising method of peopling the vacant West.

American Immigration

Especially hopeful of tapping the reservoir of European population were those whose land speculations during the Revolution had won them sizable western tracts. Many sent agents to Europe in the late 1780's in an effort to attract purchasers. But results were discouraging. The settlers recruited in Germany for the Pulteney estate in western New York, for example, turned out to be shiftless and lazy and soon became so discontented that they made off to Canada. Equally depressing in its outcome was the celebrated Scioto venture. Its leading spirit was Joel Barlow, who, as the Paris agent of the Scioto Land Company, sent some hundreds of Frenchmen in 1790 to found the town of Gallipolis upon the Ohio River. The whole enterprise was badly mismanaged. The settlers suffered many hardships and, finding that the land they had paid for was not theirs, justifiably complained of deception and fraud. By 1792 the whole project had utterly failed and the Gallipolis site was deserted.

With this fiasco ended all hopes of large-scale land promotion in Europe. The warnings of misrepresentation and insecurity of title, which the European opponents of emigration had so assiduously circulated, were now borne out. Numbers of immigrants, especially British and German, still came to the United States to acquire land, but fewer than before were prepared to commit themselves to purchase before leaving their homelands. American land promoters, for their part, were now convinced that unseasoned Europeans were unsuitable material for frontier life and henceforth concentrated their efforts upon native Americans.

For most of the 1790's, political events in Europe were the dominant influence upon the course of American immigration. The French Revolution and its resulting wars, though making it impossible for any mass exodus to take place, were nevertheless responsible for a considerable influx of immigrants into the United States. The first refugees came from France itself. By 1792 a considerable number of aristocrats and royalist sympathizers had fled across the Atlantic to escape the fury of the Paris mob, among them the future Louis Philippe, the Duc de Rochefoucauld-Liancourt, and the Vicomte de Noailles. Later they were joined by a number of Girondists and Jacobins, who in their turn had been threatened with the guillotine. But the great mass of French exiles came from Santo Domingo, where a Negro revolt had broken out in 1791. Two years later practically the whole of the white population of the island had fled, between ten and twenty thousand finding refuge in the United States. Most of the Santo Domingans arrived destitute, but generous assistance was afforded by public subscription, while Congress in 1794 voted $15,000 for their relief.

The overwhelming majority of the refugees from France and Santo Domingo settled in towns on the Atlantic seaboard. Large French colonies were to be found in Philadelphia, New York, Baltimore, and Charleston, and there was hardly a town of any size which did not receive its complement of "French dancing-masters, teachers of gentility and deportment, wigmakers, entertainers and restaurateurs." Not many exiles had any aptitude or inclination for a rural existence, since towns offered better opportunities both of employment and of contact with their compatriots. Among the few to attempt frontier settlements was the small group of émigrés and Santo Domingo creoles who in 1794 left Philadelphia to establish a royalist colony, appropriately called Asylum, on the banks of the Susquehanna. But there was no real enthusiasm for the enterprise, and in less than a decade the colony was abandoned.

About 1798 the French urban communities, too, began to disintegrate. Many of the exiles had never intended to stay permanently in the United States, and with the Directory in power and Talleyrand, a former exile, in charge of foreign affairs, they felt it was safe to return home. Others were persuaded to do so by their apprehensions of the Alien and Sedition Acts.

Though many of them remained in the United States, the French refugees left few permanent marks on American life. Not a single French-language newspaper survived the breakup of the compact refugee groups; and the vogue for French manners and fashions went out with the outbreak of the quasi-war with France in 1798. Only upon American Catholicism was the influence of the émigré movement more than ephemeral. The coming of the refugees appreciably increased the numbers and the influence of the Roman Catholic church in the United States. Moreover, an influx of French priests relieved a shortage of clergy and ultimately made French influence predominant in the hierarchy. By 1820, four of the six Catholic sees in the United States were presided over by French ecclesiastics who had earlier fled from the Revolution.

Sympathy with the French Revolution rather than opposition to it, was responsible for the arrival in the United States of a number of British radicals. During the conservative reaction that followed the outbreak of war with France in 1793 the British government severely curtailed freedom of expression and of assembly, and those who protested against the war or persisted in demanding reforms upon the French model were liable to be charged with sedition. Some, like the journalist Joseph Gales, who was to become the official reporter of congressional debates and editor of the *Raleigh Register*, fled to America to avoid arrest; others, like James Cheetham, were able to leave only after serving terms of imprisonment; and even greater numbers, though in no personal danger, were unwilling to go on living under a system of repression. Typical of this last group were the passengers of the ship "Sisters," which left Bristol in May, 1793. Intercepted in mid-Atlantic by a French privateer, they informed a boarding party that they "were leaving England because [they] abhorred the idea of contributing to a war against France, and could not avoid anticipating the extinction of liberty in [their] native land."

The two most prominent radicals to emigrate were Dr. Joseph Priestley, the celebrated scientist whose French sympathies had resulted in the destruction of his house by a Birmingham mob, and Thomas Cooper, an equally vigorous critic of the established order who had achieved notoriety by a visit to France in 1792. When they sailed to the United States in 1794, it was with the intention of establishing "a large settlement for the friends of liberty" at Loyalsock Creek on the banks of the Susquehanna. But realizing that intellectuals were "ill-qualified to commence cultivation in the wilderness," they abandoned the project. Priestley lived out his days in seclusion at Northumberland, Pennsylvania, and Cooper embarked upon a varied career that culminated in his becoming president of a southern college and a proslavery apologist.

More successful in carrying out his settlement plans was the Welsh clergyman, Morgan John Rhys, whose expressions of admiration for France in pamphlets and sermons had made him a marked man. Fleeing to the United States in 1794, he purchased 25,000 acres in Cambria County, Pennsylvania, where he founded a colony which in the next few years attracted a steady stream of newcomers from Wales.

Repression was also responsible for the flight of many of the leaders of the United Irishmen. Among the first of them to reach America was the Ulster physician James Reynolds, who had been imprisoned for contempt of the Irish House of Lords and who celebrated his departure from Ireland in 1794 by hanging George III in effigy from the yardarm of the ship that carried him to Philadelphia. By 1795 Reynolds had been joined by even more prominent United Irishmen—Wolfe Tone, Hamilton Rowan, and Napper Tandy, among others. Later, despite Federalist attempts to keep them out, a great many of the unsuccessful Irish rebels of 1798 found an American refuge.

One should not, however, exaggerate the political motive for the British and Irish influx of the 1790's. Among English immigrants, political refugees were greatly outnumbered by distressed artisans and by yeoman farmers and agricultural laborers depressed by bad harvests and low prices. Similar conditions compelled the departure of most of the Welsh farmers who joined Rhys's Pennsylvania colony or embarked upon a pioneer existence in places like Oneida County, New York, or the Paddy's Run region of Ohio. Hard times—and a desire to join relatives who had gone earlier—were also largely responsible for the continued Scotch-Irish exodus.

During the brief interval between the French Revolution and the Napoleonic Wars the volume of immigration was greater than at any time since 1783. Irishmen and Germans, particularly, flocked to the seaports in search of passage, and in 1801 and 1802 perhaps as many as twenty thousand may have succeeded in reaching the United States. But this was more than the number who came in the whole of the following decade. With the resumption of war in 1803, transatlantic trade was again disrupted, and until the downfall of Napoleon departure from continental Europe became virtually impossible.

The British Passenger Act of 1803 had almost as serious an effect upon the movement from Ireland. Ostensibly a humanitarian measure designed to reduce the evils of overcrowding during the passage, the Act's real purpose was almost certainly to check emigration. That at all events was its effect. The Londonderry and Belfast ships which had been accustomed to take four or five hundred passengers a voyage, were now limited to a few score; and with fares bounding upward in consequence, only about a thousand emigrants a year were able to leave Ireland after 1803. The withdrawal of American shipping during Jefferson's embargo added still further to the difficulties of obtaining passage, and although the immigrant traffic subsequently revived, it had a new hazard to contend with—impressment. Immigrant ships from Ireland were tempting prey to short-handed British cruisers, and between 1810 and 1812 hundreds of young able-bodied Irishmen were removed from American-bound vessels, sometimes when in sight of their destination, and impressed for naval service. The practice was spreading and becoming more flagrant when the outbreak of the War of 1812 brought immigration to a complete halt.

The limited scale of immigration during the first generation of national independence enabled those immigrants who had still been imperfectly assimilated at the time of the Revolution to take a long stride toward Americanization. Deprived of their customary accessions from abroad, non-English groups steadily lost in distinctiveness and cohesion. An especially significant sign was the snapping of those linguistic ties which more than anything else had bound together immigrants of common origin and had kept them apart from other Americans. Well might De Witt Clinton remark in 1814: ". . . the triumph and adoption of the English language have been the principal means of melting us down into one people, and of extinguishing those stubborn prejudices and violent animosities which formed a wall of partition between the inhabitants of the same land."

The decline of the French, Swedish, and Welsh tongues was already far advanced before the Revolution. Now came the turn of Dutch and German, the only remaining non-English languages that were at all widely used. In neither case was the transition to English complete; Dutch and German both lingered on for a further period as the language of the home, especially in the more remote regions. But by 1815 the public use of Dutch and German was decidedly on the wane.

The language question had its greatest impact upon the life of the immigrant churches. In New York, where commercial development had ended the isolation of the Dutch communities and made a knowledge of English essential, the Dutch Reformed Church found it increasingly difficult to resist the demand for English services. Faced with the alternative of losing the younger generation to other denominations, one congregation after another decided to make the change. In addition, English Bibles, prayer books, and hymnals were by 1815 in almost universal use in what had once been New Netherland.

A similar trend was noticeable in the German churches. In them it was hastened by the severance of ecclesiastical ties with Europe. Before the Revolution the German clergy had come mainly from Europe and had been among the staunchest defenders of the traditional tongue, believing that its decline would lead to religious indifference. But once the German churches, in common with most American religious bodies, had broken loose from their Old World parent organizations, the supply of foreign clergy abruptly ceased. The consequences became apparent after 1800 when foreign-born ministers began to be succeeded by men born and trained in the United States. In New York and Philadelphia, and in the German counties of Maryland, Virginia, and North Carolina, numerous German congregations adopted English as the language of worship, though in many places only after violent conflict and even schism. In 1815 only the churches of the Pennsylvania German country had made no concession to the "Anglicizers."

The decay of German had other repercussions. According to Carl Wittke, the German-language press experienced a marked deterioration in its "general tone, content and literary standards" during the late eighteenth and early nineteenth centuries. Despite the printing contracts and subsidies furnished by political parties anxious to win the support of German editors, the number of German-language papers steadily declined. In Maryland, in the half-century following the Revolution, not a single German paper lasted more than a few years. By 1815, Philadelphia, New York, and Baltimore, which had formerly had two or three German-language newspapers apiece, could not boast one among them. Only in the small towns of the Pennsylvania German country, like Allentown, Lancaster, and Reading, did they still survive.

As a group with no language barrier to surmount, the

American Immigration

Scotch-Irish had always found adjustment less difficult than had the Germans. After the Revolution the process should have been still easier, for the newly formed American Presbyterian church, to which most Scotch-Irishmen belonged, turned increasingly to native-trained clergy in preference to those from Ulster. Yet Americanization was less rapid than might have been expected. Immigration from Ireland, as we have seen, began to fall off seriously only after 1803, so that for most of the period there were constant infusions of new blood to keep alive the distinctiveness of the Scotch-Irish communities. Many of the newcomers, moreover, were difficult to Americanize because of their intense Irish nationalism.

When Scotch-Irishmen first began to arrive in the colonies about 1720, they were very sensitive about being confused with the native Irish, from whom they were divided by religion. But within half a century these differences had given way—temporarily at least—to a common Irish nationalism, and many of those who came to America from Ulster in the last quarter of the eighteenth century were not only proud to be Irishmen but were determined to remain so. Particularly was this true of the political refugees—drawn mainly though by no means exclusively from Ulster—who settled in Philadelphia and New York, where they formed the nucleus of distinctive and extremely self-conscious Irish communities. Their sense of solidarity was further increased by the birth of the Irish-American press, which occurred at precisely the time that the German-language press was retreating before the forces of American nationalism. Papers like the *Shamrock*, founded in New York in 1810, and the *Western Star*, which came out two years later, were an entirely new phenomenon. Unlike the German press, which simply reported American

78

news in a different language, these new Irish journals were more concerned with keeping alive the immigrant's memories of the old country than with easing his adjustment to the new.

Limited in volume though immigration was throughout this period, it was at no time a matter of indifference to Americans. But though reactions were always varied, immigration was not at first a partisan issue. It became so only when the character of the movement had revived old misgivings which had been temporarily submerged by Revolutionary idealism.

The Revolution gave new emphasis and meaning to the concept that America was an asylum for the oppressed of the world. To New Englanders, accustomed to idealizing their Puritan forefathers as fugitives from tyranny, the idea had long been familiar. Now, in the surge of philanthropy that accompanied the winning of independence it became part of the faith of Americans generally. Thomas Paine's *Common Sense* saw as one of America's unique characteristics the fact that she had been "the asylum for the persecuted lovers of civil and religious liberty from every part of Europe"; Philip Freneau's verses expressed in 1787 a widespread satisfaction that the Revolution had brought into existence a country to which the stranger could flee "from Europe's proud, despotic shores." And in reply to an address from a group of recent Irish immigrants George Washington wrote in December, 1783: "The bosom of America is open to receive not only the Opulent and respectable Stranger, but the oppressed and persecuted of all Nations and Religions; whom we shall wellcome to a participation of all our rights and privileges if, by decency and propriety of conduct, they appear to merit the enjoyment."

At least some of the eloquence the asylum theme inspired

was due to a shrewd appreciation of the material advantages that might be expected to accrue to America from immigration. Yet its main source was the universal good will that was so characteristic of the Revolutionary period. Exhilarated by their achievements in founding a new nation, many Americans were anxious to extend a general invitation to mankind to come and share the blessings of liberty they had won for themselves.

Yet even from the first there were those who had doubts about the wisdom of opening the doors to all the world. Chief among the dissenters was Thomas Jefferson. Throughout his life Jefferson's attitude to immigration oscillated between two extremes. His philanthropy and love of liberty urged him to welcome the victims of tyranny. But he could never become an enthusiast for immigration because of a fear that, by granting asylum to foreigners, America would expose herself to the corrupting influence of decadent Europe, thus endangering the success of the experiment upon which she was engaged. Most immigrants, Jefferson pointed out in the *Notes on Virginia*, would necessarily come from countries governed by despotism and would either retain the principles of the governments they had left or, if able to throw them off, would pass to the other extreme and imbibe principles of extreme licentiousness. In either event, he predicted, their influence upon the American body politic would be to "infuse in it their spirit, warp and bias its directions, and render it a heterogeneous, incoherent, distracted mass."

That Jefferson was not alone in his fears was evident when the political rights of aliens came up for discussion. In the Constitutional Convention of 1787 there was wide divergence of opinion over the question of whether foreign-born citizens should be eligible for membership in Congress. Elbridge Gerry of Massachusetts wanted to restrict membership to those born in the United States, while Pierce Butler of South Carolina and Gouverneur Morris of Pennsylvania advocated a long, qualifying period of citizenship. Echoing Jefferson's views, these speakers pointed out that the political opinions and attachments of foreigners made it dangerous to admit them too readily to office. But it was left to George Mason to give such apprehensions their bluntest expression; while he favored opening a wide door for the admission of immigrants, Mason declared that he did not choose "to be governed by foreigners and adventurers."

Other delegates vigorously attacked this position. Edmund Randolph argued, for example, that the Convention could not honorably restrict the political rights of immigrants, since many of them had come to the United States trusting in the general invitation to the oppressed that the Revolutionary leaders had extended. Alexander Hamilton, again, pointed out that only by making foreign-born citizens equally eligible with natives for holding office could Europeans of property be induced to come. To James Madison it was significant that the states which had grown most rapidly in numbers and wealth were those which had given immigrants the warmest welcome. Such views in fact prevailed, for the Constitution required only relatively short periods of residence from foreign-born citizens who aspired to enter the national legislature.

Nevertheless, a similar clash of opinion occurred when the First Congress debated the question of naturalization in 1790. The familiar argument that the monarchical and aristocratic attachments of immigrants would disqualify them for "pure republicanism" was voiced by the conservative Theodore Sedgwick of Massachusetts, who demanded that a long period of residence should precede the granting of citizenship. The radical James Jackson of Georgia not only seconded this demand but wanted barriers against the admission of "the common class of vagrants, paupers and other outcasts of Europe." In striking contrast was the eloquent speech of John Page of Virginia, who declared that Americans would be guilty of gross inconsistency if, after boasting of having opened an asylum for the oppressed, they made the terms of admission unreasonably severe. Page's remarks showed that the philanthropy of the Revolution was by no means dead. That his faith in the asylum ideal was shared by a majority of Congress was evident from the fact that the Naturalization Act of 1790 required from immigrants only a two-year period of residence before citizenship could be claimed.

During the following decade Americans came increasingly to question the wisdom of such liberality toward immigrants. The motley groups of political refugees cast upon American shores by the upheavals of the French Revolution could not fail to strengthen fears of immigration, and more especially of infection by European political ideas. "There is much to be apprehended," wrote the Connecticut Federalist Oliver Wolcott in 1794, "from the great numbers of violent men who emigrate to this country from every part of Europe." In the following year a Maryland Federalist, William Vans Murray, expressed alarm lest the newcomers, "coming from a quarter of the world so full of disorder and corruption . . . might contaminate the purity and simplicity of the American character." Accordingly, in 1795 a revised Naturalization Act was passed which raised from two years to five the period of residence that immigrants needed to qualify for citizenship.

This measure received the support of both parties. But while Federalists and Republicans were equally apprehensive of foreign influence, their fears were inspired by two entirely separate groups of immigrants. In Federalist eyes, the threat came from those "apostles of sedition"—proscribed Jacobins, United Irishmen, and British radicals—whose departure from Europe had been due to their enthusiasm for the social and political ideals of the French Revolution. These newcomers, many Federalists believed, were chiefly responsible for the growth of faction and of Jacobinism in the United States, and their purpose was nothing less than the downfall of the young republic.

Not unnaturally, Jefferson's followers warmly welcomed those whom the Federalists regarded with such abhorrence. But the Republicans had their own bêtes noires in the royalist émigrés from France and Santo Domingo. To the newly formed democratic clubs, which displayed such enthusiasm for revolutionary France, these survivals of the *ancien régime* were objects of deep suspicion and hostility. Accordingly, the Republicans insisted upon an amendment to the Naturalization Act of 1795 that required applicants for naturalization to renounce not merely their former allegiance but any titles of nobility they might hold.

Three years later a Federalist Congress took advantage of the wave of xenophobia that followed the publication of the XYZ dispatches to rush through the Alien and Sedition Acts. This time there was no answering wave of nativism from the Republican ranks. Instead, the measures were denounced by the Republicans as an encroachment on state rights, an encouragement to executive tyranny, a menace to civil liberties, and a base repudiation of the promises made during the Revolution that America would be an asylum for the oppressed.

Republicans were, perhaps, readier to revive the asylum concept now that it was apparent that from immigration they had nothing to lose and everything to gain. The fears they had formerly entertained of the French émigrés had turned out to be groundless. After the Directory came to power and had restored a measure of stability to France, many of the former counts, barons, and marquises who had fled to America took advantage of changed conditions to return home. Although considerable numbers of Frenchmen remained in the United States, the majority regarded themselves as temporary exiles and thus showed little interest in American politics.

When immigrants did become politically active, they were usually enthusiastic Republican partisans. Among the Scotch-Irish a predilection for the Republicans was simply a carry-over of earlier attitudes. The fierce anti-Federalism of the back-country Scotch-Irish, especially in Pennsylvania, had its origin in the frontiersman's dislike of strong central control. But to this long-established source of Jeffersonian strength there was added in the course of the 1790's the newer Irish elements in the eastern cities, particularly in Philadelphia and New York. These Irishmen, drawn largely from the professional and mercantile classes, instinctively hated the Federalists as would-be aristocrats and as tools of the British. Taking advantage of the wide opportunities for political expression afforded by their urban concentration, they quickly became active in the newly formed Democratic-Republican clubs and in Republican militia units.

The Irish were especially prominent in the agitation against

Jay's Treaty. At a mass meeting in Philadelphia in July, 1795, Irish-born Blair McClenachan urged his audience to "kick this damned treaty to hell." Then, placing a copy of it upon a pole, he led a mob to the house of the British minister, where the document was ceremonially burned. Among those present at the meeting was the United Irishman Archibald Hamilton Rowan, who had arrived in the United States only three days before. Rowan, like Wolfe Tone and Napper Tandy, was less an immigrant than an exile; during their stay in the United States all three were less concerned with American politics than with planning a return to Ireland. But another prominent United Irishman, Dr. James Reynolds, became one of the leaders of Philadelphia Republicanism. No sooner had he arrived in Philadelphia than he began to excite his countrymen against the Federalists. By 1798 he had the satisfaction of knowing that the Irish, not only of Philadelphia, but throughout Pennsylvania, cast an almost solid Republican vote.

The growth of this alliance between the Republicans and the Irish vote convinced most Federalists, especially those in New England, of the necessity of restricting the enfranchisement of immigrants. "If some means are not adopted to prevent the indiscriminate admission of wild Irishmen and others to the right of suffrage," wrote Harrison Gray Otis of Massachusetts, "there will soon be an end to liberty and property." Uriah Tracy of Connecticut took a similar view. Of the numerous natives of Ireland he met during a lengthy journey through Pennsylvania, Tracy wrote: ". . . with very few exceptions, they are United Irishmen, Free Masons, and the most God-provoking Democrats this side of Hell."

The first Federalist attempt to deprive the opposing party of its supply of foreign-born voters came in May, 1797, when it was proposed to levy a twenty-dollar tax upon certificates of naturalization. The measure seems to have originated with Otis, who declared that its purpose was to debar from citizenship "the mass of vicious and disorganizing characters who can not live peaceably at home, and who, after unfurling the standard of rebellion in their own country, may come hither to revolutionize ours." The twenty-dollar tax was rejected, but in 1798 a Federalist Congress adopted a revised Naturalization Act which lengthened from five years to fourteen the minimum period of residence needed to qualify for citizenship. Even this did not satisfy such extremists as Robert Goodloe Harper, who felt that "the time is now come when it shall be proper to declare that nothing but birth shall entitle a man to citizenship in this country." Otis, too, would have gone further, but his proposal that officeholding should be restricted to native Americans failed to pass.

The two Alien Acts of 1798, passed because of a Federalist belief that the country was swarming with foreign spies, gave to the President arbitrary powers to seize and expel resident aliens suspected of being engaged in subversive activities. The Federalist press fervently hoped that advantage would be taken of these powers to initiate wholesale deportations. But both measures disappointed the expectations of their sponsors. The Alien Enemies Act never became operative during Adams' administration because the expected war with France failed to materialize. The Alien Friends Act, too, remained a dead letter during the two years it was on the statute book, though this was due less to the administration's reluctance to use it than to the discovery that it was extremely difficult to enforce. Nevertheless the Alien Friends Act was not entirely without effect. Fearing that the measure would be invoked against them, several shiploads of Frenchmen left the United States in the summer of 1798 for France and Santo Domingo.

The most notorious of the 1798 measures, the Sedition Act, was not directed exclusively against immigrants. But foreign-born journalists and pamphleteers figured largely among those whom the Federalists wished to silence—not surprisingly in view of the belief, expressed by Abigail Adams in 1799, that "every Jacobin paper in the United States [was] edited by a Foreigner." Significantly, the first victim of the Sedition Act was Irish-born Matthew Lyon, a congressman from Vermont who was imprisoned for having libeled President Adams in a letter to a Federalist paper. The three most widely reported prosecutions under the Act concerned writers of foreign birth or ancestry. In the case of William Duane, the Irish editor of the leading Republican organ, the Philadelphia *Aurora*, the administration failed to secure a conviction. It succeeded, however, in jailing the English-born radical Thomas Cooper, who was editor of a Pennsylvania newspaper, and the Scottish pamphleteer James Thompson Callender, a man of unequaled vituperative talents who had long been a thorn in the flesh of the Federalists. Still another member of this "pack of imported scribblers," the Irishman John Daly Burk, who edited the New York *Time Piece*, escaped prosecution only by promising to leave the country, though in fact he took refuge in Virginia.

The nativist outburst of 1798 had diplomatic repercussions too. In London the American minister, Rufus King, intervened to prevent the departure for the United States of a group of Irish political prisoners whom the British government was prepared to pardon on condition that they went abroad. King had long felt that the contrast between his native New England, with its ethnic homogeneity, and the middle states, with their mixed population, was "a powerful admonition to us to observe greater caution in the admission of Foreigners among us." He accordingly informed the British government that the men implicated in the recent rebellion in Ireland would not be "a desirable acquisition to any nation." King's action was warmly approved by John Adams, who, though less unbalanced than many of his supporters, nonetheless shared their fears of immigrant disorganizers.

Ironically enough, each of these anti-foreign measures failed in its object and recoiled upon its authors. Many of the Irish rebels denied admission to the United States in 1798 found their way to America within a few years and, once there, played an important part in thwarting Rufus King's political ambitions. The Sedition Act completely failed to silence the foreign-born critics of the Federalists. Even from prison Callender was able to pour forth a stream of denunciatory articles against the Adams administration, and his writings, together with those of Duane, Cooper, and Burk, had an important influence upon the presidential election campaign of 1800. Nor was the revised Naturalization Act effective, since individual states continued to enfranchise immigrants after only one or two years' residence. Moreover, the effect of the Alien and Sedition Acts was to transform immigrant suspicions of the Federalists into implacable opposition. The Pennsylvania Germans, who had hitherto been apathetic and divided in their political views, now swung almost solidly into the Republican column; in New York, hundreds of Frenchmen who had never troubled to vote before, turned out in 1800 to cast their ballots for Jefferson.

The precise importance of the immigrant vote in bringing about the political revolution of 1800 still remains to be determined. But it may well have been decisive. Philip Livingston believed that Jefferson owed his majority in New York City to the votes of the Irish and French in the sixth and seventh wards; and New York was the hinge upon which the whole election turned.

To the more percipient members of the defeated party, like Alexander Hamilton, the election of 1800 gave clear notice that if Federalism was to survive it must come to terms with immigrant voters. It was evidently this necessity that led Hamilton in 1802 to describe the Naturalization Act of 1798 as "merely a temporary measure adopted under peculiar circumstances," and to approve the action of Congress in restoring the five-year residential qualification. Hamilton appears to have hoped that his proposed Washington Constitutional Society would, by affording assistance to immigrants, attach them to the Federalist cause.

Whether Hamilton, had he lived, would have succeeded in this aim is extremely doubtful. He would have been faced, first, with the persistence of nativism in the very sections in which Federalism was strongest. New Englanders still continued to fear immigrant radicalism and also resented the gain in population, and thus in federal representation, which accrued to other states from immigration. To this latter circumstance, New England was increasingly ready to attribute its loss of influence within the Union; and the resulting Yankee sense of frustration led to the revival in the Hartford Convention of the 1798 proposal to exclude the foreign-born from officeholding.

No less an obstacle to Hamilton's hopes would have been the unwillingness of the foreign-born, especially the Irish, to forget the anti-foreignism of the last Federalist administration.

American Immigration

But even without these memories the Irish would have continued to favor the Republicans as the party least disposed to knuckle under to Great Britain. This was particularly so after Irish immigrants became involved in the impressment controversy. The impressment of Irish passengers from American-bound vessels during Madison's first term brought forth heated denunciations of the British from Irish-Americans and furnished an additional reason for the enthusiasm with which they greeted the War of 1812.

Yet the Republicans, though appealing to immigrant voters, retained much of the suspicion of foreigners they had once shared with the Federalists. For this reason a succession of Republican Congresses ignored Jefferson's proposal to grant immediate citizenship to newcomers and adhered steadfastly to the five-year probationary period required by the Naturalization Act of 1802. Jefferson's presidency also witnessed Republican echoes of the uneasiness the Federalists had long felt at immigrant efforts to preserve their ties of origin. In 1795 when Governor John Jay disbanded the Irish militia regiments of New York City, he was denounced by the Republicans as a tyrant. But ten years later the Republican press was again drawing attention to the threat to American unity posed by political organizations composed of citizens of different nations. Commenting upon the growing Irish character of the Tammany Society of Philadelphia, a Jeffersonian editor remarked: "We take the liberty of feeling as national as the Irish; and though on proper occasions we would not hesitate to join the hands of St. Patrick and St. Tammany, yet we feel . . . that no man can, at the same time, be of both families."

Thus, while the more partisan Federalist views on immigration disappeared along with the party which had avowed them, the doubts that had been expressed out of a concern for the national welfare survived to influence American opinion in the period of mass immigration. By 1815 Americans had to some degree reconciled the contradictory ideas that had influenced the thinking of the Revolutionary generation and had developed a clearly defined immigration policy. All who wished to come were welcome to do so; but no special inducements or privileges would be offered them. Philanthropy and a sense of mission had been tempered by a recognition of America's practical needs.

IV

The Rise of Mass Immigration, 1815-60

The extraordinary increase in immigration to the United States in the early decades of the nineteenth century was one of the wonders of the age. The huge scale of the movement and its seeming inexhaustibility captured the public imagination on both sides of the Atlantic and inspired a flood of fascinated comment. The remark of the *Democratic Review* in July, 1852, that there had been nothing to compare with the exodus in appearance "since the encampments of the Roman Empire or the tents of the crusaders" was but one expression of a sentiment that pervaded discussion at every level. The same sense of awe was apparent in newspaper accounts of the movement's progress, in the efforts of pamphleteers and publicists to trace its origin, and in the debates of legislative bodies upon its probable outcome.

This did not mean, however, that opinion was unanimous about the new phenomenon. In Europe, some people welcomed the rise of mass emigration as a much needed bloodletting and as a safety valve for discontent, but there were others who deplored a process which seemed to them to be draining the Old World of its most vigorous inhabitants. Similarly, in America opinion ranged from the excited warnings of the nativist against the menace of foreign influence to the enthusiasm of those who, like Ralph Waldo Emerson, welcomed the spectacle of "a heterogeneous population crowding in on ships from all corners of the world to the great gates of North America."

Most of the attention the movement attracted, and not a little of the disagreement it provoked, were due to a recognition of its uniqueness. Though immigration had been a familiar aspect of American development throughout the colonial period, there was no precedent for a movement of such magnitude and persistence as that which began in 1815. In the hundred years between that date and the outbreak of World War I, no fewer than thirty million people, drawn from every corner of Europe, made their way across the Atlantic. They came in a series of gigantic waves, each more powerful than the last and separated one from another only by short periods of time.

The first of these waves began soon after the close of the Napoleonic Wars, and after gathering momentum steadily during the 1830's and 1840's, reached its crest in 1854. Its progress could be followed in the immigration statistics which the federal government began to collect in 1820. In the decade of the 1820's, the number of arrivals was only 151,000; but the 1830's brought a fourfold increase to 599,000. This figure was in turn dwarfed by the 1,713,000 immigrants of the 1840's; even more staggering was an immigration of 2,314,000 in the 1850's. Later on, the figures would climb to still greater heights, but in assessing the impact of this first great wave one should bear in mind the comparative smallness of the American population. The five million immigrants of the period 1815–60 were greater in number than the entire population of the United States at the time of the first census in 1790. Moreover, the three million who arrived in the single decade 1845–54 landed in a country of only about twenty million inhabitants and thus represented, in proportion to the total population, the largest influx the United States has ever known.

Though every country in Europe was represented to some degree in this pre–Civil War movement, the overwhelming majority of immigrants came from areas north of the Alps and west of the Elbe. Over half of the total of five million had been born in the British Isles, two million of them in Ireland and a further three-quarters of a million in England, Wales, and Scotland. Germany was the next largest contributor with a million and a half, though to this total must be added a large proportion of the 200,000 immigrants listed as Frenchmen, most of whom were in fact German-speaking people from Alsace and Lorraine. No other country sent anything like as large a number, the only ones to send sizable contingents being Switzerland with 40,000, Norway and Sweden also with 40,000, and the Netherlands with 20,000.

Comprehension of the causes of this vast movement must begin with a recognition of their complexity. To attempt to explain mass immigration by means of an all-embracing formula, or by a mere listing of European discontents, or again by a graph tracing the fluctuations of the trade cycle would be to miss its deeper significance. One must insist, first, on the infinitely varied motives of the immigrants. The "push" and "pull" of impersonal economic forces must certainly be part of the answer, but no less important were the hopes, fears, and dreams of millions of individual immigrants. Moreover, it is an error to imagine that emigration conditions were identical in every part of Europe. The situation which resulted in emigration from Ireland, for example, was quite different from that which uprooted people in England, while the German movement owed much to forces which were unknown in the British Isles. Emigration derived some of its sweep from local and temporary influences and consequently changed in character with variations in time and place. Then, too, there is a point beyond which economics and politics can no longer serve as guides to the understanding of mass movements. It was no accident that so many contemporaries spoke of emigration as a kind of fever, as mysterious in its origin as the cholera epidemics which periodically ravaged the land. The movement bore in fact a distinct air of irrationality, even of frenzy, and many of those who took part in it were simply carried along by a force they did not understand.

Having made these qualifications, one can nevertheless single out a number of social and economic factors which underlay the movement as a whole and which gave it most of its impetus. The first of these was the doubling of the population of Europe in the century after 1750. This unprecedented increase was due in the first instance to a sharp decline in the mortality rate resulting from improved medical and sanitary knowledge and the absence of serious plagues. Other contributory factors were the greatly increased food supply made possible by the introduction of improved farming methods and by the adoption of the potato as the staple diet of the European peasant. With hunger and disease in retreat, population increased by leaps and bounds, though the full extent of the increase could only be guessed at before official censuses were instituted in the early nineteenth century.

Population increase was not in itself a cause of emigration; it served merely to accentuate the effect of other changes which at the same time were transforming the social and economic life of western Europe. The most striking transformation of all resulted from the growth of the factory system. Originating in England in the middle of the eighteenth century and spreading from there to the Continent, the Industrial Revolution destroyed the old system of domestic manufacture and threw countless artisans out of employment. In Great Britain many displaced artisans moved to nearby factory towns to become wage-laborers, but a considerable number preferred emigration to America as a means of "perpetuating a rural existence." From Germany there was an even greater exodus of handicraftsmen, for the factories which had deprived them of work were not near at hand but in England. Indirectly, too, industrialism was to prove a spur to emigration in that it bound the urban worker more closely to the trade cycle and thus subjected him to repeated periods of unemployment. At such times emigration was for many the only alternative, if not to starvation, then at least to a narrowing range of opportunities.

An equally important change was the fundamental reorganization of rural economy resulting from the rise of large-scale scientific farming. The expansion of urban markets for foodstuffs called for changes in the system of cultivation and especially for the application of new agricultural techniques to large units of land. These changes appeared in a variety of forms; in England and Scandinavia in the enclosure movement, in Ireland and southwest Germany in the consolidation of estates and the transition from arable to pasture, and in the

Scottish Highlands in the conversion of farm land to sheep runs. But the social effects were everywhere the same. The old communal system of agriculture was replaced by modern large-scale production, and a large proportion of the rural population was cut loose from the soil. Nor were these displaced people the only ones affected. Because of the competition of large-scale agriculture the small farmer's difficulties multiplied and his hold on the land weakened. As for his children, only emigration offered an alternative to a reduction in status to the rank of a paid laborer.

Though economic factors predominated as causes of emigration, the influence of political and religious discontent cannot be entirely ignored. During the first half of the nineteenth century Europe witnessed a succession of political upheavals, each of which produced a wave of exiles. Some of them chose to remain in Europe in order to continue their revolutionary activities from a convenient base, but a considerable proportion made their way to the New World. By far the largest group to do so came with the failure of the revolutions of 1848 in Germany, Italy, and Austria-Hungary and the simultaneous collapse of the Young Ireland movement. Even before this the United States had granted political asylum to a motley group which included German *Burschenschaften* fleeing from the tyranny that followed the liberal demonstrations at Wartburg and Hambach, Polish and French refugees of the 1830 revolutions, and disappointed English and Scottish Chartists. Yet these earlier victims of political unrest came in mere handfuls, and even the Forty-eighters numbered only a few thousand. In short, political exiles accounted for only a tiny proportion of the total immigration of the period.

Many contemporaries in the United States tended nevertheless to attribute immigration largely to the political attraction of their country. But the falsity of this belief was evident even at the time to the more perspicacious observers of the movement. As a Belgian commentator remarked in 1846:

The influence of American institutions acts in a very indirect way upon European immigration. When the immigrants are established in the United States, they often eagerly take advantage of the privileges that are offered them; but they did not leave their native villages to seek political rights in another hemisphere. The time of the Puritans and of William Penn is past. Theories of social reform have given way to a practical desire for immediate well-being.

While religious factors alone were hardly ever responsible for emigration, they were nonetheless a significant element. They were particularly important in stimulating emigration from regions which had hitherto contributed little to the outgoing stream. Thus emigration from Norway to the United States originated in part in the anxiety of Stavanger Quakers to escape persecution at the hands of the official clergy; that from Holland stemmed in some degree from the discontent of seceders from the Dutch Reformed Church at the numerous petty annoyances to which they were subjected; and the beginning of a movement from Prussia in the 1830's can be partly attributed to the reluctance of the Old Lutherans to conform to the United Evangelical Church. Yet in all these cases religious discontent was blended with economic pressure, and one can safely say that the prospect of earthly ease was a stronger stimulus to emigration than that of heavenly bliss.

Spiritual and secular influences are more difficult to separate, however, in the case of Mormon emigrants from Great Britain and Scandinavia. While they were not unaware of the economic benefits that awaited them in the Great Salt Lake Valley, European Mormons thought of emigration as the natural consequence of conversion. With faith in the distinctive doctrine of gathering, they moved to Zion in order to live in peace, prosperity, and righteousness while they awaited the coming millennium.

No matter how it originated, discontent with existing European conditions was invariably heightened by awareness of American opportunity. The astonishing increase in popular knowledge of the United States in the early decades of the nineteenth century must rank as one of the most important influences contributing to the rise of mass immigration. The spread of public education greatly enlarged the influence of the printed word and, with the appearance of a vast flood of literature relating to the New World, the common man's ignorance and misconceptions of American geography, economic life, and institutions began to be dispelled. Books like Morris Birkbeck's *Letters from Illinois* (1818), Gottfried Duden's *Bericht über eine Reise nach den westlichen Staaten Nord Amerikas* (1829), and Ole Rynning's *True Account of America* (1838), with their descriptions of pioneer life in the West, enjoyed an immense vogue. In addition there were scores of emigrant guidebooks, compiled by travelers, land and shipping agents, and philanthropic societies, giving details of wages, prices, crops, climate, and topography in different parts of the Union. Hardly less important as a source of information were the new cheap newspapers, most of which ran regular emigration features. Indeed, so intense was the interest in emigration that there were even a number of journals, like the *Allgemeine Auswanderungs-Zeitung* of Rudolstadt, devoted exclusively to the subject. Yet it is probable that none of this printed matter was as influential as the innumerable "America letters" written by immigrants to relatives and friends at home. These communications, at once more personal and more reliable than books and newspapers, not only spoke in glowing terms of the high wages, abundant lands, and equal opportunities that America offered but contained a wealth of advice, information, and warning appropriate to the recipient's needs.

If increasing knowledge of American opportunity contributed to the emigrant's decision to leave Europe, the state of the American economy largely determined the time of his departure. The relative strength of expulsive and attractive forces naturally varied with time and place, but statistical studies have made it clear that, except in periods of unusual disaster or unrest in Europe, a close connection existed between American economic conditions and cyclical fluctuations in the flow of immigration. Periods of depression in the United States tended to be closely followed by a decline in immigration; periods of prosperity by an increase. This was less true, perhaps, of the years before the Civil War than it became subsequently, for in the earlier period immigrants responded as much to the lure of free land as to job opportunities. But the sharp falling-off of immigration after the panics of 1819, 1837, and 1857 shows that from the beginning of the movement the "pull" was a stronger influence than the "push."

Emigration from Europe was not, however, synonymous with immigration to America. Of those uprooted from their European homes in the decades after 1815 only a proportion came to the United States. It is probable that for the majority emigration involved simply a move to another part of Europe. In addition to the vast numbers who became city-dwellers without crossing any national boundaries, a considerable number chose to emigrate to other European countries. Thus 250,-000 Germans are estimated to have settled in southern Russia between 1818 and 1828; in the same period German immigration to the United States hardly exceeded 10,000. Then again, until the Irish Famine there was almost as much Irish immigration to Great Britain as there was to the United States; even as late as 1850 Great Britain had 727,000 Irish-born residents compared with 926,000 in America. There was, moreover, a substantial movement from Europe to British North America, Australia, and South America. Though none of these places attracted as large an immigration as did the United States, each had a peculiar appeal to certain groups. In the 1820's, for example, more Germans went to Brazil than to the United States; until 1832 most Irish immigrants to the New World landed in Canada and the Maritime Provinces, though not all of them stayed there; and in the early 1850's Australia was the destination of the bulk of English emigrants.

The phenomenon of mass immigration could not, of course, have occurred at all had the growing desire to move not been accompanied by greater freedom and ability to do so. Hence the removal of restrictions on emigration and the development of cheap ocean transportation were no less important than were the growth of European discontent and the spread of knowledge concerning America. The change in official attitudes to emigration came first in Great Britain. Within little more than a decade of 1815, the old mercantilist policy of outright opposition was completely abandoned. The repeal in 1825 of the laws prohibiting artisan emigration was not only a belated recognition of their ineffectiveness but an official indorsement of the view that the country was overpopulated. That all the remaining restrictions on emigration were removed in 1827 was a measure of the alarm aroused by the rising volume of Irish immigration into Great Britain. If the Irish were not allowed to depart freely for the New World, a parliamentary committee warned in 1826, they would "deluge Great Britain with poverty and wretchedness, and gradually but certainly . . . equalize the state of the English and Irish peasantry." To be sure, halfhearted attempts continued to be made for some time longer to encourage emigrants to go to British North America rather than to the United States, but with the waning of interest in colonies during the 1830's and 1840's, complete laissez faire came to prevail.

In Germany opposition took somewhat longer to dissolve. Though absolute prohibition was not attempted after the 1820's, emigration continued still to be officially frowned upon, and as late as 1836 the American consul at Bremen could report:

The different governments of Germany are, in general, not much pleased with the spirit of emigration since several years predominant in Germany, and, as is said, try by all means to keep their subjects at home. The emigrants often loudly and bitterly complain that the said Governments, before they give to people permission to depart, put as many obstacles as possible in their way.

But after the 1848 revolutions the German authorities reversed their attitude. Hopeful that emigration might prevent renewed outbreaks of disorder, they jettisoned the multitude of regulations which had hitherto hindered departure. Legal formalities were simplified, and although the obligation to perform military service remained, it became increasingly easy to evade.

In Sweden the law of 1768 restricting the right of emigration was repealed in 1840, mainly because of the need to meet the growing problem of pauperism. Though in 1843 the Swedish-Norwegian government appointed a commission to investigate emigration from Norway and to consider regulatory measures, it announced that it did "not want to hinder the emigration or to make it more difficult." By the mid-nineteenth century the thesis of overpopulation was universally accepted in Scandinavia, and with the virtual abolition of passport regulation in 1860, the last serious obstacle to departure was removed.

Before a mass movement could actually take place, however, a transportation revolution would be necessary in order to provide prospective emigrants with what had hitherto been lacking, namely, a regular, reliable, and inexpensive Atlantic crossing. In the years immediately after 1815 a revolution of this kind was brought about by an unprecedented expansion of transatlantic commerce. The most striking new development was the rise of the North American timber trade. After the close of the Napoleonic Wars, the Baltic countries gave way to Canada and the Maritime Provinces as the main source of British timber, and a vast quantity of British tonnage found new employment. As early as 1820 more than a thousand vessels were annually employed in carrying North American timber to the British Isles, and twenty years later that number had more than doubled. Simultaneously there was an astonishing increase in the amount of tonnage engaged in transporting to Europe the staple products of the United States. By the 1830's the number of freighters carrying American cotton annually to Liverpool had risen to more than a thousand, compared with only three hundred some twenty years earlier; and there were comparable increases in the amount of shipping taking cotton and tobacco from the United States to Le Havre and Bremen, respectively. On the eastward voyage across the Atlantic the timber, cotton, and tobacco vessels were generally fully laden, but when sailing in the opposite direction much of their cargo space was unoccupied, since the European manufactures they carried were much less bulky than American raw materials. With space thus available for passengers, merchants and shipowners came to look to emigrants to provide part of the return freight. In a short time the emigrant trade became a highly organized and lucrative branch of transatlantic commerce. The passenger broker made his appearance to serve as intermediary between shipowners and emigrants, and in consequence of his activities a vast network of agencies came into being to tap the emigrant stream at its various sources.

In its earliest years the emigrant trade flourished at practically every port in northwest Europe with a New World connection. Because of the difficulties and expense of overland travel in early nineteenth-century Europe, emigrants generally preferred to embark at the ports nearest to their homes. This circumstance largely accounted for the popularity with emigrants of the timber vessels, which offered passage from a score of Irish ports and from more than fifty in England, Wales, and Scotland. It explained, too, why emigrants were regularly to be found traveling on the tiny brigs which took out Welsh slate or Swedish iron to the United States. But with the improvement of European internal communications brought about by railroads and coastal steamships, the trade became gradually concentrated at the larger ports, where vessels were bigger and faster and were organized into lines so as to sail in succession on regular schedules. Liverpool became the main port of departure for the Irish and British, as well as for considerable numbers of Germans and Norwegians. On the Continent, Le Havre, Bremen, and Hamburg fought for supremacy, each port attracting to itself a portion of the movement from Germany, Switzerland, and Scandinavia. As a result of intensive competition between these ports and between brokers in each of them, fares everywhere came tumbling down. At Liverpool the cost of steerage passage to New York fell from twelve pounds in 1816 to just over three pounds thirty years later; at Le Havre the rate to New Orleans dropped from between 350 and 400 francs in 1818 to between 120 and 150 francs in the early thirties. While comparable reductions occurred elsewhere, the drop was nowhere as great or as abrupt as in Irish ports, where passage to Quebec during the 1820's could commonly be obtained for as little as thirty shillings, or only one-tenth of the rate prevailing a decade before.

Nor was this the only way in which commercial developments facilitated emigration. Since many of those engaged in the emigrant trade had personal or business connections with the United States, they were able in the late 1820's to establish American agencies for the sale of prepaid passage tickets. This enabled those who had immigrated earlier to bring over their relatives and friends, and the arrival of tickets and money from America proved an additional stimulus to emigration generally. What proportion of immigrants traveled on prepaid tickets is not known, though a sample survey conducted by the Irish Emigrant Society of New York in 1843 suggested that it might have been as high as one-third. This estimate did not, however, take into account the great numbers who, though not in receipt of prepaid tickets, had paid their fares with remittances from America.

American Immigration

Cheaper and easier to obtain though it might be, the Atlantic crossing nevertheless remained an undertaking fraught with considerable hardship and danger. Until the Civil War the immigrant trade was virtually monopolized by sailing vessels, with the result that the crossing still took between one and three months, according to the state of wind and weather. Moreover, though the vessels employed in it steadily improved in soundness of construction, sailing qualities, and seaworthiness, they remained primarily freight carriers hastily converted for passenger carrying at the beginning of each westbound voyage. Steerage quarters were in consequence cramped and ill-ventilated, sanitary arrangements were crude, and cooking facilities entirely inadequate. Although governments on both sides of the Atlantic attempted to improve conditions by enacting a series of passenger laws, these could be only partly enforced, and the evils of overcrowding and inadequate food persisted until the coming of the steamship. At every stage of the journey, moreover, the bewildered immigrant was swindled, imposed upon, and ill-treated, the victim successively of dishonest passenger brokers and their runners, lodging-house keepers, and unscrupulous ship captains. Nor was this all he had to endure, for at times ship fever and cholera broke out at sea, carrying off scores of passengers and leaving hundreds of others enfeebled.

Yet historians have tended both to exaggerate the incidence of disease on immigrant ships and to misunderstand the reasons for its occurrence. The frightful ship fever epidemic of 1847 which caused thousands of deaths among Irish immigrants and the equally severe but smaller-scale outbreaks of cholera in 1832 and 1853–54 were altogether exceptional; in every other year most ships arrived with a clean bill of health, and the

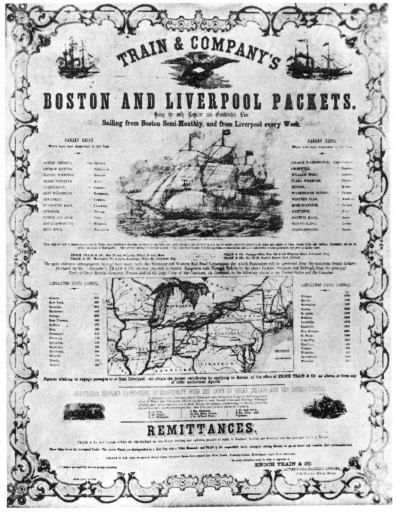

An advertising poster of Enoch Train's White Diamond Line of Boston and Liverpool Emigrant Packets, 1854. (Courtesy of the Second Bank–State Street Trust Company, Boston, Mass.)

Irish and German immigrants being recruited for the Union army at Castle Garden, 1864. (Courtesy of the Mansell Collection, London.)

mortality rate during the passage only rarely rose above one-half of 1 per cent. Moreover, the great epidemic outbreaks, on which so much emphasis has been placed, originated not in bad conditions on the ships but in the fact that immigrants were infected before they embarked. Overcrowding and lack of sanitation, not to speak of the reluctance of the immigrants themselves to co-operate in establishing minimum standards of hygiene, undoubtedly added to the virulence of an epidemic once it had started, but the real cause of the trouble lay in contemporary ignorance of epidemiology. So long as medicine remained ignorant of the causes of typhus and cholera, these diseases would continue to appear at sea and on land alike, as indeed they did long after the steamship had ousted the sailing vessel from the immigrant trade.

Though emigration had now become financially possible for a poorer class than ever before, it would be wrong to conclude that the movement we have been considering consisted wholly of the impoverished. If generalization were possible about a movement so far-ranging, protracted, and diverse, one might say that it consisted rather of people who feared a future loss of status rather than of those already reduced to the last extremity of want. But so greatly did the personnel of migration vary at different times and in different areas that one can arrive at a general picture only by considering briefly the special influences determining the character of emigration from each of the countries concerned.

Nowhere was economic change better calculated to promote large-scale emigration than in Ireland. In 1815 Ireland had a population density greater than anywhere else in Europe and, granted the existing agrarian structure, it was grossly overpopulated. An iniquitous land system characterized by absentee landlordism, rack-renting, and insecurity of tenure kept the mass of the population chained to the margin of subsistence. Increasing competition for land had led to the subdivision of holdings into tiny plots which precluded efficient farming and limited the peasant's activities to the cultivation of rent-paying crops and of the potato, upon which he relied almost wholly for food. Though in consequence the condition of Irish agriculture had long been deteriorating, the landlords decided to act only when a change in the agricultural situation after 1815 affected their personal interests. The collapse of grain prices after the Napoleonic Wars and the unrestricted opening of the British market to Irish provisions in 1826 pointed the need to convert land from arable to pasture, a process necessarily involving the amalgamation and clearing of estates for large-scale operations. Moreover, the disfranchisement of the forty-shilling freeholder in 1829 gave a further stimulus to the process of clearance. Until now, landlords had allowed small freeholds to multiply so as to increase the number of votes they controlled. Henceforth, there were to be no political motives for subdivision.

Until about 1830 the majority of Irish immigrants were small farmers whose burden of rent, tithes, and taxes had become intolerable owing to competition from large-scale agriculture. As in the eighteenth century, the bulk of these smallholders came from Ulster, where the tradition of emigration was long-established and where the custom of tenant right provided outgoing lessees with a capital which frequently supplied the means of crossing the Atlantic. But in the 1830's a significant change occurred in the character of the movement. The wholesale clearance of estates, accelerated after the Irish

The Rise of Mass Immigration, 1815–60

Poor Law Act of 1838 had placed additional burdens on the landlords, led to a large-scale emigration of cottiers—that is, smallholders—and laborers from every part of Ireland, especially from the south and west. In a number of cases landlords combined eviction with financial aid to emigrate, but for the most part the evicted had to rely on their own meager resources. What commonly happened was that families sent their younger and more able-bodied members to America in the confident hope, which only rarely was disappointed, that in a short while money would be remitted to finance the removal of those who had remained.

While the number of departures steadily increased throughout the 1830's and early 1840's, it was not until the Great Famine that the floodgates finally opened and the exodus attained epic proportions. The successive potato blights of 1845–49, leading as they did to untold deaths from starvation and fever and to appalling physical suffering even for those who survived, were a catastrophe which finally broke the Irish peasant's tenacious attachment to the soil and convinced many of the futility of further struggle against hopeless odds. As an Irish peer remarked at the time, the famine had reversed the peasant's former attitude to emigration; hitherto considered a banishment, it now came to be regarded as a happy release. The prevailing mood of despair gripped not only the laborer and the cottier but even those who in famine Ireland passed for substantial farmers. Thus all classes were represented in the million and a half people who left Ireland in the decade that followed. The panic-stricken flight from hunger that occurred in 1847 was followed by a more deliberate and sustained movement that continued even after the return of relative prosperity in the early 1850's. By now, the tide had set inexorably toward the west, and for many decades the continuing effects of the famine were to be seen in the flow of Irish emigrants into the United States.

In its general outlines the pattern of emigration from Germany closely resembled that from Ireland. Slowly gathering momentum throughout the 1830's, it reached its peak during the decade 1846–55, when more than a million Germans entered the United States. The belief that German emigration was a consequence of the failure of the 1848 uprisings and consisted largely of political refugees is now known to be a myth. Only a few thousand Forty-eighters came to America, and the great mass of German immigrants were, in Marcus Hansen's phrase, from "classes which had been little concerned with politics and with revolution not at all." Though virtually the whole of Germany was shaken by political disturbances in 1848, the overwhelming majority of emigrants, both before that date and after, came from the states of the southwest, especially Württemberg, Baden, and Bavaria, where, in contrast to the rest of Germany, small agricultural holdings predominated. After 1815 the peasants in these areas had mortgaged their farms in order to be able to modernize them, but in the 1840's crop failures and the diversion of credit from agriculture to more profitable fields like railroad-building had plunged great numbers into financial difficulties, thus swelling the volume of departures. Furthermore, while the emancipation laws passed after 1848 improved the peasant's legal status, they added to his economic difficulties by requiring annual cash payments in lieu of former feudal obligations. When, therefore, further crop failures occurred in the early 1850's, countless small farmers were ruined. Mortgage foreclosures and forced sales rose to unprecedented levels, and tens of thousands of the dispossessed made their way to America. Even greater numbers, perhaps, decided not to wait until disaster overtook them but resolved to go while something could still be obtained for their property. Not until the later 1850's, when the agricultural transformation was virtually complete and consolidated farms had supplanted the patchwork of small holdings, did the German exodus begin to lose momentum.

Though the typical German immigrant of the mid-nineteenth century was thus the small farmer, he by no means monopolized the movement to the exclusion of other social and economic groups. There was, for example, a substantial sprinkling of really wealthy farmers whom the prevailing economic difficulties barely touched but who considered the future of German agriculture to be so unpromising that they chose to migrate with their capital to the cheap and fertile acres of the New World. At the other end of the social scale were the paupers sent out annually at the expense of state and municipal authorities anxious to reduce the burden of poor relief. The practice of dumping undesirables went on continuously from the early 1830's, but it was never as widespread as many Americans believed. In response to congressional inquiries on the subject in 1836, American consuls in Germany reported that, while paupers and even criminals were being regularly shipped out by various towns and communes, only a few hundred undesirables were annually involved. Pauper immigration was in fact completely overshadowed by that of artisans, tradesmen, and professional people, who had figured continuously in the German movement from its early stages and who departed in unprecedented numbers after depression and revolution had combined by the middle of the century to cast a blight over every form of activity. The uncertainty of the times, in short, found expression in a general restlessness which resulted in emigration becoming the panacea of every class.

Probably because of the ease with which they merged with the native American population, the British immigrants of 1815–60 received less attention from contemporaries than their numbers warranted. The British influx never attained the proportions of those from Germany and Ireland; but it nonetheless totaled three-quarters of a million and accounted for about one-sixth of all the arrivals in the United States during the period. British immigration was more diverse in origin than that from any other area, with no one social or economic group predominating. It regularly included, from the late 1820's onward, a significant proportion of skilled laborers. Lancashire calico-printers, Yorkshire woolen operatives, Scottish carpet-weavers, coal-miners from Wales, the Midlands, and Scotland, Cornish copper- and lead-miners, Staffordshire potters and iron-puddlers, and Welsh stonecutters—all were represented in the outgoing stream, especially during times of depression and unemployment such as occurred during the early 1840's. But with American industrialization still in its early stages, opportunities for such men remained comparatively limited, and it was not until after the Civil War that a flood of British skilled labor poured in.

Although the exodus included also a great number of unskilled workers from the towns, the majority of British immigrants during this period probably consisted of farmers and agricultural laborers. As in Germany, some of those who went were farmers possessing large amounts of capital. The best-known was Morris Birkbeck, who in 1817 sold his property in Surrey and emigrated with a capital of £18,000 and a large quantity of prize livestock to Illinois, where he hoped to establish an English colony. Birkbeck was probably unique in his wealth but, as William Cobbett remarked after observing emigration from Lincolnshire in 1830, many farmers left for America with between £200 and £2,000 in their pockets. Yet it is probable that such men were much less important numerically than smallholders, who found agriculture increasingly unprofitable in the face of large-scale competition and who believed, however wrongly, that the repeal of the Corn Laws in 1846 implied the imminent doom of English farming. The largest stream of all, however, consisted of agricultural laborers whom economic change had plunged into redundancy and pauperism. In many English parishes, particularly in the southern and eastern counties, the ratepayers found it cheaper to promote the emigration of the agricultural poor than to continue supporting them at home. So far as the United States was concerned, this type of immigration was most common during the decade or so preceding 1834. Though the Poor Law Amendment Act of that year authorized parishes to mortgage the rates in order to subsidize emigration, it also stipulated that the assisted were in future to be sent to a British colony.

Emigration from Norway began with the departure of the celebrated "sloop party" from Stavanger in 1825. After this, however, there was no further Norwegian emigration for more than a decade, and it was not until the 1840's that the movement really began to gather momentum. Contemporary writers often attributed the exodus to religious discontent; it is a fact that many immigrants sympathized with the pietistic movement known as Haugeanism in its struggle with the state church and some of them were members of minor dissenting sects, such as the Quakers. But, as elsewhere, the underlying causes of emigration were primarily economic. Historians of the Norwegian movement tell a familiar story of rapidly increasing population and of lands being subdivided until holdings became too small to support those who cultivated them. Under these circumstances a large proportion of Norwegian emigrants consisted of *bønder*, or freeholders, who saw in emigration the only alternative to a drop in status. But as the movement developed, it drew in its wake increasing proportions both of *husmänd*, or cotters, and of laborers and servants.

The first appreciable nineteenth-century emigration from Holland to America began in 1846, when a number of clergymen, who had earlier seceded from the official Reformed Church, led groups of their followers to western Michigan and central Iowa. The movement's clerical leadership, and the fact that even in the fifties a large proportion of those who left Holland for America were *Afgescheidenen*, or Seceders, has led some students to point to religious discontent as its cause. But it is significant that the Seceders, who had been steadily persecuted ever since the middle 1830's, began to think of emigrating only when the potato blight of 1845–46 intensified a long-standing agricultural depression originating in excessive competition for land. The same period, moreover, saw the departure for Wisconsin of groups of Dutch Catholics who had experienced no religious difficulties in Holland but who resembled the Seceders in belonging to that same class of small farmers which furnished the earliest emigrants from practically every European country.

Yet immigration to the United States in the pre–Civil War period did not consist wholly of Europeans. Though statistics of overland arrivals are lacking, at least a quarter of a million people born in British America settled in the United States between 1815 and 1860. Up to the late 1830's the number of

Canadian immigrants was inconsiderable and was in any case canceled out by a similar, small-scale American movement to Canada. But after about 1837 the tide turned definitely in favor of the United States. In the van of the new movement were a number of political refugees who moved after the abortive Canadian rebellions of 1837 and 1838. A much larger group were those who were obliged to leave the Maritime Provinces when Britain's free-trade measures of the 1840's brought depression to the region's timber, shipbuilding, and provision trades. The largest exodus of all, however, was from the province of Quebec where a rapidly growing French-Canadian population was experiencing increasing difficulty in obtaining land, the unoccupied portion of which had fallen into the hands of speculators. Since Canada had no Middle West of her own, great numbers crossed the border into Michigan, Illinois, or Wisconsin; "the Laurentian Shield," as Marcus Hansen has pointed out, "deflected Canadian expansion to the south of Lake Huron and Lake Superior." But other French-Canadians went to northern New York and New England either to become farm laborers or lumbermen or to work in brickyards or textile mills.

Whether from the New World or the Old, immigrants to the United States resembled each other in traveling usually as individuals and relying wholly upon their own resources. This was not, it must be remembered, a universal characteristic of nineteenth-century migration. The contemporary British movement to Australia, for example, remained very largely a government-directed and government-financed enterprise, at least until the gold rush of the early fifties. To be sure, a great many agencies were engaged in promoting emigration to America too. As we have seen, English ratepayers, Irish landlords, and German municipalities furnished the financial aid necessary to enable various groups to depart. A number of British trade unions did likewise in an effort to rid particular industries of surplus labor. American employers, too, occasionally paid the passages of skilled workers whose services they were anxious to secure, while emigration societies, like those composed of unemployed Scottish weavers in the 1820's or of Staffordshire potters in the 1840's, appealed successfully to public benevolence for the means to finance their members' departure. Finally, the Mormon church established a Perpetual Emigrating Fund in 1850 in order to transport its poorer European converts to the Great Salt Lake Valley.

Yet the number and variety of such agencies should not be allowed to obscure the fact that, even in aggregate, they dispatched only a small fraction of the immigrants who arrived in the United States during this period. The mass immigration of the nineteenth century originated as a self-directed, unassisted movement, and this character it retained throughout. Here lies a key to the patterns both of distribution and of adjustment. That immigrants moved almost entirely as individuals or in family groups, that they received virtually no aid or direction, and that they were subject to control neither by European nor by American agencies or governments would largely determine their destination in the New World and the nature of their reaction to it.

Patterns of Distribution and of
Adjustment, 1815-60

The census of 1860 revealed that out of a total population of almost 31.5 million, the United States had 4,136,000 foreign-born inhabitants. The great bulk lived north of Mason and Dixon's line and east of the Mississippi, the largest numbers being found in New York, Pennsylvania, Ohio, Illinois, Wisconsin, and Massachusetts, in that order. The fifteen slave states had only about half a million foreign-born residents, or 13.4 per cent of the total, and of them nearly all lived in the four states of Missouri, Maryland, Louisiana, and Texas. In North and South alike the heaviest concentration of immigrants was found in the cities. New York, Chicago, Cincinnati, Milwaukee, Detroit, and San Francisco each had a population of which almost one-half was foreign-born; in New Orleans, Baltimore, and Boston the proportion was well over one-third; and in St. Louis it was more than three-fifths.

American Immigration

Between the different ethnic groups there were significant variations in distribution. Nearly two-thirds of the 1,611,000 Irish were to be found in New York, Pennsylvania, New Jersey, and New England, though there were large numbers in practically every city of any size from San Francisco to Boston, and from New Orleans to Chicago. The 1,301,000 Germans were somewhat more evenly distributed, but there were practically none in New England and more than one-half resided in the upper Mississippi and Ohio valleys, especially in the states of Ohio, Illinois, Wisconsin, and Missouri. The British-born were still more widely dispersed; practically every northern state had a share of the total of the 587,775 people born in England, Scotland, and Wales. Those born in British America, who numbered 249,970, were concentrated in the states immediately south of the St. Lawrence and the Great Lakes; more than one-half were in New York, Michigan, Wisconsin, and Illinois, and most of the remainder were in the six New England states. The smaller immigrant groups were even more highly concentrated. More than half the 43,995 Norwegians had settled in Wisconsin, and virtually all the rest were in Minnesota, Iowa, and Illinois. Likewise, of the 28,281 Dutch nearly two-thirds were in Michigan, New York, Wisconsin, and Iowa.

Analysis of the influences which determined immigrant distribution in the United States may begin with the fact, already noted, that the overwhelming mass of newcomers came on their own initiative and without assistance. A great many immigrants were completely without resources once they had paid their fares and, on reaching America, were immobilized by their poverty. The authorities in every immigrant port from Boston to New Orleans constantly complained that,

while the more prosperous and able-bodied dispersed throughout the country, the more helpless and destitute remained
wherever they happened to disembark. The complaint was
exaggerated but it had considerable basis in fact.

An equally important circumstance was the tendency for
immigrant routes to follow the paths of ocean commerce. The
Irish concentration in New England, for example, was largely
a product of the New Brunswick timber trade. Irishmen who
wanted to reach the United States often found that the cheap-
est and most convenient method was to take passage first in
vessels going out for timber to St. John or St. Andrew's. Here
the journey could be cheaply continued in one of the numerous
coasting vessels employed in carrying plaster of Paris from
the Maritime Provinces to Boston, Providence, and other New
England ports. But this was not the only method of entry, for
many pioneer Irishmen made their way from New Brunswick
into New England on foot, settling wherever employment
could be obtained and acting as nuclei around which Irish
settlements could grow. Likewise it was the Le Havre cotton
trade which helped give a German coloring to parts of the
Mississippi Valley. Most of the Germans seeking passage from
Le Havre had perforce to go to New Orleans, but as there
were excellent steamboat services up the Mississippi and its
tributaries, it was an easy matter to reach St. Louis and Cincinnati, both of which became in consequence strongholds of
German culture.

In many cases an immigrant's location was determined by
the occupational skill he brought with him from Europe.
Skilled industrial workers tended to congregate in the American centers of their crafts. Thus one found Welsh miners in
the anthracite coalfields of eastern Pennsylvania and Cornish

miners in the Wisconsin and Illinois lead region as well as in copper and iron mines of Michigan. For similar reasons Staffordshire potters made almost invariably for East Liverpool, Ohio, or Trenton, New Jersey, Welsh quarrymen for the slate areas of Vermont, New York, and Pennsylvania, and British textile workers could be found wherever cottons and woolens, silks, hosiery, and carpeting were manufactured in the United States. In the same way the wide dispersal of German Jews in the United States was directly traceable to their having been predominantly petty tradesmen and professional men.

Agricultural skills, by contrast, could not always be put to use in America. For one thing, not every immigrant farmer possessed the capital needed to embark on American agriculture; for another, the techniques of European farming differed from those required in the New World. Particularly was this so on the frontier, where conditions were unfamiliar to the European and where specialized training in the use of the ax and the rifle was an essential prerequisite of survival, let alone of success. Only rarely, therefore, did immigrants become frontiersmen or pioneer farmers; instead, their role in the westward movement was to take over farms which had already been cleared and whose original owners had moved farther west.

That the southern states attracted such a small proportion of immigrants was not due, as contemporaries sometimes thought, to the European's moral aversion to slavery. If the presence of the Negro served at all to keep white immigrants away from the slave states, it was rather because they disliked and despised him. But the fundamental reason why the South was so largely shunned was that it could offer neither the employment opportunities nor the facilities for obtaining land that were available in the free states. The unfamiliarity of the southern climate was probably a further deterrent, as was the fact that, except from Le Havre, passage to southern ports was generally more difficult to obtain than to northern ones.

For many immigrants, of course, removal to America was simply one form of participation in that country-to-town movement which was so marked a phenomenon in both Europe and America throughout the nineteenth century. But in no other group was urban concentration so complete as among the Irish. That Irishmen, though overwhelmingly of rural origin, settled so rarely on the land in the United States was for some contemporaries an inexplicable paradox. One commentator remarked in 1855 on "this strange contradictory result, that a people who hungered and thirsted for land in Ireland should have been content when they reached the New World . . . to sink into the condition of a miserable town tenantry, to whose squalors even European seaports could hardly present a parallel."

Part of the explanation lies in the poverty of the Irish, which practically ruled out the possibility of their becoming independent farmers and which made it imperative for them to obtain immediate employment on arrival. This, of course, was more readily obtainable in the towns than in rural areas. But there were other reasons. Though the Irish were generally country-dwellers, their farming experience was extremely limited, usually consisting only of potato cultivation. Then again, their experiences in Ireland, especially of the events leading to their emigration, had resulted in the land becoming for many the symbol of oppression and insecurity, of unbroken

American Immigration

want and misery. And countrymen though they were, they had been accustomed in Ireland to a gregarious existence and were unsuited by temperament and experience to the loneliness of farm life in America. Finally, as Catholics, they were reluctant to go to rural regions where churches and priests of their own faith were rarely to be found.

Numerous attempts were made, especially by members of the Catholic hierarchy, to promote Irish rural colonization in the United States. Bishop Benedict J. Fenwick of Boston established a settlement at Benedicta, Maine, during the 1830's, which he peopled with Irish Catholics residing within his diocese; Bishop Andrew Byrne of Little Rock, who had been born in Ireland, made great though largely unsuccessful efforts to plant colonies of his countrymen in Arkansas; and Bishop Mathias Loras of Dubuque founded numerous Catholic settlements, mainly Irish, in Iowa, Minnesota, and Nebraska. But the strongest advocate of Irish rural colonization was Thomas D'Arcy McGee, who had fled to America in 1848 after the collapse of the Young Ireland movement and who became editor first of the New York *Nation* and then of the *American Celt*. Seeing in rural colonization a method of elevating the moral and material condition of his countrymen and of freeing them from the Know-Nothing hostility they encountered in the eastern cities, McGee organized the Irish Catholic Colonization Convention which met at Buffalo, New York, in February, 1856. The ninety-five delegates, drawn almost equally from the United States and Canada, agreed unanimously on the necessity of removing the Irish from the demoralizing influence of the city to the open spaces of the West but proved unable to do anything to translate their wishes into action. Though the project won the support of some western members of the Catholic hierarchy, it was strongly opposed by the eastern bishops and especially by Archbishop John Hughes of New York, whose influence was so great that his opposition insured the plan's failure. Fearful lest the dispersal of the Irish should lead to a loss of faith, and not unnaturally anxious to keep his flock together, Hughes denounced the whole scheme as one devised for the benefit of western land speculators.

Just as unsuccessful as the colonization projects which aimed at breaking up the urban concentration of immigrants were those whose objective was to preserve the cultural distinctiveness and geographic isolation of particular groups. In the earliest of such schemes the Irish were once again concerned. In 1817 the Irish Emigrant Society of New York petitioned Congress to set aside part of the unsold lands in Illinois Territory for exclusive Irish settlement on extended terms of credit. But Congress saw no reason why an Irishman should be able to acquire land on easier terms than an American and was also strongly opposed to any scheme which, by permitting ethnic enclaves, threatened to slow down the process of Americanization. The only time that Congress could be prevailed upon to modify its attitude was in 1834 when it agreed to allot thirty-six sections of public land in Illinois to the refugees of the Polish revolution of 1830. Owing, however, to various delays in completing the grant the Poles dispersed to a variety of destinations and the attempt to establish a Polish colony was abandoned.

It was the Germans who were most prominently associated with attempts to preserve ethnic distinctiveness. Thwarted at home by political reaction, a number of liberals and intellectuals sought to realize the ideals of German nationalism by creating a New Germany within the borders of the American Union. "What would Philadelphia be in forty years if the Germans there were to remain German, and retain their language and customs?" asked one German in 1813. "It would . . . be a German city, just as York and Lancaster are German counties. What would be the result throughout Pennsylvania and Maryland . . . ? An entirely German state where, as formerly in Germantown, the beautiful German language would be used in the legislative halls and the courts of justice."

Such dreams, persisting for more than a generation thereafter, inspired the activities of a number of German colonization societies and other agencies. During the 1830's the *Giessener Gesellschaft* attempted to mass German immigrants along the Missouri River near St. Louis. Between 1844 and 1847 the *Adelsverein,* a colonization society founded by a group of German princes and noblemen, had similar objectives in sending thousands of German settlers to southwest Texas. In the 1850's it was hoped that by concentrating the stream of German immigration upon Wisconsin, that state might be Germanized.

Although a number of counties in each of these states became predominantly German, hopes of a New Germany in the wider sense were bound to fail. Permanent geographical isolation was out of the question in view of the speed with which the United States was being settled. But what made failure doubly sure was the fact that each venture was made in a region no less attractive and accessible to native Americans and non-German immigrants than it was to the Germans themselves. Important, too, was the opposition of German-American leaders to the New Germany idea. Men like Gustav Körner and Carl Schurz realized that German immigrants could hope neither to participate fully in American life nor to be accepted by other Americans if they insisted upon remaining a class apart.

Although, as we have emphasized, nineteenth-century immigration was predominantly a movement of individuals and families, it included a significant number of people whose location in the United States was determined by the fact that they came as members of organized groups. Among group migrations the best-known were those which resulted in the establishment of experimental communities whose members shared many things in common. Though devoted to a variety of religious, economic, ethical, and educational objectives, these communitarian settlements resembled each other in that, although they were withdrawn from the world, they hoped by their example to achieve the regeneration of society.

Communitarianism had, of course, been a feature of immigration to America long before this. From the seventeenth century onward, Labadists, Moravians, Shakers, and other persecuted European sectarians had come to settle in the New World, where their communitarian tendencies had crystallized into definite form. In the nineteenth century communitarian ideals became increasingly secularized, but the association with religion persisted and new communitarian settlements continued to be founded by immigrant religious groups consisting usually of the followers of individual mystics. George Rapp's followers established themselves at Harmony, Pennsylvania, in 1805; Joseph Baumeler led a group of Separatists to Ohio to found the community of Zoar in 1817; and six hundred Inspirationists under the leadership of Christian Metz moved in 1843 to Buffalo and later to Amana, Iowa. All these groups came directly from Germany, but in addition Wilhelm

Keil founded communitarian societies at Bethel, Missouri (1844), and at Aurora, Oregon (1856), both of which consisted of Germans who had been resident for some time in the United States. Finally the followers of the Swedish Pietist, Eric Janson, established the Bishop Hill community in Illinois in 1846.

From about 1825 onward a native communitarian movement came into existence in the United States, and during the next quarter of a century a great number of experimental communities were founded, their aim being the social rather than the religious regeneration of mankind. Only a few of the new secular communities drew personnel from abroad, but among those to do so were Robert Owen's New Harmony society, founded in Indiana in 1825, and the Icarian settlement in Texas established in 1849 by French followers of the utopian writer, Étienne Cabet. Both these ventures were short-lived, but the Owenite experiment had an important influence upon American educational methods and theories of social reform.

The largest and most successful group immigration consisted, however, not of communitarians but of Mormons. The first Mormon overseas mission was founded in England in 1837, and three years later the departure of British Saints began. Other missions were established during the 1850's in Scandinavia, Germany, and Switzerland, and by the time of the Civil War nearly 30,000 Mormons had emigrated from Great Britain and several thousand more from the Continent, especially from Scandinavia. From start to finish the movement was under close church supervision. Vessels were chartered for the exclusive conveyance of Mormon emigrants, and church officials accompanied each shipload from Liverpool to New Orleans and from there up the Mississippi. At first their destination was Nauvoo, Illinois, but after 1847, when Brigham Young led his followers to the Great Salt Lake Valley, Mormon immigrants had to make an additional thousand-mile journey on foot across the plains from Iowa. This phase of the journey was just as highly organized. Immigrants were formed into handcart companies under the leadership of experienced plainsmen, and although disaster befell two companies in the Wyoming snows of 1856, the crossings were made with remarkably little loss. Continuing beyond the Civil War, Mormon immigration was greatly facilitated by the completion of the Union Pacific Railroad in 1869, and by the end of the century, when immigration virtually stopped, the total arrivals since the movement began had risen to nearly 90,000.

Whether they came individually or in groups, whether to found communitarian societies or simply to look for jobs, immigrants faced the necessity of coming to terms with American life. Having cut themselves loose from the stable, ordered European world into which they had been born, they needed to relocate themselves in the strange new American universe. Their ability to do so was by no means uniform. It varied with the economic status and the cultural background of the newcomer himself, as well as with the economic and social structure of the regions in which he settled. Even for those whose transplantation was accomplished with a minimum of economic and psychological buffeting, the process of adjustment was painful and protracted. For all immigrants, immigration was a traumatic experience, resulting in a sense of alienation and isolation. It was nearly always the fate of the first-generation immigrant to remain a "marginal man," suspended between two cultures but belonging wholly to neither.

American Immigration

Few agencies existed to smooth the path of nineteenth-century newcomers. Until just before the Civil War immigrants could expect no help on arrival save that thrust upon them by the touts and harpies who infested the landing places. An investigating committee at New York was shocked in 1846 at the amount of outrage and fraud practiced upon newly arrived immigrants; it found "the German preying upon the German—the Irish upon the Irish—the English upon the English." The various ethnic benevolent organizations, like the Irish Emigrant Society of New York and the Deutsche Gesellschaft, did what they could to protect and shelter particular groups, but they lacked the necessary resources and authority.

Only belatedly was the task of immigrant protection assumed by the states. Initially they were concerned only to protect themselves against foreign pauperism. Led by Massachusetts and New York in the 1820's the seaboard states passed laws requiring shipmasters to give bonds for passengers who might become chargeable. But in practice the requirement was nearly always commuted in favor of a fixed rate head tax, the proceeds of which were used to provide immigrant hospitals and other services. The most elaborate reception arrangements were made by New York, which received the bulk of the immigrants. After a state board of immigration had been established in 1847, the Marine Hospital on Staten Island was set aside for infectious cases, hospitals and refuges were built on Ward's Island in the East River, and an employment exchange was opened on Canal Street. Then in 1855 an immigrant depot was instituted at Castle Garden near the Battery, where all immigrants arriving at New York had henceforth to be landed. Here, secure from exploitation, immigrants could change their foreign money, arrange for reliable accommodations, buy railroad tickets, and seek advice about jobs. Only a small percentage of the total immigration received any direct help at Castle Garden, but by the time the institution gave way to Ellis Island in 1892, many thousands of immigrants had been relieved, given temporary shelter, and directed to places where labor was wanted.

The first step in obtaining an American foothold was to find employment. For the fortunate minority with capital or industrial skill this usually presented little difficulty. To be sure, even experienced farmers and skilled artisans often found that they had to adapt their knowledge to American conditions; but within a short time of arrival such men had resumed their familiar activities, their economic adjustment completed. Other immigrants were resourceful enough to turn their European knowledge to new uses. Of the many Jews who in Europe had been traders and petty retailers, a considerable number became in America itinerant peddlers, the more successful of whom in time accumulated sufficient capital to set up retail establishments. But there were some whose previous training could not so readily be turned to account, either because of their inability to speak English or because they came in such numbers as to exceed the American demand. For these reasons many highly qualified German Forty-eighters encountered great difficulties in finding suitable work; often, according to one of the more successful Forty-eighters, "learned professors, writers and artists . . . were forced to support themselves by making cigars, acting as waiters or house-servants, boot-blacks or street-sweepers." Even so, the plight of such men, however pathetic, was hardly to be compared with that of the infinitely more numerous group who came to America with neither skill nor resources—indeed, with no asset at all save brawn and muscle. No immigrant group was without its quota of those whose employment opportunities—and whose mobility, consequently—were thus narrowly restricted. Yet none was so poverty-stricken or so lacking in previous training as the Irish, the great majority of whom therefore became an urban proletariat.

Because of their dependence upon unskilled labor, the Irish introduced a novel element of concentration into the American urban economic pattern. A New York state census in 1855 revealed that one-quarter of New York City's Irish working population consisted of laborers, carters, porters, and waiters, another quarter was made up of domestic servants, and another 10 per cent were either tailors or dressmakers. In Boston, where poor transportation facilities immobilized the laborer and the absence of large and varied industrial enterprises still further narrowed his opportunities, almost two-thirds of the gainfully employed Irish were either unskilled laborers or domestic servants. This condition had no parallel in other immigrant groups, which tended rather to reflect the dispersion of occupations characterizing the economic organization of American cities. The state census of 1855 showed that no one occupation employed more than a small fraction of the New York Germans. About 15 per cent were tailors and 10 per cent domestic servants, but only 5 per cent were laborers, waiters, or carters, the rest being distributed among a great variety of occupations.

While the Irish thus came virtually to monopolize unskilled jobs in American cities, they achieved similar prominence in construction work. Finding urban employment sporadic even when it could be obtained at all, Irishmen responded readily to the bait of high wages held out by labor agencies and contractors concerned with canal, railroad, and other construction projects in the West and South. In the construction camps working and living conditions were extremely harsh, and exploitation by unscrupulous contractors frequent; yet despite the warnings of the Irish-American press, Irishmen continued to be drawn to canal- and railroad-building, leaving their families for months at a time in the cities in which they had first settled. Toward the end of the period increasing numbers found employment in industry. During the 1840's Irish immigrants began gradually to replace native farmers' daughters in the New England textile mills, others obtained work in shoe factories, and those who had gained experience of mining during a sojourn in England scattered throughout the Pennsylvania coalfields and the lead mines of Illinois and Wisconsin. Yet even in 1860 the bulk of the Irish were still at the bottom of the occupational ladder.

The effect of immigration upon native labor was a matter of controversy among contemporaries. Some observers maintained that an influx of unskilled labor like that represented by the Irish could serve only to raise the economic status of the rest of the community. "Their inferiority," wrote Edward Everett Hale in 1852, "compels them to go to the bottom; and the consequence is that we are, all of us, the higher lifted because they are here." Though this was true enough in general, the poorer native element, such as the free Negroes in New York, certainly suffered from Irish competition for unskilled jobs, and not a few artisans were temporarily displaced by the simultaneous introduction to industry of cheap immigrant labor and machinery. Nor did immigrant competition come exclusively from the unskilled; in New York, for example, there were complaints during the 1840's that an influx of German tailors, shoemakers, and cabinet-makers had lowered wage rates and had deprived Americans of work.

Yet in the broad view the economic effects of mass immigration were undeniably beneficial. As well as contributing to the fluidity of the American economy, it hastened the construction of a transportation network and accelerated the growth of industrialism. Neither the factory system nor the great canal and railroad developments of the period could have come into existence so quickly without the reservoir of cheap labor provided by immigration.

The acceleration of the nation's economic development was, however, purchased only at the price of an intensification of its social difficulties. Mass immigration may have augmented America's working force, but it also confronted her with new problems of pauperism, disease, and criminality. Attributed by some Americans to the immigrant's inborn depravity, these evils were really a consequence of social maladjustment to the American environment. The harsh and unfamiliar conditions of life to which many immigrants were condemned by their poverty was bound to have disturbing consequences. Yet the chief sufferer from his failure to adjust was not American society but the immigrant himself.

Obliged to find housing accommodations that were both cheap and within walking distance of their employment, the majority of urban immigrants crowded into old warehouses or dilapidated mansions which had been hastily converted into tenements. Many others lived in flimsy one-room shanties erected out of whatever materials were available or sought shelter in attics and cellars. Darkness, damp, and lack of ventilation were almost universal in such dwellings, in which there was only the most primitive sanitation. These squalid and noisome surroundings proved excellent breeding-grounds for diseases like tuberculosis, smallpox, typhus, and cholera, from all of which immigrants suffered more heavily than the native population. That the immigrant death rate was also higher than that of the native population was due not only to unfavorable living conditions in America but to the fact that many immigrants were physically debilitated on arrival owing to long-continued malnutrition and to the hardships of the crossing. The assertion that immigration resulted in a shortened life-span, however, is of questionable validity. While the Boston Irish may have lived on the average only fourteen years after reaching America, one should remember that in nineteenth-century rural Ireland the average age at death was only nineteen and four-fifths of the population did not reach the age of forty.

Immigrant poverty was reflected in the fact that, wherever they congregated, the foreign-born constituted a large proportion of those dependent upon state and municipal assistance. Between 1845 and 1860 between one-half and two-thirds of Boston's paupers consisted of immigrants, and in New York City in 1860 no fewer than 86 per cent of those on relief were of foreign birth. Crime statistics, too, showed a similar disproportion between foreign-born and native offenders. In 1859, for instance, 55 per cent of the persons arrested for crime in New York City were Irish-born, and a further 22 per cent had been born in other foreign countries. Yet these statistics are misleading in that few immigrant lawbreakers committed the more serious offenses. In most cases conflict with the law resulted either from petty thievery or, still more commonly, from drunkenness and disorderly conduct.

Demoralization and degradation were not, of course, the

invariable accompaniments of immigration. One should guard against painting too black a picture of immigrant life by dwelling excessively upon the misfortunes of the poorest class of newcomers. Even Irish laborers and domestic servants, it should be remembered, were generally able to save enough out of their wages to pay the passage of relatives. Immigrant letters, moreover, were generally animated not by despair but by a sense of accomplishment. Even from the slums immigrants could write glowing tributes to America, the most eloquent of which was the continued advice to relatives to come and join them.

The persistence of feelings of alienation and isolation could not but stimulate in each ethnic group an awareness of its identity. The strange and often hostile environment in which they found themselves sharpened the nostalgia of immigrants for their homelands, led them to cherish old loyalties, and drove them in upon themselves. The most obvious expression of immigrant yearnings for the familiar was the tendency to congregate in distinct areas. American cities now became agglomerations of separate communities, the ethnic character of which was recognized in such names as Irishtown and Kleindeutschland.

The most striking examples of ethnic concentration were provided by New York City. As early as 1830 the Sixth Ward, especially the insalubrious quarter known as the "Five Points," had taken on a marked Irish coloring. From here during the next generation the area of Irish settlement was successively extended until it covered the whole of the Lower East Side as far north as the Fourteenth Ward and as far east as the Seventh.

Patterns of Distribution, 1815–60

But by 1850 a more characteristic ethnic ghetto had developed. Just to the north of the Irish district, from the Bowery to the Tenth, Eleventh, and Thirteenth Wards, lay a region known as Kleindeutschland. Until the Civil War it contained about two-thirds of New York's one hundred thousand Germans. Here, the English language was rarely heard and there was scarcely a business which was not run by Germans. Here also were to be found German churches, schools, restaurants, a *Volkstheater*, and a lending library. But what most attracted the attention of visitors was the number of lager-beer saloons. On Sundays, particularly, these establishments were thronged to overflowing, it being the common practice for people to go from the inn to church and then return to the inn again.

An equally revealing reflection of group consciousness was the banding together of immigrants in autonomous social organizations. This development, which isolated the newcomer far more conclusively than mere geographical segregation, was in most cases due to the exclusive attitudes of the natives, who tended to debar immigrants from participating in existing societies. Most of the numerous Irish militia companies, for example, came into existence only after Irishmen had been refused admission to native companies. Yet it was significant that even British immigrants, whose economic status and cultural background were passports to acceptance, often preferred their own social institutions.

What determined the nature of immigrant groupings was not national feeling, for in Europe immigrants had been hardly aware of their nationality. To most, local and regional affiliations were more important. Immigrants from England usually identified themselves primarily as, for example, Yorkshiremen or as Cornishmen, those from Ireland as Dubliners or Kerrymen, and those from Germany as Bavarians or Westphalians. The welding of such groups into national communities, which was the consequence of New World pressures, was a complex and protracted business. In the meantime, linguistic or religious links served as the basis of selection, though the pattern was varied enough to allow for many diverse combinations.

Immigrant associations sometimes represented communal attempts to meet material needs in times of crisis. Thus the numerous mutual aid societies and benevolent associations strove, with varying degrees of success, to provide sickness benefits and to pay funeral expenses. But the real function of these and similar immigrant organizations was to satisfy the desire of their members for companionship and familiar surroundings, and thus to soften the effects of contact with a strange environment. Immigrant militia and fire companies, too, were essentially social clubs; so, also, were the German *Turnvereine,* despite the political activities in which they sometimes engaged.

In addition, each group sought to preserve in America the familiar cultural pattern of the old country. For this purpose the most widely used and most effective formal instruments were the church, the school, and the newspaper. In their religious faith immigrants recognized almost the only pillar of the old life that had not crumbled in the course of the Atlantic crossing. To it, therefore, they clung both as a means of preserving their identity and as a source of security and solace in a bewildering world. Most British immigrants, of course, were fortunate in that neither linguistic nor doctrinal barriers prevented their joining existing American congregations. All other groups, however, had to rely mainly upon their own efforts if familiar forms of worship were to be re-created;

and this aim immigrants were determined to achieve even at the cost of heavy sacrifices.

Some of the difficulty of transplanting an immigrant church resulted from the fact that immigration had often disestablished it. In various parts of Europe the Anglican, Lutheran, Presbyterian, and Reformed churches had been established churches, that is, had been supported by and linked to the state. In America, where church and state were separate and where men were consequently free to join any church or none, the immigrant church had to devise a new basis of membership, reorganize its polity, and recast its attitude toward the civil power.

But equally great difficulties arose when the task of transplantation had already been accomplished by an earlier generation of immigrants. Prolonged controversy and schism were often the result of differences of opinion between newcomers and their Americanized co-religionists. Nineteenth-century German Lutheran immigrants, for example, found many features of the American Lutheran church, which had been founded by Germans in the colonial period, to be strange, distasteful, and eventually unacceptable. It was not merely that English had replaced German as the language of worship but that traditional Lutheran beliefs and practices had been profoundly altered. As a result of the Americanizing influences at work in the half-century after the Revolution, American Lutheranism had lost much of its distinctiveness. Close relationships had developed with the Anglican and Reformed churches, and the possibility of organic union with each had been considered. In addition, Lutheran preachers had copied the revivalistic approach of the Methodists and, most startling of all, the Ministeriums of New York and Philadelphia had adopted new constitutions from which "all reference either to the Augsburg Confession or to the other symbolical books had vanished."

All these changes were anathema to the German Lutherans who came to America after 1815, and violent feuds resulted. With the arrival of the ultra-conservative "Old Lutherans" from Saxony in the 1840's the battle against liberal and pietistic influences was openly joined. Finally in 1847, under the leadership of C. F. W. Walther, "the Lutheran pope of the West," the more recent Lutheran immigrants broke away and organized the rival Missouri Synod.

Similar ecclesiastical wranglings separated mid-nineteenth-century Dutch immigrants from the Reformed Church in America which in colonial days had been known as the Dutch Reformed Church. Here controversy centered upon the neglect by earlier comers of the Heidelberg Confession and the doctrine of predestination, upon the use of hymns instead of psalms, upon singing by choirs instead of by congregations, and upon tolerance of membership in Masonic lodges. But though the issues differed, the conflict, both in its causes and in its schismatic outcome, resembled that in the Lutheran church. Recent Dutch immigrants found themselves out of sympathy with the changes which had resulted from a tendency toward conformity with American conditions. Determined to establish a form of worship which would more accurately reproduce Old World patterns, they established the True Dutch Reformed Church in 1864.

The founding of separate churches by newly arrived German Lutherans and Dutch Calvinists was a consequence of their dislike of latitudinarianism. But that Norwegian and Swedish Lutherans should also insist upon their own churches and synods was an indication that, in determining religious groupings, doctrinal matters were sometimes less important than differences of language and geographical origin. For this same reason many Jewish congregations in America began to lose their earlier cohesiveness; by the middle of the century those in the larger cities tended to represent distinctive ethnic elements. Such a development among Roman Catholics would, of course, have run counter to that church's traditions of centralization and universality. Formidable problems of organization confronted the Catholic church as a result of its huge and varied gains from immigration in this period; not only were nearly all Irish immigrants Catholic, but so were perhaps half the Germans and all the French-Canadians. Geographical segregation sometimes resulted in German, French, Irish, and American Catholics attending separate churches, but all efforts at preserving ethnic exclusiveness and autonomy failed because of hierarchical opposition.

Anxiety to preserve their cultural heritage led both Catholic and Lutheran immigrants to favor the establishment of parochial schools. Yet the motives of the two groups were hardly identical. Organization of a separate Catholic school system resulted from complaints of Protestant proselytizing in the public schools, especially of daily Bible readings from a translation which the Catholic church condemned. But when German, Norwegian, and Swedish Lutherans followed a similar course, it was mainly from the belief that instruction in the mother tongue was essential to the preservation of religious belief. Neither group was wholly successful in its aims, at least in this period, principally because of a lack of funds and trained teachers. Among Scandinavian and German Lutherans, moreover, many parents were unwilling to accept church leadership on the school question and the majority probably sent their children to the public schools. The Catholic refusal to accept the common school system, on the other hand, often meant that the children of immigrants received no education at all.

In contrast to the difficulties encountered in attempting to establish autonomous school systems was the comparative ease with which each immigrant group established a newspaper press of its own. Though most immigrants had little previous experience of newspapers, they welcomed the appearance of journals that kept them in touch with happenings in the old country, acquainted them with developments in the immigrant community itself, and interpreted for them a variety of American events and issues. Because of the poverty and illiteracy of many newcomers, a stable immigrant press was slow to develop. Irish-American journalism, particularly, remained a gamble until the great influx of the forties and fifties enlarged the reading public. The leading Irish organs were the New York *Irish American*, founded by Patrick Lynch in 1849, which claimed a circulation of 40,000 in 1861, and the Boston *Pilot*, founded in 1838; but Catholic journals like the New York *Freeman's Journal*, the organ of Archbishop Hughes, had a large Irish readership. The German-language press, which had steadily lost ground during the first quarter of the nineteenth century, began to revive in the 1830's with the founding of such papers as the New York *Staats-Zeitung und Herold*, the St. Louis *Anzeiger des Westens*, and the Cincinnati *Volksblatt*, all of which had a long existence. But the greatest expansion was to come in the decade or so after 1840. As late as 1843 there was still only one German daily in the United States, but by 1850 there were a score; the total number of

German-language papers rose from forty in 1840 to 133 in 1852, and their general tone and substance were greatly improved by the arrival of a better class of editor. Among smaller immigrant groups, like the Norwegians and the Welsh, newspapers tended generally to be church journals, or at least to be edited by clergymen. These papers, however, served the same function as the immigrant press generally, namely, that of acting as a focus for the immigrant community and of facilitating its Americanization.

For the great mass of newcomers the most difficult, if not the most pressing, problems of adjustment related to their participation in American politics. Since all but a few had been denied the right of suffrage in Europe, previous experience had done little to prepare them for the exercise of political power in the country of their adoption. Whether immigrants were seriously inhibited from political activity by an acceptance of differences in rank may be doubted, for European ideas of status withered quickly in the democratic American atmosphere. Yet it remains true that immigrants were unfamiliar on arrival not only with American political issues but with the democratic process itself. The result was that many newcomers became the tools of unscrupulous politicians. While machine politics based on immigrant support was not to reach its apogee until after the Civil War, the urban immigrant tended from an early date to be bound to the machine. Open bribery was not unknown, but the machine's control of the immigrant was a result rather of its continuing attention to his practical needs. Acting through an army of ward heelers, often immigrants themselves, the machine assisted the newcomer to find accommodation and employment and afforded him a variety of services and privileges. In return, the mass of newly arrived slum-dwellers were prepared automatically to give their votes, which they otherwise valued little, to those who looked after their welfare.

Nothing could be more misleading, however, than to interpret immigrant political attitudes exclusively in terms of the ignorance and apathy resulting, respectively, from political inexperience and from the necessity of concentrating upon immediate personal problems. All-important though these factors were initially, they exercised less and less influence as immigrants gradually grasped the basic concepts of democracy and, still more, as they came to recognize their personal involvement in the political issues raised during this period. Slavery, expansion, and, above all, nativism were issues of vital concern to the immigrant and proved powerful solvents of political passivity. True, some immigrant groups usually voted in blocs. But this was due largely to a similarity of outlook resulting from a high degree of homogeneity and concentration. If political machines succeeded in retaining the allegiance of immigrants, this was because—in addition to the welfare services they provided—their political attitudes corresponded with immigrant aspirations.

All this becomes clearer, perhaps, when one attempts to explain why it was that, for most of the pre–Civil War period, immigrants gave their support overwhelmingly to the Democratic party. Only in part was this because the Democrats were more systematic and skilful—as well as earlier—than their rivals in attempting to woo the immigrant vote. Equally important was the powerful appeal to the common man of the party of Jefferson and Jackson, the latter of whom especially typified for many immigrants their own yearnings for equal-

Naturalization of immigrants at election time, 1868. (From *Harper's Weekly*, 1868.)

Steerage passengers to America, 1870. (The Radio Times Hulton Picture Library, London.)

ity. In addition the Democrats adopted a consistently friendly attitude toward immigrants. In Congress they resolutely opposed any lengthening of the residential qualifications for naturalization, and the national party platform regularly included an enthusiastic indorsement of the asylum concept. The Whigs were in contrast identified by most immigrants as the party of aristocracy, nativism, and temperance. Though the Democratic party became increasingly dominated by slaveholders, this did not at first lessen its appeal to immigrants; the Irish, indeed, because of their hatred of abolitionism, found in this new development a further cause for voting Democratic. Yet, as we shall see in the next chapter, the intrusion of the slavery issue into national politics brought to an end the Democratic near-monopoly of foreign-born votes. By the end of the 1850's the Irish were the only immigrant group which still gave the Democrats its undivided support.

Foreign-born devotion to the Democrats was one of the many factors which helped elect Andrew Jackson to the presidency in 1828. In New York, Jackson's majority owed much to a heavy Irish vote, just as in Pennsylvania it was based largely upon solid Scotch-Irish and German support. But it was not until later that immigrant votes began to have a decisive effect upon presidential elections. In 1844 Henry Clay attributed his defeat to the hostility of the foreign-born element toward the Whigs, though in fact the intervention of the Liberty party in New York was just as influential. Franklin Pierce's majority in 1852 was large enough to disprove the claim of his opponents that he had been elected by immigrant votes, but in the much closer contest four years later James Buchanan may well have owed his election to immigrant support, especially in key states like Pennsylvania.

American Immigration

It was in local politics that immigrant influence was most marked. As early as 1820 the Irish had captured control of Tammany Hall, and before the end of the decade were the dominating force in New York City politics. Moving steadily up the political ladder from ward boss to alderman and then to state legislator, the Irish also gained an appreciable number of federal offices during Democratic administrations. The Germans, though just as consistently Democratic as the Irish—at least until the 1850's—received less political recognition. This was a consequence partly of their language difficulties but also because, in comparison with the Irish, German immigrants were less concentrated and more heterogeneous.

While they thus became increasingly involved in American politics, immigrants continued to agitate European issues. The Irish, especially, retained a lively interest in the politics of their homeland and, wherever they congregated in the United States, formed organizations favoring Irish causes. During the struggle for Catholic emancipation in Ireland during the 1820's, Irish-American associations known as the Friends of Ireland sent money and addresses of encouragement to the Catholic Association in Dublin. Daniel O'Connell's repeal agitation in the early 1840's attracted still more Irish-American support; the repeal associations formed in many American cities collected a "rent" of twelve cents a month from their members for transmission to Ireland, and a National Repeal Convention held in New York in 1843 attracted delegates from thirteen states and one territory. The Young Ireland movement, too, aroused tremendous enthusiasm among Irish-Americans, at least until its radicalism incurred the denunciation of the Catholic hierarchy, and the 1850's brought into being a great number of Irish nationalist clubs pledged to work for the independence of Ireland. In similar fashion German and Hungarian Forty-eighters established revolutionary societies in the United States to plan renewed insurrection in their homelands and to agitate for American intervention against the despotic monarchies of Europe.

It has been argued that the agitation of Old World causes does not demonstrate the divided allegiance of immigrants, as contemporaries so often charged; it proves instead the strength of their Americanism. Concern for the liberty of all peoples was a long-established American tradition, the validity of which newcomers acknowledged by demanding freedom for their European compatriots. But this interpretation did not apply universally. While a few enlightened spirits may have been familiar with and sympathetic to American democratic traditions, the mass of the immigrants had narrower horizons. The Irish, for example, were generally so little imbued with the spirit of universal liberty that they could clamor for Irish freedom while applauding the efforts of European reaction to suppress the uprisings of Garibaldi and Kossuth. In such cases there was some substance to the nativist complaint of a conflict of loyalties. Furthermore, there was a tendency among Irish political refugees, as well as among German Forty-eighters, to look upon themselves as exiles and to use the United States simply as a base for promoting European causes. That the mass of immigrants supported such causes was due partly to sentimental attachment to the homeland, partly to the need to discharge an emotional debt toward her, but most of all to the fact that they afforded a means of group identification and self-assertion. Significantly enough, the groups most inclined to perpetuate Old World interests were those whom American society was most adamant in rejecting.

American Immigration

During the 1850's the European past became increasingly overshadowed by the American present. With the simultaneous growth of nativism and of sectional tension the immigrant was confronted with issues that were immediate, personal, and unavoidable. A period of national crisis would now remold his political attitudes and would significantly alter his whole adjustment to America.

VI

Nativism, Sectional Controversy, and Civil War, 1830-65

In considering nativism it is important to distinguish between a general dislike of foreigners resulting from a recognition of cultural difference and a similar but more deep-seated antipathy based upon emotions of fear and hatred. The former, present to some extent in all societies, has been a constant factor in America from colonial days to the present. Using stereotypes of the foreign-born which only rarely corresponded to reality, this sentiment has been essentially passive, probably reflecting no more than a general ethnocentrism. Much more, however, has been involved in the usually short-lived but highly concentrated outbursts of mass xenophobia which have erupted in America from time to time. These have been the product of a loss of national confidence owing to internal stress of one kind or another. Cyclical in character, strongly marked by hysteria and irrationality, and generally inspired by a specific political purpose, such nativistic movements have been essentially attempts to safeguard American nationality from the foreign influences which were believed to threaten it.

The first of these anti-foreign outbursts came, as we saw, in the 1790's when, at a time of deep political cleavage closely related to the prevalent international conflict, the Federalists sought to guard the new nation against revolution by proscribing immigrant radicals. That the generation preceding the Civil War witnessed a recrudescence of nativism was not so much because the period was one of heavy immigration but that it too was one of internal crisis, when national unity was increasingly threatened by sectionalism. The intensity of the hostility to immigrants was therefore a measure less of their number than of the nativist's need to strengthen American institutions against them.

Pre–Civil War nativism was, as always, a complex phenomenon, drawing its strength from a great variety of sources and only rarely finding expression in a single straightforward formula. Its most prominent theme was that of hostility to the Roman Catholic church. The astonishing growth of American Catholicism, mainly as the result of immigration, revived the fears of popery that had been so widespread in America in colonial days. The steady expansion of Catholic membership, reflected in the amount of church-building, the creation of new dioceses, and the rise of a Catholic press, produced in the 1830's a mounting wave of anti-Catholic literature and oratory. The outcry was more than a mere consequence of differences in religious belief. The characteristic feature of Protestant nativism was rather its constantly expressed fear that the Catholic influx threatened American institutions. The Catholic church, because of its authoritarian organization and its close connection with the despotic monarchies of Europe, was regarded by many Americans as the inveterate enemy of political liberty, and there were not a few who believed in the existence of a far-ranging popish plot to subvert free government in the young republic. Such fears were expressed, for instance, by Samuel F. B. Morse, the future inventor of the telegraph, in a series of widely publicized letters written in 1834 to the New York *Observer* and subsequently published as a pamphlet entitled *A Foreign Conspiracy against the Liberties of the United States*. Morse's attack was directed especially against the Leopold Association of Vienna, a Catholic missionary society whose efforts were concentrated upon the United States; the sending of financial assistance by this body to American Catholic bishops was, Morse believed, the first step in the papal conquest of the United States. Particularly alarming to Protestant nativists were the alleged designs of the Pope and the Holy Alliance upon the Mississippi Valley. Thus in *A Plea for the West* (1835), the Reverend Lyman Beecher described an alleged plot to win the United States for Catholicism by sending Catholic immigrants to the West in such numbers as ultimately to dominate the region.

Equally characteristic of the no-popery agitation was its suspicion of Catholic religious houses. True, the burning of the Ursuline Convent at Charlestown, Massachusetts, in 1834 was not indicative of widespread anti-Catholicism but was due mainly to the local brickmakers' resentment of Irish economic competition. Although the outrage was almost universally condemned, it inspired a whole series of propaganda works purporting to reveal the truth about nunneries and thus significantly affected the pattern of Protestant nativism. The most celebrated exposé was Maria Monk's *Awful Disclosures of the*

American Immigration

Hôtel Dieu Nunnery of Montreal (1836), which, allegedly on a basis of personal experience, depicted convents and monasteries as dens of iniquity and vice. This piece of scurrilous sensationalism greatly stimulated popular anti-Catholicism and continued to be a best-seller long after its author had been discredited.

During the 1830's fears of Romanism remained for the most part vague and intangible. They took on clearer shape, however, during the prolonged school controversy of the next two decades. Catholics had long complained of the sectarian nature of the instruction in New York City's state-supported school system, but when in 1840, with Governor Seward's encouragement, they demanded a share of the state school fund, they met with vehement Protestant opposition. In the impassioned debates that followed, nativist speakers expressed indignation at Catholic opposition to the use of the King James version of the Scriptures in the schools. To many Protestants, the Bible was doubly sacred—as a patriotic symbol and as Holy Writ; an attack on it was thought to be both disloyal and blasphemous. The entire episode was viewed by Protestants as a dangerous manifestation of foreign influence. Particularly alarming to Protestant opinion were the political activities of Bishop John Hughes of New York, whose action in running a separate Catholic ticket in the fall elections of 1841 was denounced as a violation of the American principle of the separation of church and state. Nor was the agitation confined to New York. There were similar controversies in other cities, one of them resulting in the Philadelphia Riots of 1844, in which several Catholic churches were burned and many Irish Catholics were killed and injured.

A further source of nativist hostility to Catholicism lay in the recurrent controversies within the Catholic church over the question of trusteeism. In a number of places conflict and schism resulted from the efforts of the hierarchy to recover control of church property from boards of lay trustees, some of which had become so indifferent to ecclesiastical authority as to attempt to appoint their own pastors. The most celebrated case concerned the congregation of St. Louis' Church in Buffalo, which was placed under an interdict in 1851 and whose recalcitrant trustees were subsequently excommunicated. Because this particular controversy centered upon Hughes, now elevated to the archbishopric of New York, the hostile attention of nativists was insured. But the real basis of criticism lay deeper. Regarding the issue between the hierarchy and the trustees simply as one between autocracy and democracy, Protestants were strengthened in their belief that Catholicism was incompatible with American traditions and ideals. Fears of foreign influence were, moreover, greatly stimulated in 1853 when a papal nuncio, Monsignor Gaetano Bedini, arrived in the United States to settle trusteeism conflicts at Buffalo and Philadelphia. Because of his part in suppressing the Italian revolutions in 1848, Bedini appeared to many Americans as a personification of European reaction, and riots and disorder greeted him wherever he went in the United States.

While anti-Catholicism was the most prominent theme of pre–Civil War nativism, it was far from being synonymous with it. Some of the most rabid supporters of the "Protestant Crusade" were themselves recent immigrants. In Philadelphia in 1844, for example, the anti-Catholic rioters included a considerable Scotch-Irish Presbyterian element, and in Cincinnati nine years later the demonstrations against Mgr. Bedini were led mainly by German Forty-eighters. Then again, from the participation of native Catholics in the outcry against immigrants, it is evident that nativism was not simply a matter of religious bigotry. It owed not a little, for instance, to the notion that immigration was flooding the United States with large numbers of foreign paupers and criminals. Greatly adding to American resentment on this score were persistent reports—exaggerated but nonetheless widely believed—that great numbers of undesirables were being systematically deported by European governments and municipal authorities. The powers of Europe, complained a congressional committee in 1856, were making the United States the "receptacle for the dregs and offscourings of their population . . . thus relieving themselves of the burden of pauperism and crime."

As might have been expected, complaints of the poverty and criminality of immigrants were loudest in the states and cities through which the bulk of immigration flowed. In 1848 a committee of the Massachusetts legislature drew attention to the mounting evils of foreign pauperism in the state, whereby an enormous and unfair tax was placed upon the industry of the thrifty and law-abiding. In New York City, every mayor from Aaron Clark in 1837 to Fernando Wood in 1855 complained bitterly of his powerlessness to prevent a constant influx of destitution and lawlessness. Repeated investigations showed that complaint was all too well founded. In 1835, it was reported that more than one-half of the paupers in the almshouses of New York, Philadelphia, Boston, and Baltimore were foreign-born, and in later years the proportion was even higher. Crime statistics, too, revealed a disproportionate number of foreign-born offenders; in 1850 there were three times as many foreign-born inmates of the New York state prisons as there were natives. The efforts of several states to check undesirable immigration by requiring bonds from ship captains proved unsuccessful; and since repeated applications for federal legislation were equally fruitless, the burden of supporting the foreign-born poor remained with local authorities.

Yet it would be wrong to imagine that nativist opposition developed simply from the intensification of problems of poor relief and law enforcement. What contributed most to nativist fears of an influx of paupers and criminals was its wider implications. It was upon these, rather than upon local problems, that attention was focused in 1856 by a congressional Committee on Foreign Criminals and Paupers. The immigration of such classes, the committee believed, was a matter

affecting not only the fiscal affairs of the nation, but the morals, habits and character of the people, and the safety of our institutions. . . . A nation of freemen, no matter how great and powerful, cannot long continue as such without religion and morality, industry and frugality; for these are indispensable supports of popular government. Crime and pauperism are the bane of a republic and they cannot be too seriously considered, nor too stringently guarded against.

To many nativists an equally grave and more immediate threat to republican freedom stemmed from the political role of the foreign-born. In places the proportion of foreign-born voters had so increased as to hold the balance of electoral power; this of itself was a source of alarm, for most immigrants remained ignorant of American institutions. In addition, the electoral violence and voting frauds, which had come to characterize immigrant participation in politics, were believed to be sapping the very foundations of the American political system. There were numerous complaints of native voters being kept from the polls by organized mobs of foreign laborers, of immigrants voting on the very day of their arrival in America, and of hired witnesses and false testimony as the commonplaces of naturalization proceedings. In 1845 a congressional committee investigating naturalization frauds reported that, in New York, New Orleans, and Philadelphia, it was the common practice on the eve of elections for immigrants, many of them not yet qualified by residence, to be naturalized in droves at the instigation of the political machines. Such abuses could serve only to swell the chorus of nativist anger. To an already existing belief that the immigrant was the tool of the priesthood was now added the conviction that he was the dupe of unscrupulous politicians.

Criticism of immigrants as a corrupting influence upon American political life was leveled chiefly against the Irish. But German immigrants aroused even more apprehension because of their supposed revolutionary tendencies. Though the anti-revolutionary tradition of nativism was never as prominent in the pre–Civil War period as it had been during the 1790's, the impact of the German Forty-eighters kept it from dying out completely. Even among Americans with no nativistic inclinations the Forty-eighters were an unpopular group because of their agnosticism and rationalism, their unconcealed contempt for American culture, and their criticisms of such social customs as the Puritan Sabbath. But when Forty-eighters plunged headlong into the battle for social and political reform, American reaction became palpably sharper. Resentment of German arrogance gave way to excited warnings against the machinations of a disaffected and turbulent element to whom America had unwisely given asylum. The most widely publicized example of German radicalism was contained in the Louisville platform of 1854, which was the work of such political refugees as Karl Heinzen and Bernhard Domschke. This document demanded the abolition of slavery, the enfranchisement of Negroes and women, and a flood of social legislation; it also advocated the abolition of the Senate and the presidency, which were to be replaced by a unicameral Congress elected by popular vote. Obnoxious though this platform was to conservative Americans, it was moderate in comparison with the demands of Communist Forty-eighters like Wilhelm Weitling, who advocated complete social revolution and the establishment of an American "republic of the workers."

Fear of immigrant labor competition, so prominent a feature of later outbursts of anti-foreignism, was not an important cause of pre–Civil War nativism. Occasionally, however, native tradesmen and mechanics complained that immigration lowered wage levels, contributed to the decline of the apprenticeship system and generally depressed the condition of labor. Such complaints occurred particularly during the hard times that followed the panic of 1837. In some of the eastern cities an incipient workingmen's nativist movement appeared, with organizations like the American Laboring Confederacy and newspapers like the *Champion of American Labor* to demand that workingmen be given the same protection against foreign competition as the tariff afforded to capitalists. But the movement was never strongly supported and disappeared altogether with the return of prosperity in the early 1850's.

Concern for national homogeneity, prompted by the conviction that immigrants were an unassimilable element, was to receive its fullest expression in later nativist movements. Yet these were the grounds upon which many pre–Civil War nativists based their fears that immigration would prove to be the Trojan horse of the American republic. The basic complaint was against immigrant clannishness, which expressed itself most obviously in a tendency to mass together in distinct foreign quarters. Ignorant of the true causes of this practice, nativists persisted in interpreting it as a deliberate effort to resist Americanization. The practice of forming separate foreign-born militia units, too, seemed to show a reluctance to allow old associations and influences to yield to new. But the final proof to many a nativist of the immigrant's imperviousness to his new surroundings was the prevalence of foreign nationalist organizations, membership in which seemed to imply at best an unwillingness to give to America more than a divided allegiance and at worst a readiness to use her simply as a base for revolutionary activity abroad. So long, therefore, as Irish immigrants continued to work for an Irish republic and Germans for the abandonment of American neutrality in the interest of European liberty, the nativist reaction would be not only a fear of the foreign entanglements that might result but an insistence that "the obligations of citizenship [could] not exist in favor of different nationalities at the same time."

For all the intensity of feeling it reflected, nativism was slow to develop any widespread political expression. Not until sectional controversy had disrupted the existing parties did the movement become a significant factor in national politics. The ephemeral nativist parties which appeared during the 1830's at places like New York and New Orleans were essentially local organizations, and even the Native American Party founded in 1845 had only minimal support in the fourteen states in which it claimed branches. Nevertheless, the many nativist secret societies of the 1840's, such as the Order of United Americans, showed a persistent tendency to develop political offshoots; and finally about 1850 there appeared a new nativist organization, the Order of the Star-Spangled Banner, which was still secret in character but avowedly political in aim. Metamorphosed into the Know-Nothing, or American, Party by 1854, the new organization quickly won support and in the next two years enjoyed astonishing success. Know-Nothingism reached its peak in 1855, when it elected six governors, dominated several state legislatures, and sent a sizable delegation to Congress. But the party's decline was just as sudden as its rise, and the heavy defeat in 1856 of its presidential candidate, Millard Fillmore, marked its virtual demise.

Know-Nothing aims were expressed succinctly in the slogan "America for the Americans." By this the party did not, however, intend a repudiation of the traditional asylum ideal. On the contrary, leading Know-Nothings protested their devotion to a liberal immigration policy. The only immigrants they wanted to exclude, they claimed, were the pauper and criminal element. Everyone else was welcome to come subject only to the proviso that they must not expect to participate in American political life. Thus, not only did the Know-Nothing platform call for the restriction of officeholding to native Americans; it also advocated extending to twenty-one years the residential qualification for naturalization.

For their failure to translate this program into legislation Know-Nothing leaders could blame their lack of a congressional majority as well as the constitutional objections of their state-rights supporters to a congressional ban on particular classes of immigrants. But, even where they had absolute power, the Know-Nothing record of accomplishment was meager. Though they controlled six states for varying periods of time, the only legislative results of their rule—apart from literacy tests for the franchise in Massachusetts and Connecticut, which were not specifically anti-immigrant measures—were a Massachusetts law disbanding foreign militia units and an amendment to the constitution of that state prohibiting immigrants from voting until two years had elapsed since their naturalization.

Explanation lay in the fact that the rise of Know-Nothingism had been due less to concern at the evils of immigration than to bewilderment and alarm resulting from the controversy over the Kansas-Nebraska Act. At a time of party disintegration and mounting sectionalism, the Know-Nothing movement seemed at once to afford a political refuge and a basis of national unity. Opposition to immigrants was thus not an end in itself but rather a means of expressing national sentiment, and many politicians who rode to power on the Know-Nothing hobby felt no compulsion to legislate against immigrants once they had been elected.

Even so, to account for Know-Nothingism simply in terms of a revived nationalism is to tell only part of the story. Equally significant was the involvement of the immigrant in a number of local and sectional conflicts which coincided with, and were in part reflections of, the larger crisis of the 1850's. Southern Know-Nothingism, for example, had a strongly Unionist flavor, but many southerners supported the movement because of their conviction that the South's dwindling influence in national affairs was due largely to the continuing influx of immigrants into the free states. But for the heavy immigration into the North in the decade 1840–50, alleged Senator Stephen Adams of Mississippi in 1856, the South would have gained in population and representation upon the North, instead of the reverse being the case; furthermore, if immigration continued on the same scale, the North would soon have a sufficiently large majority in both houses of Congress to initiate amendments to those provisions of the Constitution relating to slavery. Southern fears were due just as much, however, to the supposed antipathy of immigrants to slavery as to the effect of their presence upon the sectional balance. To quote Senator Adams:

The whole education of foreigners and their prejudices when they come to this country are against the institution of slavery; and everything they hear at the North confirms that prejudice, and establishes them in opposition to the South; and in such a contest as I have supposed [i.e., over amending the Constitution] I have no doubt that nine-tenths of them would vote the Republican ticket.

In Massachusetts, on the other hand, Know-Nothingism was closely linked with antislavery and reform. Indeed, the movement's astonishing electoral success in that state was largely a recognition by the natives that the Irish were an obstacle to the success of these allied causes. Two factors brought Yankee xenophobia to a head. First, the apparent Irish support of the slave system, as revealed in their approval of the Fugitive Slave Act and, more graphically, in the use of Irish militia companies to thwart attempts to rescue the escaped slave Anthony Burns. Just as important was the frustration felt in 1853 at the Irish role in defeating a revised state constitution incorporating many radical reforms. The reform impulse was always the strongest factor in Massachusetts Know-Nothingism, and although the party was elected ostensibly to curb the foreign vote, its main concern was to enact its reform program.

From these examples it is clear that while some Americans supported Know-Nothingism because they wanted to uphold slavery, others did so because they desired its abolition. And there were yet others who were attracted to the movement because it offered a prospect of putting an end to agitation of the slavery question.

If these contradictory attitudes contributed in part to the rise of Know-Nothingism, they were even more responsible for its decline. The hope that the party would afford a rallying point for Unionists of all sections could survive only so long as commitment could be avoided on the slavery issue. Yet the moment that northern and southern Know-Nothings attempted to combine on a national basis, sectional differences over slavery destroyed party unity and with it all prospect that nativism could overcome the power of sectionalism. In the 1856 presidential election, many northern Know-Nothings bolted to the Republicans, many of those from the South voted Democratic, while the party's own candidate, Millard Fillmore, carried only a single state. Thereafter, political nativism survived only at the state level, and even there the demands of sectionalism soon proved too much for it. By 1860, hostility to immigrants was everywhere a dead issue.

An important contributory factor in the decline of nativism was the continuing strength of traditional American values. The Know-Nothing movement, it should be remembered, not only remained the creed of a minority; it also produced a countervailing response from the defenders of democratic ideals. To Abraham Lincoln, for example, Know-Nothingism was a repudiation of the principles of the Declaration of Independence, and to Emerson immigration was an essential part of the process of creating a democratic society. "The energy of Irish, Germans, Swedes, Poles, and Cossacks, and all the European tribes," wrote Emerson, ". . . will construct a new race, a new religion, a new state, a new literature, which will be as vigorous as the new Europe which came out of the smelting-pot of the Dark Ages. . . ." A similar faith in the dynamic character of American democracy led Theodore Parker to argue that the New World should be "the Asylum of Humanity for this century as for the seventeenth." Even if Know-Nothingism had not perished of its own contradictions, it would have been hard put to survive at a time when the American democratic faith could be so vigorously reasserted.

Northern and southern nativists may have differed over the precise role of the foreign-born in the slavery controversy, but they shared a common belief that on this, as on political issues generally, each immigrant group tended to vote as a bloc. In judging political issues, it was charged, immigrants allowed ties of common origin to transcend all other considerations. While there were certainly grounds for such an accusation with regard to some groups, the fact is that immigrants generally were no more united on the slavery question than were native Americans. Nor could it be otherwise when the outlook of each group, never entirely uniform to begin with, was significantly affected by a whole host of conflicting influences, among which the most important were geographic location, economic interest, religious affiliation, and, not least, the attitudes of other groups.

The failure of some historians to take these factors into account has led to widespread misunderstanding of the role of the foreign-born, especially of the Germans, in the presidential election of 1860. It has repeatedly been claimed that the decisive factor in Lincoln's success in winning the doubtful states of the Middle West was a solidly Republican German vote. But recent investigations have made it clear that the German vote was neither as large nor as undivided as this claim would imply. In some German-settled areas, it is true, there was strong support for Lincoln; the German wards of Cincinnati and Chicago, for example, gave him large majorities. But throughout the Middle West substantial numbers of Germans remained faithful to the Democratic party, and in Wisconsin the majority of German votes appear to have gone to Douglas. Only in Illinois, apparently, was German support decisive; elsewhere Lincoln would probably have won even if all the Germans had voted against him.

To refute the myth of a unified German vote for Lincoln is not of course to dispute that Germans played a prominent part in the growth of Republicanism. Some Germans were strongly opposed to slavery on moral grounds; others feared that "the Africanizing of the West" would necessarily close that section to free labor. The Kansas-Nebraska Act outraged large sections of German opinion and led many German-language newspapers to embrace the antislavery cause. Prominent Forty-eighters, like Friedrich Hecker, Friedrich Hassaurek, and Carl Schurz, welcomed Republicanism as a suitable outlet for their idealism and political talents, and they were joined by such representatives of an older German element as Gustav Körner and Friedrich Munch. The extent of German influence in the Republican party was revealed in 1860 when the Republican platform incorporated the so-called Dutch planks. Drawn up at the Chicago Deutsches Haus convention of German Republicans, these called for homestead legislation and for equality of treatment for native and foreign-born citizens. One of the highlights of the ensuing campaign was Schurz's attempt to win the votes of his countrymen for Lincoln by a 21,000-mile speaking tour which took him from the Middle West to the Pennsylvania Dutch country.

The limited success of Republican efforts to woo the German vote was due in the first place to the notorious conservatism of many Germans, particularly in the rural areas. However vocal and partisan the Forty-eighters might be, they were not typical of the mass of German immigrants. As recent arrivals for whom slavery was not a vital concern, the latter tended to concentrate on securing a livelihood and to be apathetic toward public affairs. Even more important was the disinclination of German Catholics to follow the political lead of the Forty-eighters, whom they detested as anticlericals and freethinkers. Catholics and Forty-eighters had remained two distinct and antagonistic groups, and the association of men like Karl Heinzen and Schurz with Republicanism had led the entire German Catholic press to identify the new party with irreligion and extreme radicalism. It was no accident that such a center of German Catholicism as Milwaukee should have been overwhelmingly Democratic in 1860.

The German Lutherans, by contrast, were not a distinct element politically. In the Wisconsin Synod a split over the slavery question resulted in most of the younger generation joining the Republican ranks. But the older Lutherans generally remained in the Democratic party, particularly in the congregations belonging to the Missouri Synod, whose leaders had found biblical justification for the institution of slavery. Significant, too, was the widespread belief among middle western Germans that the Republican party was deeply tainted with nativism. They had been particularly alarmed at eastern Republican support for the Massachusetts two-year amendment, and although repeated disavowals of nativism by Lincoln and other Republican leaders had done something to repair the damage, German suspicions had not been entirely allayed. In Wisconsin there was a further cause for German distrust in that many Republicans in the state had also been leading Prohibitionists. Finally, throughout the North, most German merchants and bankers were opposed to Lincoln because they feared, as did northern commercial circles generally, that a Republican victory would mean secession, war, and the loss of the valuable southern market.

In the South most Germans seem initially to have been indifferent to the slavery issue. Even those who were averse to slavery on moral grounds kept their opinions to themselves for fear of incurring social ostracism and of provoking fresh outbursts of nativism. If few Germans were slaveholders this was not because of humanitarianism but because the overwhelming majority were either city-dwellers or, as in southwestern Texas, had settled in regions unsuitable for cotton cultivation. It is true that in 1854 a group of Texas Germans at San Antonio, led by Adolf Douai, an old Forty-eighter, drew up a platform denouncing slavery as "an evil the removal of which is absolutely essential according to the principles of democracy." But the Forty-eighters were no more typical of German opinion in the South than they were in the North. Virtually the whole of the German-language press in the South joined in denouncing the San Antonio platform, and Douai's own paper, the San Antonio *Zeitung* lost so much support that it went out of existence in 1856. Only in Baltimore, where German artisans saw in abolition a means of eliminating the competition they suffered from slave labor, was there appreciable German sympathy for the antislavery movement. Elsewhere in the slave states the Germans were inclined to adopt the southern point of view. Wanting only to pursue their callings in peace, and believing that agitation of the slavery question could result only in disunion and war, they became bitter critics of the Republicans, especially those of German origin.

By 1860 the Germans of the South had become almost completely sectionalized. In such German strongholds as New Braunfels, Texas, voting was overwhelmingly for Breckinridge; in the German wards of New Orleans it was largely for Douglas, though some Germans swallowed their dislike of the nativist element in the Constitutional Union party and supported Bell. Of the four presidential candidates, only Lincoln failed to win a share of the German votes in the South.

Another group to react in a variety of ways to the slavery controversy consisted of immigrants of the Jewish faith, most of whom were of German origin. Since individual congregations were autonomous and their rabbis enjoyed freedom from hierarchical control, personal background and local allegiance rather than Jewish teaching determined Jewish views. Thus the southern rabbis were unanimous in upholding the slave system, and the two Jewish senators from the South, Judah P. Benjamin and David Yulee, were deeply committed to the views of their section. In the North, on the other hand, Jewish opinion was completely disunited. The most highly publicized Jewish pronouncement upon the slavery question was that of Rabbi Morris J. Raphall of New York City, who, during the secession winter of 1860–61, preached a celebrated sermon which found scriptural justification for slavery. Few northern Jews agreed with Dr. Raphall, but there were many who, without being proslavery, held with Rabbi Isaac Mayer Wise that the abolitionists were demagogues and fanatics who were likely to lead the nation into ruin. At the other extreme were abolitionist rabbis like Bernhard Felsenthal of Chicago and David Einhorn of Baltimore.

This diversity of rabbinical opinion stemmed from differing assessments of the effect of abolitionism upon the status of the Jew. Men like Wise distrusted the religious fanaticism that inspired the antislavery extremists, and feared that its next victim after the South had been crushed would be the Jews. Rabbi Einhorn, on the other hand, insisted that in fighting for Negro rights he was defending those of the Jew; no minority, he held, could feel safe from persecution so long as American society permitted the enslavement of any one group. Yet extremism was untypical of Jewish opinion. Many rabbi-editors like Samuel M. Isaacs, the editor of the *Jewish Messenger,* were opposed to any Jewish discussion of political issues, and the mass of Jewish laymen were inclined to agree. Preoccupied with problems of economic and social adjustment, and anxious, as a minority group, to remain neutral in a controversy where participation would inevitably bring down upon them the wrath of at least one of the antagonists, most Jews were neither proslavery nor antislavery.

The political attitudes of Scandinavian and Dutch immigrants were molded by influences similar to those which operated upon the Germans. About 1854 these groups began to transfer their allegiance from the Democratic to the Republican party. Yet, except among the Swedes, the process was by no means complete in 1860. The strength of Swedish Republicanism was due partly to the Republican promise of free lands by means of a homestead law, partly to the reluctance of the fiercely anti-Catholic Swedes to ally themselves with Irishmen in the Democratic party, and partly to the antislavery stand of the Reverend

T. N. Hasselquist, a Lutheran minister who edited *Hemlandet,* the only successful Swedish-language newspaper to appear before the Civil War. Clerical leadership was not always as effective, however, as it evidently was among the Swedes. Though they were solidly Lutheran, most Norwegian laymen refused to indorse the proslavery position of leading Norwegian Lutheran clergymen who had fallen under the influence of the German Missouri Synod. Likewise, though Lincoln's candidacy in 1860 was championed by Albertus C. Van Raalte and Hendrik P. Scholte, the two Dutch clergymen who had organized and led the exodus from Holland a dozen years before, a large proportion of their countrymen, especially in Iowa, refused to abandon the Democratic party. Many Norwegians and Dutchmen continued to suspect that nativism still lurked in the Republican ranks and were concerned at the threat to national unity posed by antislavery agitation.

Only among the Irish, a group of exceptional uniformity both in composition and in distribution, was political diversity the exception rather than the rule. The concept of "the Irish vote," it must be conceded, was not the product of a fevered nativist imagination but a reflection of reality. With rare exceptions Irish-Americans were bitterly hostile to the antislavery movement. Most Irishmen associated abolitionism with the worst excesses of European radicalism, distrusted it for its connection both with nativism and with temperance reform, and were suspicious of the close connection between British and American antislavery leaders. In such Irish-American journals as the Boston *Pilot* and the New York *Freeman's Journal* intemperate criticism of abolitionism was a commonplace; the abolitionist leaders were denounced as enemies of religion, as hypocrites indifferent to the welfare of white labor, and as fanatics who threatened the stability of the Union. These were also the sentiments of the Catholic hierarchy in the eastern states, many of whom, like Archbishop John Hughes of New York, were of Irish origin. The Catholic bishops would have tended in any case to remain aloof from a movement calculated to promote sectional differences among their followers; and they were markedly unsympathetic to abolitionism, whose emphasis upon material advancement ran counter to the whole tenor of Catholic social thought.

Closely connected with Irish antipathy to abolitionism, and in part responsible for it, was a hostility to free Negroes so notorious that even the Irish leader Daniel O'Connell had felt obliged in 1843 to rebuke his countrymen in America for being "among the worst enemies of the colored race." Some Irish-American leaders, like John Mitchel, editor of the New York *Citizen*, carried their Negrophobia so far as to become unqualified proslavery apologists. The explanation is to be sought in a deep-seated fear of Negro labor competition. In cities like New York, Irishmen and Negroes had competed directly for employment as laborers, waiters, servants, porters, and longshoremen. The use of Negroes as strikebreakers, both in railroad-building and in the docks, had added further to Irish bitterness. There was thus a solid basis for the concern constantly expressed in the Irish-American press lest emancipation, by flooding the northern labor market with freed Negroes, should depress the status of Irish workingmen.

In the South, where Irish laborers were widely employed in arduous work from which Negro slaves were carefully shielded, Irish hostility to the colored race was even more intense. There, too, competition for jobs was a powerful stimulant to ethnic rivalry. In New Orleans, for example, Irishmen had ousted free

Negroes as laborers, draymen, and rivermen and were constantly on the alert for signs of renewed Negro competition. Such situations, combined with the immigrant laborer's natural desire to have someone beneath him in the social pyramid, explained why the Irish in the slave states became vehement defenders of the South's peculiar institution. After making an extended journey through the slave states on the eve of the Civil War, Frederick Law Olmsted was moved to comment that "no native can exceed in idolatry to Slavery the mass of the ignorant, foreign-born laborers. Their hatred of the Negro is proportionate to the equality of their intellect and character to his; and their regard for Slavery to their disinclination to compete with him in a fair field."

Neither in the North nor in the South, therefore, was there much prospect during the 1850's that antislavery sympathies would tempt the Irish to abandon their traditional allegiance to the Democratic party. In fact most Irishmen supported the Kansas-Nebraska Act, blamed the troubles in Kansas on the abolitionists, and loudly condemned John Brown's raid. Since, moreover, Irish leaders continued to associate the Republicans with nativism, Lincoln received practically no Irish support in 1860, the bulk of their votes going to Douglas and Breckinridge.

The outbreak of war in 1861 simplified at one stroke the complex pattern of immigrant thought. The moment that union replaced slavery as the burning issue, sectional feeling became the sole determinant of attitude. Irrespective of its views on slavery each ethnic group simply gave its loyalty to the section of which it was a part. In the North the response of the foreign-born to Lincoln's call for volunteers was as immediate and as enthusiastic as that of older Americans, and foreign-born soldiers and sailors played an honorable, and at times a distinguished, part in the struggle. In Missouri in the spring of 1861 the bulk of the Union forces consisted of German militiamen, whose loyalty may well have been decisive in thwarting secessionist attempts to take the state out of the Union. Especially during the first half of the war many foreign-born soldiers served in distinctive military units under their own officers. Irish and German companies and regiments were particularly numerous; there was even an Irish brigade which, under the command of General Thomas Francis Meagher, fought with great gallantry at Fredericksburg. Yet, as the war wore on, these units increasingly lost their identity. Ethnic distinctions proved impossible to maintain in face of the need to replace casualties with whatever recruits were available, and in forming new regiments the military authorities found it simpler and more efficient to mix foreign-born and native soldiers indiscriminately.

South of Mason and Dixon's line the immigrant population showed just as much enthusiasm in rallying to the defense of the Confederacy, and there were tens of thousands of foreign-born soldiers in the Confederate army. On occasion, men of similar origin found themselves face to face on the battlefield. At Fredericksburg it was a largely Irish regiment from Georgia which withstood Meagher's charge upon Marye's Heights. As was the case in the Union army the Confederate forces included a number of foreign-born military companies, such as the New Orleans Jägers and the Emerald Guards. But Confederate opinion, doubtful of immigrant loyalties, was hostile to the formation of such companies, and most foreign-born soldiers were to be found in mixed units.

Only among the Texas Germans did the South's suspicions

of its foreign-born find justification. But Texas German resistance to the Confederate draft of 1863 was probably due less to Union sympathies than to a desire to remain neutral. And while much has been made of the fact that some Texas Germans were to be found in the Federal army, the Confederate general Richard Taylor could still report of the Louisiana campaign that "none of my regiments did better than General Büchel's regiment of Texas Germans, raised near New Braunfels."

Foreign-born support for the South was necessarily limited by the relatively small numbers of immigrants who settled there. Since the great bulk were concentrated in the North, the overwhelming reaction of the immigrant to the Civil War was one of intense devotion to the Union. This stemmed largely from a deeply felt gratitude for the benefits it had conferred upon him. Thomas D'Arcy McGee had asserted in 1855 that not even the natives of New England had a greater interest in the preservation of the Union than had the Irish, who had received in America the equality of treatment they had been denied by England. In December, 1860, the New York *Irish-American* warned the South that Irishmen could never "countenance the destruction of the government which [had] naturalized, enfranchised and protected them." Moreover, as a Norwegian visitor to the United States had pointed out in the 1840's, the loyalty of immigrants was concentrated wholly upon the Union, since, unlike native Americans, they had no narrow local attachments to compete for their affection.

The fierce nationalism of the foreign-born does not entirely account for the alacrity with which they sprang to arms in 1861. What led many to enlist was the offer of a bounty greater than an unskilled laborer's annual earnings. Large numbers, too, joined the army because the trade depression at the beginning of the war, and its consequent unemployment, left them no choice save starvation or military service. Such cases were common, for example, in New York where Horace Greeley, struck in April, 1861, by the high proportion of foreigners among the recruits, wondered whether "the applicants [were] actuated by the desire of preserving the union of the states or the union of their own bodies and souls." The hostility of the British government to the Union cause was a further cause for Irish support of the war. Some Irish-American leaders, like Meagher and General James Shields, repeatedly stressed that the military experience Irishmen would gain in fighting for the Union would ultimately prove useful in the fight for Irish independence.

The proportion of foreign-born soldiers in the Union ranks has been the subject of almost as much controversy as the relative strengths of the Union and Confederate armies. During the Civil War itself many southerners were firmly convinced that the overwhelming majority of Federal soldiers were of foreign origin, and it was to this fact that in later years they often attributed the defeat of the Confederacy. But it is probable that the number of foreign-born soldiers in the Union army did not much exceed half a million, which was only about one-fifth of the total number of enlistments. This proportion was slightly higher than that of foreign-born persons in the Union population but it should be remembered that the foreign-born contained, relatively, much larger numbers of men of military age than did the rest of the population.

Also firmly implanted in the southern mind was the notion that the United States was enlisting soldiers abroad. So concerned was the Confederate government at this alleged practice that in 1862 it dispatched two emissaries to Ireland to counter the activities of Federal recruiting agents. Union Secretary of

State Seward repeatedly denied, however, that any soldiers had been enlisted abroad by accredited representatives of the United States or that any official inducements had been offered in Europe to those who had enlisted on reaching America. All that he had done, Seward claimed, had been to encourage voluntary immigration in the hope of relieving the wartime shortage of labor. In 1862–63 he circularized American diplomatic and consular representatives in Europe, authorizing them to publicize the high rates of wages prevalent in the United States and to draw attention to the advantages of the Homestead Act. It was only to be expected that these circulars should have been interpreted in Europe as an attempt to win recruits for the army under false pretenses, and it is difficult to believe that Seward can have been unaware of the relevance of increased immigration to the problem of replenishing the ranks. At all events, a systematic recruiting program was instituted among newly arrived immigrants. As immigrants arrived at Castle Garden they were met by recruiting officers with the offer of large bounties and other inducements. Especially during the latter half of the war, when the volume of immigration sharply increased, great numbers of foreigners became soldiers immediately on arrival.

The unanimity with which immigrants rallied to the support of the Union in 1861 was far from implying the repudiation of their prewar attitudes toward political and social issues. Most of those who had been Democrats in 1860, for example, continued throughout the war to dislike Lincoln and to oppose abolitionism. This was particularly true of the Irish, whose unchanged attitude to the Negro was graphically illustrated in July, 1863, by the New York draft riots, in which a largely Irish mob terrorized the city for three days. The immediate cause of the outbreak was the attempt to enforce the Conscription Act passed in the previous March. To Irish immigrants it seemed outrageously unfair that the measure should allow wealthy draftees to escape military service by paying the sum of $300, a choice which most immigrants were denied by their poverty. It was widely and correctly believed, moreover, that the draft law, administered by Republican officials, bore unfairly upon Democratic wards. Yet the wholesale attacks made by the rioters on Negroes and the fact that they destroyed a Negro orphanage showed that conscription was not the only cause of discontent. What largely prompted the riots was the long-established Irish fear of labor competition. The Emancipation Proclamation, followed shortly in New York by the use of Negroes to break a strike of Irish longshoremen, revived for Irishmen the specter of economic extinction. Conscription merely added insult to injury, since it compelled Irishmen to fight for the freedom of the very class which threatened to deprive them of work.

The anti-Irish reaction provoked by the New York draft riots seemed momentarily to presage a revival of nativism. So, too, did General Grant's order of December, 1862, expelling Jews as a class from the Department of the Tennessee, an act which made Jews the scapegoat for all the illicit cotton trading that was being conducted through the Union lines. But neither of these incidents produced prolonged nativistic repercussions. Even the bitterest critics of the Irish rioters acknowledged that their loyalty was not in question, and Grant's notorious order was revoked after three weeks, on instructions from Lincoln. Dislike and distrust of foreigners did not entirely disappear; nor did the practice of identifying ethnic groups by stereotypes. But hatred and fear of foreigners was now definitely on the wane, and most of the surviving non-political nativist associations followed the Know-Nothing Party into oblivion. There were other evidences, too, of a lessening of ethnic discord. Massachusetts repealed both the two-year amendment and the law making Bible-reading compulsory in schools, and New Yorkers were able to marvel in 1862 at the spectacle of an "Anti-Abolition States Rights Society" supported jointly by Irish Catholics Richard O'Gorman and Charles O'Connor and the erstwhile nativist Samuel F. B. Morse. These signs of the decline of nativism were due to the realization that, in the new situation brought about by the war, immigrants were not a menace to the existing order but one of its stoutest props. Accordingly, with rebellion and Copperheadism taking the place of foreign influence as the main threat to the status quo, popular hostility was transferred from the foreign-born to the native nonconformist.

For the foreign-born the war years brought something more than a mere lessening of nativist hostility. It brought also a new prestige, an improved status, and a reoriented cultural outlook. The many thousands who fought for the Union did so upon terms of equality with the native population, and thus lost the sense of inferiority which had dogged them since their coming to America. But even those who remained on the farms and in the factories shared in this wartime Americanization. The general prosperity of the war years facilitated their economic adjustment and in doing so began to transform their economic and social position and thus to remove the barriers which had divided them from older Americans. Moreover the anxieties and stresses of the struggle had so filled the mind as to dim immigrant memories of what had been left behind. The nationalizing effect of the struggle must not, of course, be exaggerated. Each immigrant community remained a distinct group, fully conscious of its identity and its separateness. The Germans, for example, persisted throughout the struggle in regarding Union generals like Carl Schurz, Franz Sigel, and Ludwig Blenker as symbols of their personal contributions to the war and in interpreting the criticism these well-known Forty-eighters incurred as slights upon themselves. While these tendencies were widespread, the war left an ineffaceable mark. Tested in their adjustment to America, immigrants showed by their response that they had captured her ethos and rhythm. For them as for the nation of their adoption the Civil War was both an ending and a new beginning.

VII

New Sources of Immigration, 1860–1914

A single assumption ran through the forty-one-volume report of the Dillingham Commission set up by Congress in 1907 to investigate the question of immigration. This was that the early 1880's had seen a fundamental change in the character of American immigration. Up to that time immigration had come almost exclusively from the countries of northern and western Europe and, according to the Commission, had been very largely a movement of families seeking a permanent home in the New World. Those who had constituted this "old" immigration had, it was claimed, "entered practically every line of activity in nearly every part of the country," a considerable number having taken up farming. And despite the fact that a large proportion had been non-English-speaking, they had "mingled freely with . . . native Americans" and had therefore been quickly assimilated.

American Immigration

Far different, however, was the Commission's view of the movement which had begun about 1883 from the countries of southern and eastern Europe. This "new" immigration had consisted, it declared, largely of unskilled male laborers, a large proportion of whom had come to the United States not as permanent settlers but simply as transients. Almost entirely avoiding agriculture, they had flocked to the industrial centers of the East and Middle West, where they had "congregated together in sections apart from native Americans and the older immigrants to such an extent that assimilation [had] been slow."

For half a century these sharply drawn distinctions have been almost universally accepted. The concept of an "old" and a "new" immigration, differing from each other in many essentials, has exerted a decisive influence upon American immigration policy and has served as a framework for a great deal of historical writing about nineteenth-century immigration. Historians have in fact often been more emphatic than the Immigration Commission in distinguishing the "new" immigration from the "old." The two movements, it has been claimed, differed from each other just as much in their motivation as in their composition. Whereas the immigration from northern and western Europe is accepted to have been largely spontaneous and self-directed, that from southern and eastern Europe is alleged to have been involuntary and artificially induced. The rise of the "new" immigration, we have been led to believe, was due mainly to steamship and railroad advertising and to the efforts of American employers to import cheap labor.

That there was a significant shift in the geographical origins of American immigration toward the end of the nineteenth century is beyond dispute. Of the three great waves which made up the century-long mass migration, the first two—covering the years 1815–60 and 1860–90, respectively—came from the same general areas in Europe. Both the five million immigrants who composed the pre–Civil War wave and the ten million who arrived in the succeeding thirty years were predominantly from the British Isles, Germany, Scandinavia, Switzerland, and Holland. But the last and greatest of the three waves, which brought to the United States a total of fifteen million immigrants between 1890 and 1914 was drawn very largely from Austria-Hungary, Italy, Russia, Greece, Rumania, and Turkey.

The extent of the change can be measured by comparing the immigration of 1882 with that of 1907, the years in which the two post–Civil War waves reached their respective crests. Of the 788,000 immigrants who arrived in 1882, 87 per cent came from the countries of northern and western Europe and 13 per cent from the countries of southern and eastern Europe. But in 1907, when 1,285,000 immigrants reached the United States, the proportions were 19.3 and 80.7 per cent, respectively. The "old" immigration had thus declined absolutely as well as relatively. Yet the shift came both later and with less suddenness than we are sometimes told. Not until 1896 did the volume of the "new" immigration exceed that of the "old," and the disparity between the two groups became really marked only after the turn of the century.

Despite the fact that the period saw a marked change in the sources of the movement, the interpretation favored by the Dillingham Commission and by many historians is open to serious objection. The coming of the southern and eastern Europeans did not reflect a change in the pattern of immigrant recruitment; steamship lines, railroad companies, and American industry were no more responsible for the "new" immigration than they had been for the "old." Moreover, as we have already shown, urban concentration and clannishness were by no means unknown among pre–Civil War immigrants. The fundamental weakness of the traditional interpretation, however, is that it is based upon a completely artificial distinction. In no real sense could either the immigration from northern and western Europe or that from southern and eastern Europe be regarded as a collective entity possessing common attributes; on the contrary, each of the two groups of immigrants was composed of a great variety of contrasting types who deserve to be treated as such. Any other approach is not only unobjective but misleading.

This much is glaringly evident from an examination of the data upon which the Dillingham Commission based its distinctions. The Commission attempted to show statistically that the "new" immigration differed from the "old" in having a higher percentage of males and of unskilled laborers, in being more illiterate, and in having a greater tendency to impermanence. But the Commission's own data did not bear out these conclusions. Had specific groups of immigrants been considered individually, instead of being lumped together in two arbitrarily chosen categories, a very different picture would have emerged. It was undeniable that Italian and Slavic immigrants, for instance, were predominantly male, unskilled, illiterate, and transient. But there were larger percentages of males among German, Scandinavian, and English immigrants than there were among Jewish, Bohemian, and Portuguese; Bohemians, Moravians, and Finns had lower percentages of illiteracy than had the Irish and Germans; Englishmen, Germans, and Scandinavians showed a greater tendency to return to Europe that did Armenians, Dalmatians, Jews, and Portuguese; Jews had a higher percentage of skilled laborers than any group except the Scots, and the Irish had a smaller percentage than the Italians.

The Commission also neglected to take into account the duration of settlement of each of the immigrant groups. Had it done so, it could not have failed to notice a marked correlation between the percentage of males and the recency of immigration. There was a much higher proportion of males among the Greeks, whose immigration had begun on a large scale only about 1900, than among the Italians, who had been coming for a decade longer; the Italians in turn had a much higher proportion than the Bohemians, whose immigration had begun in the 1860's. In this respect, therefore, what the Commission's statistics tended to show was that post–Civil War imigration adhered closely to the pattern established by Irish immigrants at the very beginning of the nineteenth century. That is to say, the initial phase of immigration from any given area was generally composed largely of unaccompanied males; but as soon as the firstcomers had established themselves, they were usually joined by their wives and families.

Still another defect in the Commission's reasoning resulted from the narrow chronological limits of its inquiries. The Commission drew attention to the fact that in the period 1899–1909 the percentage of skilled laborers among immigrants from northern and western Europe was twice as great as among those from southern and eastern Europe. But this was a misleading comparison to make for the simple reason that, in the period named, the proportion of unskilled laborers from northern and western Europe was as low as it was only because of the extent of the competition from south and east Europeans. A more proper comparison would have been between the "new" immigration in the period 1899–1909 and the "old" immigration in the period 1871–82—that is, before the "new" immigration had begun. This would have shown that the "old" immigration had only a slightly higher proportion of skilled laborers than had the "new"—22.9 per cent as against 18.1 per cent.

The belief that the "new" immigration was artificially induced in some distinctive way rested in large part upon a mistaken view of the promotional activities of steamship companies in southern and eastern Europe. The Dillingham Commission reported that, although steamship company propaganda circulated in every European country, "the attempted promotion of emigration by steamship ticket agents" was carried on chiefly in Austria-Hungary, Greece, and Russia. In those countries a vast army of agents and sub-agents was said to be feverishly at work to induce the peasants to leave; in Galicia alone, it was reported, two of the leading steamship companies employed no fewer than five thousand agents in "a great hunt for emigrants." By means of "highly colored posters," circulars, and other advertising matter attempts were being made to impress the peasants with the belief that employment at high wages could promptly be secured on landing in the United States. Some lines, indeed, had even established their own labor bureaus in American cities to assist immigrants in finding work. Such activities, the Commission believed, proved that the steamship lines were largely responsible for "this unnatural immigration."

But it was not the case that the steamship lines adopted novel methods to drum up custom in southern and eastern Europe; they simply used the same advertising techniques there that had proved successful elsewhere. Steamship labor bureaus, for example, were first advertised not in Austria-Hungary or Italy during the eighties, but in Scandinavia during the sixties. In any case job inducements were nowhere a regular feature of steamship advertising, except perhaps in the earliest stages of immigration from any given area. Individual sub-agents may well have continued to hold out the bait of high American wages —just as they had done from the beginning of mass emigration; but the steamship companies themselves soon found it both impossible and unnecessary to encourage emigration. Impossible, because the practice was strictly forbidden by nearly every European government; unnecessary, because emigrants offered themselves in sufficient numbers without solicitation. The highly colored posters in nearly every case simply gave particulars of sailings. As for the thousands of agents whom the Dillingham Commission pictured as working surreptitiously to flood the United States with an "unnatural immigration," these were for the most part inoffensive storekeepers who sold steamship tickets on commission as a profitable and not very demanding sideline. Similar agencies existed also in northern and western Europe; they had done so ever since the immigrant trade had first become organized in the 1830's. Thus to ascribe the "new" immigration simply to steamship advertising was, as a shrewd contemporary remarked, a mere "rhetorical commonplace," which appealed to observers in inverse ratio to their knowledge of the subject.

Nevertheless, the transition from sail to steam in the transatlantic immigrant trade was an event of enormous significance for the history of immigration. It meant, first, that the Atlantic crossing lost virtually all of its hazards and that the perils of the journey were much less of a deterrent than before. More than this, the opening-up of new steamship routes made immigration possible for the peoples of the entire European continent. By the beginning of the twentieth century, passage to the United States was as easy to obtain from Odessa as from Queenstown, from Palermo as from Bergen. Finally, by introducing the possibility of seasonal migration across the Atlantic, the steamship altered the whole character of the movement to the United States.

The entry of the steamship into the immigrant trade dates from the early 1850's, when Inman Line steamships began carrying steerage passengers from Liverpool to Philadelphia. But the bulk of the trade remained firmly in the hands of American sailing packets until the Civil War, when the threat of Confederate commerce-raiders like the "Alabama" virtually drove the Stars and Stripes from the sea lanes. Seizing their opportunity, British and German shipowners built a great quantity of steamship tonnage specially designed for passenger-carrying. Existing lines, like the Inman and Cunard from Liverpool, the Hamburg-Amerika from Hamburg, and the North German Lloyd from Bremen, were thus able greatly to expand their services in the sixties. The same decade also saw the birth of new lines like the Guion and the National from Liverpool, and the Compagnie Générale Transatlantique from Le Havre, while the seventies brought into being the White Star, Holland-America, Red Star, Dominion, and other lines. In little more than a decade, steamships almost completely ousted sailing vessels from the immigrant trade. The annual reports of the New York Commissioners of Immigration show that, as late as 1856, 96.4 per cent of the immigrants arriving in New York came in sailing vessels; but by 1873 an even higher proportion traveled in steamships.

A drastic reduction in the length of passage was the outstanding benefit brought about by this transportation revolution. Whereas the crossing had taken between one and three months in sailing vessels, it now took a mere ten days. Unlike the sailing packets the new steamers were built primarily as passenger-carriers, and therefore had better steerage accommodations. To be sure, there was still room for improvement. The steerage remained dark and poorly ventilated, access to the deck was restricted, and overcrowding was still a problem, especially in rush seasons. Moreover, epidemics did not completely disappear. An outbreak of cholera caused hundreds of deaths among German immigrants traveling from Rotterdam on National Line steamers in 1866; and a similar outbreak in 1892 among Russian Jewish immigrants traveling on Hamburg-Amerika liners forced the United States to apply quarantine measures which brought all immigration to a halt for a time. But these were isolated occurrences which in any case were not attributable to conditions on board the ships. As early as 1873 a congressional investigation of the immigrant trade could find no serious abuses; the general opinion of the investigators was rather that "the cruelty, ill-usage, and general discomfort of the steerage belong to the history of the past."

In the eighties the emigrant trade became the subject of fierce international competition, especially between British and German steamship lines; and although by 1900 the establishment of the North Atlantic, Continental, and Mediterranean Steamship Conferences had put an end to rate wars, rivalry persisted right down to the outbreak of World War I. The German lines were, of course, better placed than the British to tap the newer sources of immigration in central and eastern Europe. But it was not until after the cholera epidemic of 1892, when the German government established a series of control stations along the Austrian and Russian frontiers that German superiority in these areas became clear-cut. Though the original purpose of the control stations was to enable medical inspection to be carried out, the German government allowed the Hamburg-Amerika and North German Lloyd companies to use them for their own purposes. Thus immigrants arriving at the control stations with British or other non-German steamship tickets often found themselves delayed or even sent back unless they agreed to travel by one of the two German lines. The British lines nevertheless managed to retain a substantial proportion of the south and east European traffic. They worked out routes whereby immigrants from Austria-Hungary and Russia could reach Liverpool without crossing the German frontier; they even ferried Russian immigrants direct to Liverpool from Libau (Lepaya) and other Baltic ports; and they started services to New York, Boston, and New Orleans from Naples, Genoa, Palermo, Fiume, and Trieste—a practice which the German lines copied. Largely out of this Anglo-German commercial rivalry was woven the modern steamship network which did so much to "grease the wheels of immigration."

The steamship not only bridged the Atlantic from areas which until then had contributed little to the westward flow; it led to a tremendous expansion of the prepaid passage system. By 1890 hardly a town of any size in the United States was without its steamship agencies where passages for relatives and friends could be purchased; the Hamburg-Amerika Line alone had 3,200 American agencies, the Red Star Line 1,800, the Anchor Line more than 1,500. In that year, according to the testimony of passenger agents before a congressional Committee on Immigration and Naturalization, between one-quarter and one-third of all immigrants were arriving on prepaid tickets. In 1901 the United States Industrial Commission found that between 40 and 65 per cent of all immigrants now came either on prepaid tickets or on fares paid for with money sent to them by relatives in the United States. The proportion, incidentally, was the same among "new" immigrants like the Italians as among "older" groups like the Irish and Swedes.

It is also important to recognize that it was the steamship, and not the shift in the sources of immigration, that was responsible for the beginning of temporary European immigration to the United States. No sooner had the Atlantic crossing become regular, fast, and tolerably comfortable than a substantial transient movement set in. British and German skilled workers began in the seventies to shuttle back and forth across the Atlantic in response to wage movements in America and the homeland. Great numbers began to go out to the United States each spring with the fixed intention of returning in the fall. This was the practice of house decorators and quarrymen whose trades shut down in the American winter, and also of miners, potters, and textile workers whose purpose in migrating was simply to obtain temporary employment at high wages. Thus the transatlantic steerage traffic became for the first time a two-way movement. There were even times during the long American depression of the seventies when the eastbound movement exceeded that in the opposite direction.

Though the steamship companies did little directly to stimulate immigration, there were a number of agencies which did. The most active were those established by individual American states and by the land-grant railroads. The northwestern states had a double reason for trying to attract immigrants; they were anxious to dispose of their unsold lands, and they recognized that increased population was essential to material growth. Though some states—Michigan and Wisconsin, for instance—

attempted even before the Civil War to turn the immigrant stream in their direction, it was not until later that their example was at all widely followed. After 1865, however, practically every northwestern state and territory from Wisconsin to Oregon embarked upon a policy of encouraging immigration. State immigration bureaus advertised extensively in the press of the eastern states and of Europe, published and distributed many thousands of pamphlets and maps, and dispatched immigration agents to numerous places in Europe and America. Just how effective these efforts were is impossible to judge, but Wisconsin, Minnesota, and Iowa particularly seem to have owed a significant part of their foreign-born population to the vigor of their advertising campaigns.

Most of the southern states, too, joined in the postwar scramble for immigrants. The South had practically no unsold land to dispose of, but it wanted cheap foreign labor to replace its allegedly inefficient Negroes. Unlike the northwestern states, the South received comparatively little return for its efforts. The failure of the anticipated mass influx to materialize was proof that slavery had not been the reason that earlier immigrants had shunned the southern states. The truth was that the absence of free land and—until the twentieth century—of large-scale industry deflected the current of immigration elsewhere.

Less sporadic and more systematic than those of the states were the colonizing activities of the land-grant railroads. For them, it was vital that the empty lands contiguous to their tracks should be settled as soon as possible. Accordingly, many of them spent large sums of money in efforts to attract immigrants, both from Europe and from longer-settled regions in the United States. First in the field was the Illinois Central, whose promotional campaign was initiated as early as 1855. But the heyday of railroad colonization did not come until the seventies and eighties, when the Northern Pacific, Burlington and Missouri, Santa Fe, Southern Pacific, and many other roads operated land and immigration departments. Apart from being conducted upon a more lavish scale, railroad advertising in Europe and the eastern states closely resembled that of the state immigration bureaus. But the railroads were able to offer immigrants greater inducements than could the states. Free "land-exploring" tickets, reduced steamship and railroad fares, liberal sales policies, and long-term financing plans were only some of the baits the railroads held out to prospective land-purchasers. Many of the roads built immigrant houses on the plains where buyers could stay free of charge while they selected suitable tracts; some, like the Great Northern, offered to educate settlers in plains agriculture, and a few roads even went so far as to build churches and schools for the communities they planted. Altogether the colonization activities of the railroads were marked by a benevolence which contrasted strangely with some of their other contemporary practices.

Railroad colonization, characterized as it was by a tendency to establish compact, homogeneous settlements, did more than a little to determine the ethnic pattern of the trans-Mississippi West. The Burlington planted numerous German, British, and Scandinavian colonies in Nebraska and Iowa; the Northern Pacific fathered an even greater number in Minnesota, Dakota, and the Pacific Northwest; and the Santa Fe was responsible for bringing to Kansas some thousands of Russo-German Mennonites. Each of these colonies, moreover, acted in succeeding decades as a lodestone for immigrants of similar background.

Yet it is all too easy both to exaggerate and to misinterpret the role of railroad and state immigration promotion. Both types of agency directed their European advertising almost exclusively toward the British Isles, Germany, and Scandinavia; the "new" immigration owed virtually nothing to their efforts. And even their attempts to attract immigrants from northern and western Europe were less a matter of stimulating the movement than of directing it. Neither state bureaus nor railroad land departments undertook grass-roots campaigns to induce Europeans to leave; instead they stationed agents at strategic points along immigrant routes with the object simply of tapping a movement already under way.

Still less concerned with the process of immigration was American industry which, together with the steamship lines, occupied a prominent place in nativist demonology. Not only nativists but the mass of contemporary opinion assumed that between 1864, when Congress legalized contract labor, and 1885, when the Foran Act forbade it, American industry imported on contract vast numbers of unskilled laborers from southern and eastern Europe for the purpose of lowering wages and breaking strikes. This, too, has been the view of most historians. But recent research has disclosed an entirely different situation. It has been shown that, although mine operators and railroad contractors were glad enough to employ those immigrants who found their own way to America, they did not import masses of unskilled labor on contract. Contract labor was in fact extremely rare in America in the post–Civil War era, largely because manufacturers found it too unreliable. On the comparatively few occasions when it was used, it was for the purpose of bringing in highly skilled workers—usually from Great Britain or Germany—for particular jobs or for introducing new processes. As for the Italian and Slavic immigrants used as strikebreakers in Pennsylvania in the early eighties, these were not contract laborers but voluntary immigrants supplied to industry by labor agencies in the larger American cities.

Somewhat akin to contract labor was the *padrone* system, a method of immigrant recruitment which first developed in connection with the movement from southern Italy. During the eighties some *padroni*, or labor bosses, collected children from the hillsides of Italy and carried them to America, practically in the condition of slaves, to be employed as wandering musicians and street acrobats. This practice was soon prohibited by law, however, and by 1880 had virtually ceased to exist. Yet the *padrone* system, even from the first, was concerned less with child labor than with that of adults. Either on his own initiative, or in association with an Italian immigrant "bank"—an institution which combined banking with the sale of passage tickets and also acted as an employment agency—a *padrone* would go to Italy to recruit unskilled labor on contract at a fixed wage, usually paying the fares of those he engaged. On arrival in the United States the recruits were supplied in gangs to American employers at rates which gave the *padrone* a substantial profit. In this form the *padrone* system flourished only during the early stages of Italian immigration. After about 1890 the movement from Italy reached such proportions that it was no longer necessary for contractors to go abroad to import labor. By this time, the *padrone* had become, for Italian immigrants at least, simply a special kind of employment agent. Newly arrived Italians, ignorant of American conditions, were glad enough to place themselves in the hands of a *padrone* who, though he often exploited them, could be relied upon not only to find them work but to supply them with food and lodging. As Italians became better acquainted with American conditions, however, and learned how they were being exploited by the *padrone*, they tended to dispense with his services.

The *padrone* system was also a feature of Greek and Syrian immigration. Among the Syrians it flourished chiefly in merchandising, the practice being for Syrian merchants to control a number of immigrant peddlers. These they lodged and boarded, and sent out daily to peddle notions and dry goods in the larger cities. There seems to be no evidence that Syrian *padroni* were responsible for the immigration of those they employed; and in any case the system soon declined because Syrian immigrants preferred factory or railroad work to peddling. Among the Greeks, on the other hand, *padroni* often financed the immigration of youths whom they employed as fruit and candy peddlers or, more often, as shoeblacks. That by 1910 practically every American city had its Greek-operated shoeshine parlors was due to the steady importation of youths during the previous fifteen years from the Greek province of Arcadia.

Though all these agencies, from steamship lines to *padroni*, did much to stimulate immigration in the post–Civil War era, the essential forces underlying the movement were to be found elsewhere. These forces were precisely those which had brought to the United States the first great wave of mass immigration in the decades immediately after 1815. Among them were political and religious discontent, as well as increasing knowledge of American opportunity. But the successive extension of the frontiers of European emigration in the period between 1860 and 1914 was due basically to the widening impact of economic change. In northern and western Europe, as we saw earlier, the collapse of the old agrarian order and the rise of the factory system had transformed social and economic life and, in conjunction with the pressure of mounting population, had provided the impetus for emigration. Now, in the later decades of the nineteenth century, the same thing happened in other parts of Europe.

Although between 1860 and 1890 the bulk of the immigrants to the United States came as before from the British Isles, Germany, and Scandinavia, from none of these regions was the geographical source of the movement quite the same as in pre–Civil War days. The Irish exodus, though still considerable, was very much smaller than during the famine and, in the movement from the British Isles, Englishmen, Welshmen, and Scots replaced Irishmen as the most numerous element. In Scandinavian emigration, Swedes came to the forefront at the expense of Norwegians, and in that from Germany, Bavarians and Württembergers gave way to Prussians and Saxons. In each of the three main areas of emigration, therefore, the center of gravity of the movement moved appreciably to the eastward.

Mainly responsible for the change was the competition of cheap foreign grain. England, Sweden, and Germany east of the Elbe were all grain-producing regions which were hard hit in the sixties and seventies by the sweep of technical progress. Thanks to the railroad and the cargo steamer the cost of transporting grain fell dramatically, with the result that the wheat farmers of the United States, Russia, India, and other distant countries could for the first time compete successfully in the European market. Upon European farming the effect was immediate and catastrophic. Germany, now linked by rail to the Russian black earth zone, the Polish and Hungarian plains, and the Rumanian wheatlands, changed within a single decade—1865–75—from a grain-exporting to a grain-importing country. In England a searing agricultural depression in the seventies, originating in the competition of American wheat, spelled the doom of the old agrarian economy; between the sixties and the eighties the price of wheat and the acreage of land under wheat both fell by almost 50 per cent. In Sweden, which turned to free trade in 1865, the agrarian crisis was heightened by disastrous crop failures between 1861 and 1869 which produced famine conditions in many areas.

In each of the areas affected tens of thousands of farmers and agricultural laborers were driven to emigrate. To be sure, the agricultural crisis does not wholly explain the exodus. In Sweden the decline of the timber industry caused by the transition from wooden to iron ships, and the depression of the iron and steel industry as a result of American tariff policy, both helped to swell the number of departures. Special factors were at work in Germany, too, such as the widespread hostility to military service after 1866 when the formation of the North German Confederation brought into being a centralized military system under Prussian control. Industrial depression, particularly in the early eighties, had a marked effect upon the character of German immigration, which at all times included a substantial proportion of artisans. From the Ruhr came thousands of coal-miners and iron and steel workers; from the textile districts of Saxony, Bavaria, and Silesia a steady stream of weavers and spinners; and from Westphalia and Rhenish Prussia great numbers of glassworkers, cutlers, and leatherworkers. From Britain, a sizable part of the outflow bore a similar character. In the late sixties began a large-scale movement of Lancashire textile workers, followed shortly afterward by one of Yorkshire woolen operatives and a smaller but no less significant exodus of Macclesfield silkworkers, who felt the pinch after Cobden's treaty of 1860 had admitted French silks to Britain free of duty. Yet the most numerous group of British industrial emigrants were probably coal-miners from Durham, Scotland, and Wales, and iron puddlers and rollers from the Black Country.

Even so it was the European agricultural crisis which was mainly responsible for the postwar wave of emigration from Germany, the British Isles, and Scandinavia. That the wave should reach its crest in the early eighties was a consequence less of industrial depression than of a steadily worsening agricultural situation. German farming had been under a blight for almost a decade, Swedish commodity prices were the lowest for half a century, the English farmer was reeling under a succession of disastrous harvests, and Ireland had just been revisited by famine. In 1882, therefore, with the American economy booming, the volume of immigration rose to an unprecedented 788,000. German arrivals amounted to 250,000, an all-time record, British and Irish immigrants to 179,000, and those from Sweden, Norway, and Denmark to 105,000.

After 1890 immigration from all these countries showed a sharp decline. During the succeeding quarter of a century the annual arrivals from the British Isles only rarely exceeded 100,-000 and in many years came to less than half that figure. Scandinavian immigration showed an even greater drop, and that from Germany became almost negligible. After 1894 the annual movement from Germany never exceeded 40,000, and by 1912 had fallen below 20,000.

One reason for the decline was that the countries of northwestern Europe now had fewer men to spare. The fall in the birthrate, which began in the last decades of the nineteenth century and which became precipitate after 1900, brought to an end a period of more than a century of rapid population increase in that area. In Germany and Scandinavia, moreover, rapid industrialization created new employment for those displaced from the land. So tremendous was the absorptive capacity of German industry that after 1890 German agriculture experienced a labor shortage which was met only by the large-scale importation of foreign labor for harvesting and other seasonal work. Then, too, the international rivalries of the late nineteenth century brought a new awareness of the military and economic value of manpower, a change which was reflected in official attitudes to emigration. Germany now made strenuous efforts to keep her people at home; some of Bismarck's social legislation as well as the laws to broaden landownership were inspired partly by this aim. Sweden pursued a similar course, with the government giving its blessing to a society for the prevention of emigration which sought to achieve its object by promoting land reform. Britain, by contrast, did nothing to check departures but attempted to divert her emigrants away from the United States and toward her own dominions and colonies. How successful she was is shown by the fact that between 1901 and 1912 the proportion of British and Irish emigrants choosing the United States declined from 61 per cent to 25 per cent—Canada, Australasia, and South Africa now claimed the great majority. Finally, there were now fewer opportunities in the United States for north and west Europeans. After 1890 the empty lands of the American West were no longer there to beckon the would-be farmer. Equally important, the unskilled labor market was now being pre-empted by south and east Europeans.

New Sources of Immigration, 1860–1914

Even if other circumstances had been favorable, emigration from southern and eastern Europe could hardly have begun before it did because of official hostility. For the first two-thirds of the nineteenth century most countries in this region strictly forbade their subjects to emigrate, the prohibitory laws being especially severe in the states of southern Italy and in those areas of the Balkans under Turkish rule. The growth of more liberal attitudes was closely related to major European political changes. In Italy it was the success of the unification movement in 1859–60 which brought about the removal of existing restraints. In Austria-Hungary freedom of emigration was officially conceded in 1867 in the course of the political reorganization marked by the *Ausgleich;* this concession, however, did not prevent the Austrian and Hungarian governments from attempting to impede emigration for more than a decade longer. For large parts of the Balkans the right to emigrate came after the Russo-Turkish War of 1877, when large Slavic areas—Serbia, Bulgaria, Montenegro, Bosnia, and Herzegovina—were emancipated from Turkish rule. Although by the beginning of the twentieth century there was a general tendency to deplore emigration as a drain upon national resources and military strength, all European countries, except perhaps Russia and Turkey, had come to recognize the right of their peoples to emigrate freely. Even the Russian and Turkish prohibitory laws were largely dead letters.

With the disappearance of official restraint and the simultaneous development of new transportation facilities, emigration to the New World was free to develop to the extent determined by local conditions. As economic change spread southward and eastward in the last decades of the nineteenth century, it was thus able to have the same expulsive effect that we have already noted in other regions. First to be affected was the sprawling, ramshackle empire of the Hapsburgs with its ethnic hodgepodge of Germans, Magyars, Rumanians, and half a dozen varieties of Slavs. Though conditions in Austria-Hungary varied from province to province the basic situation producing emigration was everywhere the same, namely, one of dislocation resulting from the breakup of the age-old peasant economy. The abolition of feudal dues in 1848 transformed the peasant into a free proprietor, thus ending the medieval conditions which had hitherto persisted. But it was not until the sixties that the emancipated peasant was given the right to divide his land. Once that happened subdivision took place at an extremely rapid rate so that the land became split up into tiny holdings quite incapable of supporting those who lived on them. Then, as had happened elsewhere, the peasant emigrated to avoid an inevitable fall to the status of a propertyless day laborer.

In its earliest stages, during the sixties and seventies, the bulk of Austro-Hungarian emigration consisted of Bohemians and Moravians, or Czechs as they later became known. But as the movement from Austria-Hungary increased, rising from 17,000 in 1880 to 114,000 in 1900 and reaching a peak of 338,000 in 1907, it became increasingly heterogeneous. By the eighties the stream included considerable numbers of Poles, Jews, and Ruthenians from Galicia, and Slovaks and Magyars from Hungary; a decade later these groups were being accompanied by Rumanians from Bukovina and Croats, Serbs, Slovenes, and Dalmatians from the southern provinces of Carniola, Carinthia, and Styria. In each of these areas local economic difficulties helped swell the outgoing throng. In Bohemia the McKinley Tariff of 1890 destroyed the local pearl-button industry, causing its transplantation to the United States; in parts of Carniola and Croatia, the destruction of the vineyards by phylloxera proved to be the last straw for the struggling peasants; in Dalmatia, emigration was stimulated by the Italian-Austrian treaty of 1890, which admitted Italian wines free of duty, thus crippling local vineyards. But these were minor influences. The outflow was in essence one of displaced peasants and agricultural laborers, whose departure could be attributed to more widespread and permanent economic influences.

Similar forces were at work in Italy, particularly in the South, which groaned under a vicious land system reminiscent in many respects of that prevailing in Ireland in pre-famine days. Southern Italy was predominantly a region of large estates owned by absentee landlords who made little effort to return profits to the soil or to make capital improvements; short leases and high rents encouraged tenants to exploit the land and precluded the introduction of modern agricultural methods. Nor were matters any better on small estates cultivated by their owners, for here excessive subdivision—*frazionamento* the Italians called it—produced its usual results. Throughout the region obsolete and unscientific methods of cultivation kept productivity low, and the wholesale deforestation which followed upon the abolition of feudalism and the secularization of church lands added still further to the difficulties of cultivation. Considering also that southern Italy had only recently emerged from centuries of Spanish and Bourbon neglect and misrule, and that in the latter half of the nineteenth century population was increasing by leaps and bounds, it was hardly surprising that the region as a whole presented a picture of chronic poverty unparalleled in Europe.

In the late eighties the precariously balanced rural economy of southern Italy sustained a double shock. Owing to a rapid increase in subtropical fruit production in Florida and California, American imports of Italian lemons and oranges fell precipitately, ruining thousands of growers in Calabria, Basilicata, and Sicily. Simultaneously, France built a prohibitive tariff wall against the Italian wines, thus depriving Apulian, Calabrian, and Sicilian winegrowers of their chief export market. These events ushered in a period of unprecedented hardship and set in motion the first large-scale Italian emigration to the United States. A substantial exodus from northern Italy to South America was already in progress, and the movement from southern Italy would probably have taken the same direction but for the fact that South American conditions in the late eighties were temporarily uninviting. A yellow fever outbreak in Brazil had carried off 9,000 Italian victims and had led the Italian government temporarily to ban emigration to that country; in Argentina, political disturbance, financial crisis, and a war with Paraguay brought economic life almost to a halt. Hence the south Italian current set toward the United States and, having once chosen its course, rapidly gathered momentum. Italian arrivals in the United States rose from 12,000 in 1880 to 52,000 a decade later; by 1900 the figure had passed 100,000 and after averaging over 200,000 in the succeeding decade reached a peak of almost 300,000 in 1914. From about the turn of the century, when emigration to Brazil declined as a result of a crisis in coffee-growing, the north Italians too tended to choose the United States. But their numbers were never more than a fraction of those from southern Italy.

Emigration from Russia differed from the Slavic and Italian movements in that its origin was not primarily economic but political and religious. The first sizable group to leave Russia for the United States consisted of Russo-German Mennonites from the Volga and Black Sea areas. These people had settled in Russia at the end of the eighteenth century in response to the invitation of Catherine the Great, who had granted them immunity from military service, freedom of worship, and a substantial degree of autonomy. But with the withdrawal of these privileges in 1870 as a result of rising Russian nationalism, the Mennonites determined to seek homes elsewhere. Thanks to the attraction of railroad lands, several thousand of them settled in Kansas, Nebraska, the Dakotas, and other western states during the seventies and eighties, and here they were subsequently joined by even larger numbers of non-Mennonite Russo-Germans.

This exodus was completely overshadowed, however, by that of Russian Jews for whom the rise of Pan-Slav nationalism betokened a renewal of persecution. The assassination of Tsar Alexander II in 1881 set off a wave of anti-Jewish riots and led to strict enforcement of the requirement that all Jews must reside within the Pale of Settlement, an area bordering on Germany, Austria, and Rumania. A year later came the notorious May Laws, which placed restrictions upon Jewish worship, virtually debarred Jews from agriculture, industry, and the professions, excluded them from public office, and denied them educational opportunities. Persecution now became systematic, persistent, and ruthless; worst of all there were the frightful pogroms of 1881–82, 1891, and 1905–6 in which countless Jews were massacred. Largely in consequence, Russian arrivals in the United States rose from 5,000 in 1880 to 81,000 in 1892 and then bounded upward to a peak of 258,-000 in 1907.

After 1900, however, the Russian outflow was more varied. Between 1899 and 1910, Poles accounted for fully a quarter of the total immigration from Russia, and Lithuanians, Finns, and Russo-Germans together made up a similar proportion. But Jews were still easily the largest single group, comprising 43.8 per cent of the total. Immigration from Russia to the United States was thus composed almost entirely of what was known as the "alien element" in the Russian population. During the period named less than 5 per cent of the westward exodus could be classified as Russian. This was not because Russians proper were averse to movement; vast numbers of them moved eastward both before and after 1900 in order to colonize the empty wastelands of Siberia.

While Austria-Hungary, Italy, and Russia were by far the most important sources of the "new" immigration, substantial numbers came from other areas. The collapse of the French market for Greek currants in the early nineties, resulting from France's adoption of a protective policy, gave the initial impetus to emigration from Greece, more particularly from the currant-producing regions around Tripolis and Sparta. From Portugal, a backward, densely peopled, agricultural country, emigration took place chiefly to Brazil, on account of the linguistic, historical, and religious ties between the two countries. But a steady trickle of Portuguese emigrants found their way to the United States. They came not only from Portugal itself but from the Azores—whence emigration first developed out of the circumstance that American whalers had long called there to recruit sailors—and from the Cape Verde Islands. In Rumania and Bulgaria the transition from a peasant economy to large-scale modern agriculture gave emigration its usual stimulus, and in Finland the same result was brought about by a declining demand for agricultural labor, coupled with Russia's repressive policy from 1899 onward. It was oppression, too, in the form of the "Armenian massacres" of 1894–96, which set emigration in motion from Armenia, a Christian island in the Mohammedan world of the Ottoman Empire. Turkish misrule also brought about the wholesale expatriation of another Christian minority, the Syrians, about a million of whom emigrated between 1870 and 1900. Most of them went to Egypt, South America, and India, but in the 1890's, thanks mainly to the influence of American Protestant missionaries who told of the opportunities America offered, discontented Syrians began to go to the United States.

Not all of those who immigrated to the United States in this period came from across the Atlantic. A very large though indeterminate number came overland from Canada, both from the Maritime Provinces and Quebec, whence the movement had been in progress continuously since before the Civil War, and to an increasing extent from Ontario, where the limit of desirable agricultural settlement was reached in the seventies and where the competition of western wheat brought about a major shift in land use. For a generation after the Civil War, emigration to the United States took place on such a scale as to threaten the Dominion with depopulation; only at the very end of the century, when the frontier of settlement reached the prairie provinces of Manitoba and Saskatchewan did the human tide at last begin to flow in the opposite direction.

Finally, there was a relatively small but highly significant influx from across the Pacific. The first Oriental arrivals were the Chinese, of whom 300,000 came to the Pacific coast of the United States between 1850 and the passage of the Chinese Exclusion Act in 1882. Though contemporaries generally referred to Chinese immigrants as coolies, implying that they had been imported in a servile state, those who came to the United States were voluntary immigrants who had paid their own fares from Hong Kong to San Francisco. Large-scale Chinese immigration, like that of the Irish, originated in economic catastrophe; the great Taiping rebellion, beginning in 1848, paralyzed trade and industry in southeastern China and brought famine and ruin to millions. News of the high wages paid to laborers in gold-rush California was thus all that was needed to start an exodus from the hard-hit province of Kwangtung. Having once begun, Chinese emigration from this region to California went on uninterruptedly until the law of 1882 brought it virtually to an end.

Three years later a second Oriental movement got under way when the Japanese emperor removed a long-standing ban on the emigration of his subjects. For the first time Japan had men to spare, as a result of a population increase without parallel in the Western world. In the eighties and nineties most Japanese emigrants went to Hawaii as contract laborers to work on American sugar plantations. But after Hawaii had been annexed in 1898, the Japanese were free to move to the continental United States, which they did at the rate of about 10,000 a year. The Gentlemen's Agreement of 1907–8, whereby Japan undertook not to issue passports to unskilled laborers wishing to enter the United States, checked without halting the influx. Since the agreement permitted Japanese residents in the United States to send for their wives, thousands of Japanese women continued to come, many of them as "picture brides" who had been married by proxy in Japan to men they had never seen.

It is thus apparent that the widening of the frontiers of emigration, which was perhaps the outstanding feature of migration history in the latter half of the nineteenth century, implied no fundamental change in the pattern of the movement to the United States. With the exception only of the east European Jews, the Armenians, and the Syrians, who were driven from their homes by persecution, post–Civil War immigrants were everywhere uprooted by a common set of economic influences and had much the same objects in coming to America that men had had for centuries. The belief that the motives of the "new" immigrants were more sordid and mercenary than those of their predecessors runs quite contrary to the facts. And if immigrants tended in the late nineteenth century to revisit their homelands more frequently than before, this was largely because such a practice had hitherto been impossible.

Though immigrant motives were pretty much alike, the immigrants themselves were not. In refuting the traditional view that nineteenth-century immigrants to the United States can be divided into two mutually exclusive categories, one should not lose sight of the fact that the bulk of the southern and eastern Europeans were culturally very different both from native Americans and from immigrants born in northern and western Europe. The fact and the extent of cultural difference shaped much of the new immigrant's experience in the United States. One must not forget, though, that while the type of immigrant was changing, so was America herself. And from the point of view of immigrant adjustment, perhaps the latter circumstance was the more important.

VIII

Immigrants in Industrial America,
1865-1920

Nothing so forcibly impressed commentators upon early twentieth-century America as the increasing prominence of the immigrant. In all the larger American cities, and in scores of smaller ones too, there were great masses of immigrants speaking strange languages, following strange customs, and, with their children, outnumbering the native population by as much as two to one Henry James, returning to America in 1907 after a twenty-five-year absence, experienced a "sense of dispossession" and in New England felt himself to be almost in a foreign country. The British novelist H. G. Wells, visiting America about the same time, saw little sign of a nation but only a welter of contending nationalities. Small wonder that, with immigrants still pouring in at the rate of almost a million a year, some Americans should have begun to fear that the national culture was being submerged beneath a sea of for-

American Immigration

eigners, or that they should have looked back nostalgically to the relatively homogeneous society that had existed in Lincoln's day.

Despite appearances, the foreign-born proportion of the American population was hardly greater in 1910 than it had been in 1860. In the year of Lincoln's election, America's four million immigrants accounted for 13.2 per cent of her population; fifty years later, though the number of immigrants had grown to more than thirteen million, they still represented only 14.5 per cent of the total. Nor had the over-all pattern of immigrant distribution shown much change over the fifty-year period. As in 1860, so in 1910, the southern states could claim only a tiny proportion of the foreign-born; in many parts of the South, indeed, the period saw a decline in the number of immigrants. And despite the large immigration to the Pacific Coast and the Great Plains, the great bulk of the foreign-born was still to be found east of the Mississippi and north of the Ohio River and of Mason and Dixon's line. Four states, in fact, now contained almost half the total foreign-born population; New York had nearly two and three-quarter million, Massachusetts, Pennsylvania, and Illinois more than one million each.

The real change the half-century had brought lay in the origin of the foreign-born population. In 1860 natives of Ireland, Germany, and Great Britain had made up more than four-fifths of the foreign-born total; by 1910 the proportion contributed by these countries was less than two-fifths. But natives of Russia, Austria-Hungary, Italy, and other southern and eastern European countries, who in 1860 had accounted for only 1.2 per cent of the foreign-born population, now made up no less than 37.5 per cent of the total. Admittedly, the largest single foreign-born group in 1910 was from Germany;

208

it contained more than two and a half million. But second and third places were occupied by natives of Russia and of Austria-Hungary, each of whom numbered well over a million and a half. Natives of Ireland and of Italy came next, each with more than one million, three hundred thousand, while the Scandinavian countries, Great Britain, and Canada could each claim almost a million and a quarter. It was not so much their numbers, therefore, as their cosmopolitanism that made immigrants so conspicuous.

Between the various immigrant groups significant differences in distribution had persisted. The largest German concentrations were still in the Middle West, especially in the states of Illinois, Wisconsin, Ohio, and Minnesota; but there were very large numbers in New York, Pennsylvania, and New Jersey. Norwegians, Swedes, and Danes were also fairly heavily concentrated, especially in Minnesota, Illinois, Wisconsin, the Dakotas, and the state of Washington, and the Finns were to be found chiefly in Michigan, Minnesota, and Massachusetts. Of those born in Canada, almost half had settled in New England, and most of the rest in New York, Michigan, and other states bordering on the Great Lakes. The Irish-born were largely in the middle Atlantic states and New England, though there were large contingents in Illinois and California; these regions also contained the great majority of the immigrants from Italy. Finally, immigrants from Russia and Austria-Hungary were clustered mainly in New York, Pennsylvania, and New Jersey, with considerable numbers also in Illinois and Massachusetts.

According to the Dillingham Commission, immigrants from southern and eastern Europe were more prone to congregate in cities than were those from northern and western Europe.

American Immigration

Yet the difference between the two groups was comparatively slight, the relative proportions living in urban communities in 1910 being 78.6 per cent and 68.3 per cent, respectively. While, moreover, there was considerable variation between one ethnic group and another in the proportion of city-dwellers, this hardly warranted the drawing of a sharp distinction between "old" immigrants and "new." At the top of the list of city-dwellers were natives of Ireland and of Russia, of whom more than five-sixths lived in urban communities. Next came immigrants from Italy and Hungary, among whom the proportion was more than three-quarters. Among those born in England, Scotland, Austria, Greece, and China, it was above seven-tenths; among natives of Germany it was almost exactly two-thirds, and among the Swedish-born, three-fifths. Less than half the native American population was urban, however, and the only immigrant groups with a lower percentage of urban-dwellers than the natives were the Norwegians and the Montenegrins.

The high proportion of Norwegian, Swedish, German, Dutch, Swiss, and British immigrants in rural communities resulted from their arrival in the United States at a time when abundant quantities of cheap and free land were available. These were the groups, moreover, on whom the land-grant railroads and the immigration bureaus of the northwestern states had concentrated their advertising campaigns. Important, too, was the fact that these were relatively prosperous groups, many of whose members possessed the capital necessary to embark on American farming.

In contrast to other immigrants from northern and western Europe the Irish showed in America a marked aversion to a rural existence. The reason for this, as we saw earlier, was that

Embarkation for America, Liverpool, 1870. (The Radio Times Hulton Picture Library.)

The American River Ganges. Anti-Catholic cartoon by Thomas Nast, 1871. (From *Harper's Weekly*, 1871.)

Immigrants in Industrial America, 1865–1920

Irish immigrants lacked funds and farming experience, that they were reluctant to deny themselves the ministrations of their priests, and that their Old World experiences had taught them to look upon the land as the symbol of insecurity and suffering. Even after the Civil War, continued efforts were made, especially by Catholic organizations, to break up the urban concentration of the Irish and to spread them out on the rural frontier. The Irish Catholic Benevolent Union, founded in 1869 to co-ordinate Irish Catholic activities in the United States, embarked upon a colonization program which resulted seven years later in settlements in Virginia and Kansas. Unsound financing, however, together with factional quarrels among those in charge of the colonies soon led to their collapse.

No more successful was the Irish Catholic Colonization Association organized in 1879 with the support of a number of Catholic prelates, some of whom believed that "the religious mission of the Irish people" was to spread Catholicism throughout the West. A fund-raising lecture tour of eastern cities by Bishops Spalding of Peoria, O'Connor of Omaha, and Ireland of St. Paul aroused great enthusiasm but failed to raise the $100,000 the Association needed. Ironically enough, Irish-Americans were ready a few months later to contribute many times that sum in response to Parnell's appeals on behalf of the Irish Land League. But colonization schemes failed to stir Irish-Americans and the Irish Catholic Colonization Association, having established three small colonies in Nebraska and Minnesota, was wound up in 1886. Bishop Ireland, on his own initiative, succeeded between 1876 and 1881 in founding ten Catholic rural colonies on railroad land in southwestern Minnesota. Ireland's settlers were not, however, industrial laborers from the eastern cities, as he had originally hoped; they were small farmers from Pennsylvania, Ohio, Indiana, and even eastern Minnesota, who had left thriving farms in order to obtain better ones.

That western lands could be successfully farmed only by those experienced in agriculture was shown by the complete failure of attempts to settle destitute Connemara peasants in the trans-Mississippi West after the Irish famine of 1879. Some were brought to one of Bishop Ireland's colonies, others to the Sweetman colony planted in Minnesota by the Irish philanthropist of that name. But although they had been given free passages, frame houses, farming implements, seeds, and provisions these hapless people displayed neither industry nor initiative and seemed quite content to let their benefactors keep them. Bishop Ireland soon gave up the attempt to make farmers of them, whereupon nearly all made off to St. Paul, where they found work on the railroad more congenial than waiting for farming's slow returns.

Another group whose leaders endeavored to promote agricultural colonies were the Jews. Even before the Civil War there had been proposals for Jewish land settlement, and a number of short-lived agricultural colonies were actually established, like Moses Cohen's Shalom in Ulster County, New York, in the late 1830's. But it was not until the mass movement of east European Jews got under way in the 1880's that rural colonization was undertaken with any determination. Enthusiasts like Michael Heilprin and Jacob Schiff, reflecting a long-established Jewish tendency to idealize the land, urged a systematic plan of rural colonization in the United States and Canada. Many Jewish rabbis and newspaper editors welcomed the proposal both in order to promote the welfare of the refugees and as a "means to refute the oft-muttered calumny that our people are unfitted by habit, nature and sentiment for honest toil." Assistance from various Jewish relief bodies and from American Jewish communities enabled several colonies to be planted in the West and South between 1881 and 1883; among the earliest were Sicily Island, Louisiana, New Odessa, Oregon, and Cotopaxi, Colorado. Under similar auspices a group of colonies was established in New Jersey in the course of the following decade: Alliance, by the Alliance Israélite Universelle; Carmel, by the Montefiore Agricultural Society; Rosenhayn, by the Hebrew Emigrant Aid Society; and Woodbine, by the Baron de Hirsch Fund.

These efforts were largely unavailing. Most of the colonies lasted only a short time, and even those which survived, like Alliance and Carmel, could probably not have done so had the colonists not supplemented their income by working in cigar and clothing factories. Many reasons have been adduced for failure: that American Jews did not support the colonies as much as had been hoped, that many of the colonies were thoughtlessly located on land that was infertile or liable to flooding, and that the wrong type of settler was chosen. But these circumstances were of only incidental importance when compared with the fact that, in eastern Europe, nearly all Jews had of necessity been town-dwellers and thus had no experience of agriculture. Like the Irish, moreover, Jewish immigrants seem to have been temperamentally unsuited to the loneliness of farm life; nor were they less immune than other immigrants to the attractions of the cities. Rather the contrary, for only the cities could offer Jews the educational opportunities they sought for their children and the facilities for orthodox observance which most were determined to retain.

While there were thus special cultural and economic factors to explain the almost complete absence of Jews from agriculture, the mere fact that they arrived late on the scene would have tended to produce the same result. It was significant that of all the south and east Europeans, the only groups to enter agriculture on a large scale were the Czechs and the Russo-Germans, whose immigration began while there was still abundant land available. By 1910, almost one-third of all Czech immigrants, and an even higher proportion of the second generation, were engaged in agriculture, mostly in the prairie states of the Mississippi Valley and in Nebraska and Texas. The Russo-Germans, finding the soil and climate of the plains to be not dissimilar to those of their native steppes, were clustered together in hundreds of small communities in Kansas, Nebraska, Iowa, Minnesota, and the Dakotas.

Nevertheless, other factors beside that of time deterred Slavic, Italian, and other "new" immigrants from taking up farming. The Dillingham Commission was content to attribute the urban concentration of southern and eastern Europeans to their reluctance to become separated from members of their own groups, and to the fact that a large proportion did not intend to remain permanently in the United States. Though this might well have been the case, the great mass of late-nineteenth-century immigrants could not possibly have become farmers on arrival because they were almost completely without capital. Nor was the position of farm laborer attractive to them; the language difficulty was more serious on the farm than in the factory, employment was more intermittent and the pay lower than in other forms of employment. Finally, both the Slavs and the Italians had been accustomed in Europe to the intimate contacts of village life and were repelled by the loneliness of rural existence in America.

Apart, therefore, from the Czechs and the Russo-Germans, southern and eastern European immigrants usually shunned the Great Plains. Not only were the limitless expanses forbidding, but plains farming called for reapers, binders, wire fences, and a variety of other expensive equipment. When they did take up American farming, most "new" immigrants chose thickly settled areas where highly specialized, intensive agriculture could be practiced with little capital outlay. After 1900 there was a small but significant movement of Poles from American mines, factories, and steel mills into the semi-abandoned farms of the East. In western Massachusetts and Connecticut, Polish farmers began to cultivate onions and tobacco, crops requiring special soils, intensive hand-labor, and not a little technical skill and business ability. Likewise, Italians took up truck and vegetable farming in New Jersey and New York, vine-growing in California, and cotton and fruit farming in Louisiana and Texas. Finally, numbers of Portuguese immigrants operated small farms on Cape Cod and in Rhode Island, where they grew potatoes and other vegetables for local consumption.

Some southern and eastern European immigrants found seasonal employment as agricultural laborers. In late summer when the schools were on vacation and some factories were closed, Italian and Polish families from Baltimore, Philadelphia, and other eastern cities moved into southern New Jersey to follow the berry crops northward. Other Italians, especially Sicilians, migrated annually from the North to Louisiana and Mississippi at the beginning of "la zuccarata," the season of sugar-cane cutting; in the spring they went north again to find construction or factory work. In New England Portuguese dock laborers from New Bedford and Greek and Syrian mill hands from Fall River and Lowell moved each fall into the cranberry bogs, and in rural Michigan and Wisconsin, Poles and other Slavs from Detroit and Milwaukee took on the task of hoeing and weeding beets.

Thus to refer, as contemporaries often did, to the "new" immigrant's "failure" to settle on the land was to pose the question of his economic adjustment in unreal terms. What else but urban concentration was to be expected from new-comers at a time when even the children of native Americans were leaving the farms in droves for the cities? Nor was it true, as is sometimes still implied, that the bulk of south and east Europeans came to the United States in the hope and expectation of obtaining land, only to find themselves trapped in their cities by their poverty and their consequent need to obtain immediate employment. On the contrary, it was American industrial development which had attracted them in the first place; had they not known that work awaited them in the mines, mills, and factories, they would not even have crossed the Atlantic.

Not merely the phenomenal expansion of American industry but its changing character accounted for the huge volume of the "new" immigration. The introduction of additional mechanical devices and processes eliminated much of the need for industrial skill and experience and made it possible, even essential, for manufacturers and mine-operators to employ cheap, unskilled labor. In the bituminous coal fields the skill and experience which had been necessary for pick or hand mining became superfluous once mechanical cutters began to

be employed on the coal face; in cotton manufacturing, unskilled and inexperienced immigrants could, after brief training,
operate automatic looms and ring-spinning frames which took
over work formerly performed by mule frames and highly
trained weavers.

In these and other industries the late nineteenth century
brought a remarkable change of personnel. Before 1890 most
of the miners in the Pennsylvania bituminous coalfields had
been either American-born or English, Scottish, Welsh, Irish,
and German immigrants; thereafter they were largely Slovak,
Magyar, Polish, and Italian. In New England textile centers
like Fall River, New Bedford, and Lowell, where the labor
force had hitherto been almost wholly British, Irish, and
French-Canadian, the same period brought a significant influx
of Poles, Portuguese, Greeks, and Syrians. In the garment
trades of New York, Chicago, and Baltimore, where the majority of employees had originally been German, Bohemian,
or Irish, they became Russian Jewish and Italian.

To what extent the entry of southern and eastern European
immigrants into industry displaced earlier comers is a question which has aroused considerable controversy. The conclusion of the Dillingham Commission was that in certain industries, such as bituminous and anthracite coal mining and iron
and steel manufacturing, "new" immigrants had ousted both
native Americans and older immigrant employees. But it is
unlikely that this occurred to any considerable extent. One
reason why there were fewer native Americans and northwestern Europeans in the Pennsylvania coalfields after 1890
is that many of them had been drawn to the newer mines in
the Middle West. Moreover, many of those who had stayed
had been able, when the "new" immigrants arrived, to move

into executive and technical positions. Indeed, since it was the unskilled labor provided by the "new" immigrants which alone made possible America's phenomenal industrial expansion in the late nineteenth century, it was to them that native Americans and older immigrants were indebted for the increased opportunities available for skilled, white-collar, and professional workers.

By the early twentieth century the foreign-born formed the mass of the wage-earners in every area where manufacturing or mining was practiced. They were to be found in the textile factories of New England, in the mines, mills, and factories of Pennsylvania, New Jersey, and New York, in the coal mines and factories of the Middle West, and in the iron ore and copper mines of Michigan and Minnesota. In 1910 the Dillingham Commission reported that in the twenty-one industries it studied, 57.9 per cent of all employees were foreign-born, some two-thirds of them from the countries of southern and eastern Europe. In some industries, such as clothing manufacture, textiles, coal mining, and slaughtering and meatpacking, the proportion was even higher. In railroad and construction work, too, the Commission found a similar preponderance of the foreign-born.

Although in every industry the labor force was varied, a tendency toward ethnic concentration was apparent. This is at first sight surprising, for, unlike many of the older immigrant groups, southern and eastern European immigrants had virtually no experience of industry and could not take up familiar work. Contemporaries believed that the physical and mental characteristics of immigrants determined the type of industrial employment they sought. Thus it was suggested that the concentration of Poles, Lithuanians, and Slovaks in heavy industry was due to their physical strength, stolidity, and sub-missiveness; that of Jews in the clothing industry to their light physique and individualism. But cultural and economic factors were also important, as were ethnic rivalries and the particular time of arrival of each group.

The presence of so many French-Canadians in the textile industry, for example, originated in the proximity of New England to Quebec and in the fact that the beginning of French-Canadian immigration coincided with a greatly in-creased demand for labor in the cotton mills of Massachusetts, New Hampshire, Maine, and Rhode Island. A further attrac-tion to a group in which large families were common was that the looms afforded employment to women and children as well as to men. By the 1870's French-Canadian women sup-plied a high proportion of all the female labor in the New England mills, and their offspring outnumbered every other group among child operatives. So eager were French-Canadian parents to put their children to work that they frequently falsified their ages in order to evade school attendance laws.

The concentration of Russian and Polish Jews in the cloth-ing trade owed little to previous experience; only about 10 per cent had been tailors in Europe. Nor was it particularly significant that the garment industry offered openings for all members of the family. Unlike Polish and Italian women, Rus-sian Jewish women did not usually remain at work after mar-riage; and in contrast to the French-Canadians, Russian Jews preferred to see their children at school instead of in the fac-tory. The real attraction of the garment trade to Jewish im-migrants was that it opened an avenue to commerce. Earnings in the clothing shops were more closely related to individual effort than in factories, and capital was more readily amassed.

American Immigration

Because, in addition, the unit of industrial production in the garment industry was small, there was a better chance than anywhere else of being able to set up on one's own.

Because Italian and Slavic immigrants were largely male they enjoyed greater mobility than did Russian Jews, and were thus more inclined toward railroad and construction work. But the concentration of these and other groups in particular industries was due also to the immigrant's desire to be with his own kind. Only thus can one account for the high proportion of Finns in iron ore and copper mining, of Greeks and Syrians in peddling, of Portuguese in textiles, and of Bulgarians in steel towns like Hungry Hollow, Illinois, which by 1910 had about fifteen thousand of them.

Before the Civil War the mobility of immigrants had been limited by the comparatively primitive character of the American transportation network and by the almost complete absence of job-finding agencies. But the growth of the railroads and of a number of specialized agencies to supply labor to industry meant that immigrants became a kind of mobile reserve force which could be concentrated wherever the demand summoned them. During the 1890's, a number of states and cities established employment bureaus, and the Immigration Act of 1907 created a Division of Information in the Federal Bureau of Immigration for the purpose of gathering information about employment opportunities in all parts of the Union. Yet neither these official agencies nor the labor bureaus established by the benevolent and philanthropic societies of the various ethnic groups were particularly effective, and the bulk of the work of finding places in American industry for immigrants was done by private labor agencies. These began to multiply in New York, Chicago, and other large cities in the late 1860's, supplying labor on commission to railroads, contractors, and a variety of industrial enterprises. Although exploitation and abuse were not unknown, they performed a valuable function in linking together immigrant and industry. To the former the labor agency was a kind of sieve which shook him around until he found a permanent place; to the latter it was a means both of expansion and, not least, of checking the growth of labor unions.

In the early development of the American labor movement immigrants played an outstanding part. In 1888 the well-known American economist, Francis A. Walker, remarked that ". . . the main impulse toward the formation of labor organizations among us has been of foreign derivation, and . . . alien elements have contributed by far the greater part of the membership." This comment, reflecting as it did the contemporary nativist tendency to stigmatize trade unions as foreign importations, by no means overstated the case. Two years earlier the Illinois Bureau of Labor had analyzed the ethnic composition of the state's trade unions and had found them to be 21 per cent native, 33 per cent German, 19 per cent Irish, 10 per cent British, 12 per cent Scandinavian, 5 per cent Polish, Bohemian, and Italian. Even more striking was the predominance of immigrants in the leadership of the labor movement. During the generation after 1865 an extraordinarily large proportion of the founders, organizers, and executives of American trade unions had been born abroad, more particularly in the British Isles. In nearly every industry British and Irish immigrants were among the first to undertake the work of organization; Richard Trevellick, John Hinchcliffe, John Siney, and Daniel McLaughlin in coal mining; Robert Howard and George Gunton in textiles; and John Jarrett in iron and steel. British and

American Immigration

Irish immigrants also occupied many of the top positions both in the National Labor Union of 1866–72 and in the Knights of Labor. Then again, Samuel Gompers, the chief founder and president of the American Federation of Labor, was himself an immigrant.

While the trade-union proclivities of northern and western European immigrants aroused nativist ire in the 1880's, southern and eastern Europeans were equally criticized a generation later for their reluctance to become trade unionists. The opinion of the Dillingham Commission was that the "new" immigrants had tended to undermine the American labor movement and had made it difficult to unionize the occupations and industries in which they were engaged. It seems highly probable in fact that the use of immigrant strikebreakers materially contributed to the decline of the Knights of Labor. Strike after strike in the Pennsylvania coalfields in the 1870's and early 1880's was smashed when employers brought in Slavic, Hungarian, and Italian labor. Nonetheless the New York Bureau of Labor could remark in 1885 that, although immigrants might be prepared to work for low wages on arrival in the United States, they soon became "sufficiently Americanized" to go on strike themselves. Indeed, Hungarians and Poles played a leading part in the bitter strikes in the Pennsylvania coke regions in the 1880's.

It was nonetheless true at the beginning of the present century that proportionately few southern and eastern Europeans were to be found in trade unions. But this was largely because most of them were unskilled workers, among whom labor organizations were notoriously weak. Because of ethnic antipathies, moreover, the leaders of unions composed of native Americans and older immigrant workers made few attempts to organize newer arrivals. When such attempts were made, as by the leaders of the United Mine Workers, the result was a large southern and eastern European membership. In the clothing industry, meanwhile, the "new" immigrants organized their own unions. By 1910 the International Ladies Garment Workers' Union and the Amalgamated Clothing Workers of America, each of which was composed largely of Russian Jews, Italians, and Poles, were among the strongest labor unions in America. In other industries the employers' policy of "balancing nationalities" hampered union growth, but it failed to prevent the great textile strike at Paterson in 1912, when nearly a score of ethnic groups acted in unison.

The trade union was perhaps the only institution in which immigrants mixed with others of different origin. For the rest, immigrant life was organized almost wholly along the lines of nationality. Each group exhibited strong tendencies to live in separate areas and to move elsewhere whenever newcomers appeared. Thus in the generation after the Civil War, New York's Lower East Side experienced an almost complete change of population. Formerly the stronghold of the Irish and the Germans, its character changed as these groups retreated northward or to Brooklyn in the face of Russian Jewish and Italian invasions; while the Italians took possession of the old Irish neighborhoods, Russian and Polish Jews pressed into the German districts. In Chicago, Bohemians and Poles took over areas which had hitherto borne an Irish, German, or Scandinavian character.

Yet to refer to the new ethnic ghettos, as contemporaries usually did, as, say, a "Little Italy" or a "Little Poland" was to tell only half the story, for immigrant clannishness was based on provincial rather than on national loyalties. Among New York's Italians, for example, Neapolitans and Calabrians clustered together in the Mulberry Bend district; a colony of Genoese occupied Baxter Street and one of Sicilians a part of Elizabeth Street; west of Broadway in the Eighth and Fifteenth wards north Italians predominated, and a small group of Austrian and Tyrolese Italians was to be found on Sixty-ninth Street, near the Hudson.

The congested, decayed districts into which the "new" immigrants swarmed exemplified the worst evils of city life. Living conditions in the slums had been bad enough in the fifties, but thirty years later they were infinitely worse. New York, with its huge aggregations of immigrants, provided the most conspicuous example of poverty and overcrowding. The erection in the eighties and nineties of a new type of slum, the "dumb-bell" tenement, involved immigrants in new levels of compression and degradation. Five or six stories high, and honeycombed with tiny rooms lacking both light and proper sanitation, these grim structures became focuses of disease, crime, and immorality.

But New York was far from being the only place scarred by immigrant slums. Boston, Pittsburgh, Kansas City, Buffalo, and Jersey City all had notorious black spots. So, too, had smaller places like Lowell, Massachusetts, where the tenement district known as "Little Canada" was said to have a population density greater than anywhere else in the United States outside the Fourth Ward of New York City. Hardly any better were housing conditions in the mining and industrial towns of Pennsylvania, Ohio, and Illinois, where Slavic, Magyar, Italian, and other immigrants lived in male boarding houses notorious for their dirt, darkness, and overcrowding.

Slums, in short, could be found wherever recent immigrants congregated. And they could be found almost nowhere else. The Dillingham Commission, anxious in 1910 to compare immigrant and native tenement conditions, was unable to locate a single tenement occupied by a native American.

The clannishness which produced the ethnic ghettos manifested itself also in the character of immigrant institutions. Like their predecessors, the "new" immigrant groups established their own churches, schools, and newspapers, as well as fraternal and benevolent associations. The various mutual aid societies were at first organized on the basis of local or regional affiliation, but in time they federated along the lines of nationality. In this way there developed bodies like the Order of Sons of Italy (1905), the Polish National Alliance (1880), the Pan Hellenic Union (1907), and L'Association Canada-Américaine (1896).

As earlier groups had done, southern and eastern European immigrants attempted to reconstitute in America the precise forms of their old religious life. But large numbers of them were Catholics and their ability to create autonomous religious institutions was limited by the need to conform to a single, centralized authority. Furthermore, the Catholic hierarchy in America, many of whom were of Irish origin, were opposed to any attempt to organize national parishes, which they regarded as a threat to the church's essential unity. German Catholic immigrants had long resented Irish dominance of the American Catholic church, and Polish, Italian, and French-Canadian Catholics came to share their feelings. In consequence many local controversies developed over the nationality of the priest, the language of worship, and the nature of the religious festivals to be observed.

American Immigration

German Catholic discontent received open expression in 1886 when the Reverend Peter M. Abbelen, the German-born vicar-general of the diocese of Milwaukee complained to the Vatican—on behalf of the German priests of Milwaukee, St. Louis, and Cincinnati—about the alleged hostility of Irish-born bishops to the German language and customs. Four years later controversy reached a peak with the submission to Rome of the Lucerne Memorial by the St. Raphael Society, a European organization concerned with the welfare of Catholic immigrants. Largely the work of a German philanthropist, Peter Paul Cahensly, the Memorial did not, as is often stated, advocate that Catholic dioceses in the United States should be organized upon the basis of nationality rather than of geography; but it did suggest that each group should be represented in the episcopate and that each should have separate parishes with priests of its own nationality.

The response of the Vatican was a refusal to contemplate any change in the method of choosing the American episcopate; in practice, however, it tacitly accepted the national parish. But this concession failed to assuage the discontent of those groups who felt they were being discriminated against. Bitter feuds persisted in New England between French-Canadian parishes and Irish bishops. Elsewhere schism sometimes resulted. After conflict with Irish bishops in Scranton, Buffalo, and Chicago, a number of Polish parishes cut loose from Rome to form the Polish National Catholic Church, which still followed the Roman rite but adopted Polish as the language of worship. Similar "Cahenslyite" controversies led groups of Lithuanian and Italian Catholics to form independent churches, though the seceders made up only a small proportion of the total of each group.

Immigrants in Industrial America, 1865–1920

The amount of "leakage" from the Catholic church through immigration has been frequently disputed and may never be precisely determined. But though the position varied between one Catholic group and another, practically none of them was transplanted intact and the total numbers lost to Catholicism cannot have been negligible. In some cases lack of churches and priests caused immigrants to drift away from the old faith. In others, Protestant proselytizers won over disaffected Catholics. The growth of Cahenslyism in the 1890's, for instance, led Presbyterian, Methodist, Baptist, and Episcopalian denominations to establish missions in the Italian quarters of eastern cities, and by 1916 over fifty thousand Italians belonged to American Protestant churches.

Of Czech immigrants a considerable proportion seem to have seceded from their old country faith. Though in Bohemia virtually all Czechs had been Catholics, about half of those who emigrated to America became Protestants or freethinkers. Partly responsible was the rationalism of Czech immigrant leaders like Joseph Pastor and F. B. Zdrubek, who edited, respectively, the anticlerical journals *Pokrok* (Progress) and *Svornost* (Union), both of which had large circulations, especially in Chicago. But the principal cause of alienation lay deep in Bohemia's history. Until the Thirty Years' War Bohemia had been a Protestant country, and although Protestantism had been practically stamped out during two centuries of Austrian oppression it burst forth again as part of the reviving national consciousness of the Czech-American.

Among Polish immigrants history produced a contrary effect. After the partition of Poland in the eighteenth century, Polish Catholicism became patriotic as well as religious in character; having a form of worship different from that of their Russian and German, if not of their Austrian, oppressors, Poles were able to keep alive a sense of national identity. And since in America Polish nationalism could at last be given free expression, it was only to be expected that Polish immigrants would remain steadfast in their Catholicism.

The late nineteenth and early twentieth centuries were the heyday of another immigrant institution, the foreign-language newspaper. Between 1884 and 1920 more than thirty-five hundred additional foreign-language papers came into existence, though only a fraction of them survived and the total number increased during the period only from 794 to 1,052. In 1884 more than six hundred of the foreign-language papers had been German, and nearly all the rest either Scandinavian, French, or Spanish. But by 1920 many more nationalities were represented and the total was more evenly divided. While the number of German papers had shrunk to 276, there were 118 in Spanish and Portuguese, 111 in the Scandinavian languages, 98 in Italian, 76 in Polish, 51 in Bohemian, 46 in French, 42 in Slovenian, and 39 in Yiddish, besides others in Magyar, Finnish, Lithuanian, Japanese, Greek, Dutch, Russian, Ukrainian, and other languages.

At first foreign-language newspapers were simply the organs of religious, fraternal, radical, and nationalistic bodies, and in style and format they modeled themselves upon European patterns. But in the American environment significant modifications crept in. To make themselves understood to the simple, uneducated people who formed the mass of their readers, immigrant editors had to adopt a popular literary style and to substitute the vernacular for the formal, recondite language they initially employed. Gradually, too, immigrant journals became less doctrinaire and propagandist in tone, tending instead to conform to the prevailing type of American newspaper, namely, a commercial paper published entirely for profit and concerned less with opinion than with circulation. Hence lengthy editorial columns were replaced by sensational news stories; advertisements of all kinds began to appear; market reports, sporting items, and women's pages were introduced. All these, of course, were features of the American press in general so that the exotic titles of dailies like the Magyar *Szabadsag* (Liberty), the Albanian *Dielli* (The Sun), and the Slovenian *Glas Narodna* (People's Voice) concealed the fact that they were essentially American newspapers, though published in different languages.

During the forty-year debate on immigration that culminated in the enactment of the restrictive laws of the 1920's, nativists repeatedly linked immigrants as a class with extreme political radicalism. The charge was not lacking in plausibility, for each of the revolutionary and extreme radical movements which arose in the United States during this period possessed a large foreign-born membership. It was significant, for example, that of the seventeen Socialist papers in existence in the United States in 1876, ten were German, three Bohemian, and one Swedish. Then again, the Socialist Labor Party, founded in 1878, was composed largely of German immigrants, as was the anarchist movement which took root in Chicago in the 1880's. In the twentieth century the Socialist Party of America relied heavily and increasingly upon foreign-born support and was especially strong among Finnish, Jewish, and Slavic immigrants. Two of the party's best-known leaders, Morris Hillquit and Victor Berger, had been born abroad, and by 1919 more than one-half of its membership belonged to the various foreign-born federations. Finally, both the Communist and the Communist Labor parties derived much of their support, initially at least, from the foreign-born and especially from those born in Russia.

Even so the stereotyped picture of the immigrant as a wild-eyed radical corresponds hardly at all to reality. Only a tiny fraction of the immigrant population gave its support to socialism, anarchism, or communism; the great majority were staunchly, even narrowly, conservative. Most immigrants were markedly hostile not only to revolutionary programs of European derivation but to all political reform movements, even of the comparatively moderate kind brought forth by American politics in the latter half of the nineteenth century. In rural regions neither the Granger Movement nor Populism attracted appreciable immigrant support; nor, in the cities, did the reforms demanded by Progressivism strike a responsive chord among the foreign-born.

To some extent this was due to the peculiar characteristics of the reform movements themselves. The failure of the Grange to attract immigrants was due largely to its being a secret society. On this account it was condemned both by the Roman Catholic church and by the German, Swedish, and Norwegian Lutheran churches, whose opposition kept many immigrant farmers from joining the Order even when they sympathized with its purposes. Some of the tenets of Populism, too, were repellent to newcomers; not a few immigrants retained in America the European peasant's hostility to inflationary schemes, and still more of them were antagonized by the barely concealed nativism of leading Populists. Nor was Progressivism entirely free of the taint of nativism, and its proponents, particularly in the social settlements, were often guilty of a condescension toward immigrants that could hardly fail to produce an unfavorable reaction.

The basic causes of immigrant conservatism were to be found, however, not in the nature of the various reform movements, but in the newcomer's fundamental patterns of thought. With few exceptions, nineteenth-century immigrants did not share the ebullience, the faith in progress, that characterized their native American contemporaries. Their European antecedents had taught them rather to be pessimistic, resigned, unhopeful of changing the existing order of things. As strangers to democracy, they still looked upon government primarily as an evil to be kept at arm's length, rather than as an instrument lying conveniently to hand. These tendencies were, perhaps, particularly marked among Catholics, whose religion stressed both the acceptance of authority and the subordination of earthly to spiritual values. But in addition to the Catholic church, most of the other religious organizations to which immigrants belonged were generally to be found on the side of conservatism and orthodoxy. The reason for this was that, as a group, immigrant clergymen were congenitally suspicious of any organization which threatened to compete with them for the loyalty of their flocks; Lutheran pastors and Catholic priests vied with each other, therefore, in denouncing reform movements as materialistic, pagan, even sacrilegious.

In addition to all this, the circumstances of immigrant life were such as to breed a political attitude which was wholly at variance with that of the native, middle-class reformer. To the Progressive of Yankee Protestant stock, politics offered both a challenge and an opportunity to remake society by the application of moral principles; but to the immigrant, struggling to establish himself in a strange environment, the

American Immigration

Progressive's talk of municipal reform, antitrust legislation, and women's rights, not to speak of devices like the referendum and the recall, were meaningless abstractions. What the immigrant sought in politics was not long-range, comprehensive solutions to the problems of civic government but practical help in meeting his immediate needs. In a contest for the immigrant's loyalty, the reformer could never hope to outbid the political boss who was ready to supply a job, protection from the law, financial help, and the innumerable other services and privileges that immigrant slum-dwellers were sorely in need of. It seemed to immigrants not only fair but essential that they give their votes to their benefactors and moreover that all attempts by reformers to overthrow the boss should be strenuously resisted. That politics was a field for disinterested service was to newcomers incomprehensible; their whole experience in America taught them to think of it rather as an area wherein personal interests might be realized.

The relationship which thus developed between immigrant and boss contributed largely to the growth of the great urban machines and to the corruption and inefficiency which so marred American municipal government in the late nineteenth century. Small wonder that native Americans in general, and frustrated municipal reformers in particular, should complain that "it was the ignorant foreign riff-raff of the big congested towns that made municipal politics so bad." Yet it was unfair to put the blame exclusively upon the immigrant. Given the speed with which American cities grew, and the lack of administrative experience of those who were called upon to govern them, civic anarchy and boss rule were almost bound to develop. And although immigrants certainly became the instruments of municipal corruption, they were not responsible for its introduction.

Immigrants, particularly the Irish, were remarkably adept, nonetheless, in learning the tricks they had been taught by such native practitioners of boss rule as Fernando Wood and William Marcy Tweed. How the Irish came virtually to monopolize political leadership in the cities is easy enough to explain. They formed a large proportion of the urban population and, as the first immigrants to congregate in the cities, were able to enter politics a generation or so before any other group. The Irish also possessed other advantages over newcomers from continental Europe; they were English-speaking, and in Ireland they had been used to "the forms if not the realities of representative government." They also had a natural flair for politics and were able as immigrants themselves to appreciate the needs and problems of other newcomers. Accordingly, they acted as a bridge linking immigrants generally with the world of American politics.

Even before the Civil War, Irish bosses like Mike Walsh and John Morrisey had risen to prominence from the brawling atmosphere of New York's gang wars. But the heyday of Irish boss rule was the half-century beginning in 1870; "Honest John" Kelly, Richard Croker, and Charles F. Murphy reigned in turn over Tammany Hall, "Hinky Dink" Kenna and "Bathhouse" John Coughlin dominated Chicago, and men of similar origin ruled most of the other great American cities. By the 1890's, the "Irish conquest of the cities" was virtually complete. Most of the large municipalities had become the private domain of Irish bosses, and many of them had Irish mayors as well, among the earliest being Hugh O'Brien, who became mayor of Boston in 1885, and William P. Grace, who had been elected mayor of New York five years earlier. To round off the pattern of Hibernian control, the police forces and fire departments of nearly all the major cities were controlled by men of Irish origin.

Lacking the political advantages enjoyed by the Irish, and having alternative avenues of opportunity open to them, other pre–Civil War arrivals were less prominent in the struggle for political power. Still, as each group gained in voting power, and as they developed a middle class to provide leadership and financial backing, they invariably made their impact on American politics. One should not, perhaps, make too much of Carl Schurz's career as evidence of the political rise of the Germans. Schurz's election as senator from Missouri in 1869 and his appointment as Secretary of the Interior in Hayes's cabinet were a tribute primarily to his own abilities. More significant for our purposes was the sharp increase in the late 1870's in the number of congressmen of German birth; in the decade before 1875 there had been only four German-born congressmen, but in the next ten years fourteen were elected, most of them from German-settled areas in Illinois, Missouri, Minnesota, New York, and Texas. Then, in the 1890's, the election of two governors of German origin, Altgeld of Illinois and Goebel of Kentucky, signified that German-Americans had moved still further up the political ladder. Likewise, the election of Knute Nelson as governor of Minnesota in 1892 denoted the political coming-of-age of Norwegian-Americans.

During the half-century that followed Appomattox there was no great change in the political affiliations of the immigrant groups which had arrived earlier in the century. Most of the Irish remained firmly attached to the Democratic party, in whose counsels they occupied an increasingly prominent place. There were, however, repeated Republican attempts to woo the Irish vote. Both in 1868 and in 1872 the Republicans published special Irish campaign newspapers, admitted Irishmen to a share in federal patronage, and appealed to Irish veterans to support their old commander, Grant. But even in 1872, when Grant's opponent was Horace Greeley, whose temperance views, reform aspirations, and general eccentricity were offensive to Irish voters, comparatively few of them could be induced to cast Republican ballots. Apart from a natural disinclination to break with the urban Democratic machines, fear of Negro competition was still strong enough to deter Irishmen from supporting the party which had enacted Emancipation; moreover, both of Grant's running mates, Schuyler Colfax and Henry Wilson, were suspect because of their earlier Know-Nothingism.

In the 1884 presidential contest the Republicans made their greatest effort to wean the Irish away from the Democratic machines. The Republican candidate, James G. Blaine, had already commended himself to the Irish when, as Secretary of State, he had adopted an aggressive attitude toward Great Britain; in addition, the Republicans made much of Blaine's Irish origins and of the fact that his mother had been a Catholic. These arguments, coupled with Cleveland's advocacy of a lower tariff, which made it possible for the Republicans to christen him "the British candidate," did in fact bring into the Republican camp a number of prominent Irishmen, notably Patrick Ford, editor of the *Irish World*, and John Devoy of the *Irish Nation*. But Blaine's failure to repudiate the Reverend Samuel D. Burchard's celebrated reference to the Democrats as the party of "Rum, Romanism, and Rebellion" lost him much of the Irish support he had gained, a fact which may have been decisive in bringing about Cleveland's narrow victory. The Irish Republicans whom the campaign had brought into being held together for a time, sustained during Harrison's presidency by a generous share of consular posts and other diplomatic appointments. But the group was never numerous and by the end of the century had practically disappeared.

Like their Irish co-religionists, German Catholics tended to regard the Republican party as a vehicle for intolerant Puritans bent on prohibition, Sunday-closing, and immigration restriction. Most other German-Americans, however, were usually Republican, but the promptness with which many of them followed Carl Schurz into the Liberal Republican movement in 1872 showed that their commitment to the GOP was less than absolute. German voters were always quick to assert their political independence whenever their personal interests were involved. Thus in Milwaukee in 1890 Republican indorsement of the Bennett Law, which required English to be used in the parochial schools, alienated enough Lutheran German Republicans to permit the election of a Democratic mayor.

In general, however, particular issues had less influence upon the shaping of immigrant political attitudes than had ethnic rivalries and antipathies. The Democratic affiliation of the Irish was in many places simply a reflection of their cultural conflict with the native voters who dominated the Republican party. That the Irish were the backbone of the Democratic party was in turn responsible for the alienation of other groups. Swedish, Norwegian, and Welsh immigrants, for example, remained staunchly Republican, less because of their devotion to GOP policies than because of distaste for the Catholicism of the Irish. Likewise, it was rivalry with the New England Irish, both for jobs and for control of the Catholic church, which led French-Canadians, almost to a man, into the Republican fold.

In their political rivalry with the Irish the French-Canadians were for a time handicapped by the reluctance of many of their number to become naturalized. But in the 1880's after a vigorous agitation by their leaders in favor of naturalization the number of French-Canadian voters increased sufficiently to bring political rewards. In places where they were heavily concentrated, like Manchester, New Hampshire, Lewiston, Maine, and Woonsocket, Rhode Island, French-Canadians soon came to dominate local politics; in the 1890's they began to win representation in state legislatures, and in 1908 they elected their first governor, Aram J. Pothier of Rhode Island.

For most of the period we are considering, immigrants from southern and eastern Europe remained a negligible quantity in American politics. Though their numbers grew steadily from the early 1880's onward, the great majority were at first too absorbed in the task of gaining an economic foothold to develop political interests. Right up to the 1920's, they remained for the most part politically backward and leaderless.

Nonetheless, there were clear signs in the early years of the twentieth century of a stirring of political consciousness among the newer immigrant groups. The restrictionist demand for a literacy test for immigrants brought organized opposition not only from German and Irish organizations but also from those composed of Russian Jews, Slavs, and Italians. After 1900, moreover, Republican politicians began to bid for the favor of south and east European voters in order to offset the advantage the Democrats derived from their vast Irish following. As early as 1902–3 Theodore Roosevelt was attempting to win Jewish support by making diplomatic gestures against the ill-treatment of Jews in Rumania and Russia. And when, in 1906, William Randolph Hearst threatened to capture the Jewish vote of the Lower East Side in his campaign for the governorship of New York, Roosevelt promptly appointed a Jew, Oscar Straus, as Secretary of Commerce and Labor, with control over the administrative aspects of immigration. About the same time, Senators Matthew S. Quay and Boies Penrose, together with other leading Republicans, began to manipulate the immigrant press in the interest of Republican candidates. Their shrewdest and most successful move was to finance a new advertising agency, the American Association of Foreign-Language Newspapers; under the direction of a Polish editor named Louis Hammerling, this organization distributed advertising contracts to the immigrant press in return for political support.

The political effects of Republican control of the foreign-language press are difficult to gauge. But that they had very clear limitations was abundantly demonstrated by the outcome of the 1912 presidential campaign. As in the two previous presidential elections, Hammerling supplied pro-Republican editorials to the foreign-language newspapers under his control, and in this fashion an estimated twenty million readers became acquainted with the virtues of Taft. Yet the bulk of the voters of south and east European origin appear to have voted for Theodore Roosevelt, possibly on personal grounds, but more probably because the platform of his Progressive party included a pledge to protect immigrants from exploitation and advocated a program of immigrant education and assimilation.

Whatever the cause, it was significant that in three of the four districts Roosevelt carried in New York City, the electorate was very largely Russian Jewish and Polish.

Woodrow Wilson, on the other hand, probably gathered fewer votes in 1912 from south and east European immigrants than did either Taft, Roosevelt, or even Debs. A decade earlier he had written in his *History of the American People* that the "new" immigration had consisted of

multitudes of men of lowest class from the south of Italy, and men of the meaner sort out of Hungary and Poland, men out of the ranks where there was neither skill nor energy nor any initiative of quick intelligence; and they came in numbers which increased from year to year, as if the countries of the south of Europe were disburdening themselves of the more sordid and hapless elements of their population. . . . The Chinese were more to be desired, as workmen if not as citizens, than most of the coarse crew that came crowding in every year at the eastern ports.

These remarks first returned to plague Wilson when he became a contender for the Democratic presidential nomination in 1912, when they received wide publicity from the supporters of his chief rival, Champ Clark, and especially from Clark's leading backer, William Randolph Hearst. During the election campaign itself the offending passages were translated by Wilson's opponents into Czech, Yiddish, Italian, and other languages, and were brought to the attention of the southern and eastern European voters by a committee of the publishers of the foreign-language press. In response to the angry protests of Polish-, Italian-, and Hungarian-American societies, Wilson attempted to explain away his *faux pas*. But his belated expressions of admiration for the "new" immigrants were anything but convincing and probably did little to undo the harm he had earlier done himself.

American Immigration

The outbreak of the European war in the summer of 1914 began a new era in the history of immigrant political activity. Of the thirteen million foreign-born people in the United States, nearly all were from countries now engaged in mortal combat with one another; and a further nineteen million Americans were the children of European immigrants. When, therefore, Wilson appealed to Americans in 1914 to be neutral in thought as well as in action, he can hardly have expected that his advice would be followed literally. In fact, the war was to show that Old World ties were still remarkably influential; for most immigrant groups these ties now took the place of immediate personal and local needs as the mainspring of political action.

Immigrants had shown themselves even earlier to be extremely sensitive to happenings in Europe. The German defeat of France in the war of 1870–71 had, for example, aroused tremendous enthusiasm among German-Americans, who had held victory celebrations in all the larger American cities; even Forty-eighters had sent messages of congratulation to their old persecutor, King William I of Prussia, whose assumption of the title of Emperor in 1871 signaled the achievement of German unity. And the Kishineff massacres of 1903, in which great numbers of Jews were put to death in Russian Bessarabia, had led to protest meetings of Russian Jewish immigrants, who had urged President Theodore Roosevelt to remonstrate officially with Russia.

Yet in intensity of devotion to the old country, no immigrant group could compare with the Irish, whose sympathies with Ireland had been constantly in evidence from the very beginning of large-scale Irish immigration. Perhaps the most extraordinary manifestation of this feeling came at the close of the Civil War, when the anxiety of demobilized Irish soldiers to strike a blow for Irish independence led to the Fenian invasions of Canada. Only a minority of Irish-Americans joined the Fenian movement and still fewer belonged to the Clan-na-Gael, an extreme revolutionary organization whose adherents were under oath to promote republicanism in Ireland. But the movement to bring about Irish land reform produced an almost universal response from Irish-Americans. Within a few months of Parnell's American tour on behalf of the Irish Land League in 1880, hundreds of branches of the organization were functioning in the United States, a national convention had been held in Chicago, and Irish-Americans had contributed hundreds of thousands of dollars to the cause.

In the period between the Civil War and World War I, Irish Anglophobia was a constant and complicating factor in American relations with Great Britain. Considerable embarrassment resulted to the State Department, first from the Fenian imbroglio, then from a Clan-na-Gael plot to torpedo British warships visiting New York harbor in 1883, and last from the sending of a group of Irish-American sharpshooters to South Africa during the Boer War in the guise of a Red Cross corps. Moreover, because of the size of the Irish vote, successive administrations had constantly to be on their guard against giving the impression of submitting to British dictation. Cleveland's peremptory dismissal of the British minister, Sir Lionel Sackville-West, after the publication of the Murchison letter during the 1888 election campaign was clearly due to his anxiety not to lose Irish support. Irish-Americans also loudly opposed the Bayard-Chamberlain agreement of 1888 and the Olney-Pauncefote Treaty of 1897 on the ground that they tended, in the words of the Boston *Pilot*, "to place this re-

public before the world as a mere colony of Great Britain."
But contrary to what many Irish-Americans liked to believe,
the rejection of the two treaties by the Senate was due to
causes other than their opposition. While politicians might be
prepared at election times to gratify the whims of Irish voters
by "twisting the lion's tail," they were not prepared to base
American policy upon Irish interests. That Irish-Americans
had in reality little influence upon the course of American
diplomacy was proved by the fact that the late 1890's witnessed the growth of a warm Anglo-American rapproche-
ment.

The outbreak of World War I brought renewed manifesta-
tions of Irish-American Anglophobia. The Clan-na-Gael executive committee sent a secret address to the Kaiser expressing its hope "for the success of the German people in the
unequal struggle forced upon them"; even the more moderate
Irish-American organizations openly sympathized with the
Central Powers and complained of the alleged pro-Allied bias
of the American press. At the same time a new concern for
Ireland's future became apparent. In March, 1916, an Irish
Race Convention, meeting at New York, dissociated itself
from John Redmond's moderate Home Rule program and
went on record as demanding Irish independence. The failure
of the Easter Rebellion in Dublin shortly afterward, and the
execution of a number of its leaders, still further embittered
Irish-Americans toward England. Wilson's refusal to intervene
on behalf of the rebels turned many Irish-Americans finally
against him. A majority had already been affronted by his
criticisms of hyphenated Americans and by his administration's pro-British leanings.

Wilson's foreign policy during the period of American

neutrality came under fire also from German-Americans, with whom the Irish tended increasingly to act in concert. Not unnaturally, the outbreak of war found the great mass of German-Americans wholeheartedly on the side of the Fatherland. German-American orators and newspapers defended the invasion of Belgium, refuted the charge that Germany was to blame for the war, and confidently predicted her success. Simultaneously, German-American organizations undertook relief work, subscribed to the German Red Cross, and promoted the sale of German war bonds. From an early date in the war, German-Americans protested Wilson's partiality for the Allies. They complained that the supply of munitions to Britain and France was a violation of the spirit, if not of the letter, of neutrality, and demanded an embargo and a prohibition of American loans to the belligerents. Such protests, and the arrogance and tactlessness with which they were sometimes made, led many Americans to question the loyalty of the German element and of course made the situation of German-Americans more difficult once America had entered the war.

For many voters of German and Irish origin, the major issue in the 1916 presidential campaign was Wilson's policy toward the European war. But much as German-Americans disliked Wilson they were still more hostile to Theodore Roosevelt, who had been characteristically extreme in his denunciations of hyphenism. Accordingly, when Hughes received the Republican nomination in preference to the Rough Rider, on a platform of "straight and honest" neutrality, he won the support of virtually the entire German-language press and a large number of German-American organizations. Yet on election day German-Americans divided their votes between the two chief candidates. In Oregon, Minnesota, and

Illinois most of them supported Hughes, and in the first two of these states they may even have contributed significantly to his success. But elsewhere, Hughes's equivocations and Roosevelt's warlike speeches in his support seem to have scared the Germans away. At all events, Wilson carried such German centers at Milwaukee and St. Louis, and received a large German-American vote in Ohio and Maryland.

The Irish, on the other hand, deserted Wilson en masse, and he failed to carry a single state in which they were strong. So bitter had the Irish now become toward the President, that the Democratic city machines in places like Boston, Chicago, and New York, "either knifed the national ticket or else made only half-hearted campaigns." But at least part of Wilson's losses among Irish voters were offset by his gains among other ethnic groups. The President's firm stand against the literacy test had done much to retrieve his reputation among southern and eastern Europeans. His efforts to help war sufferers, intensified in the summer of 1916, had been greatly appreciated by voters from countries overrun by the Central Powers. Polish-Americans, for example, having almost unanimously opposed Wilson four years earlier, voted for him in overwhelming numbers in 1916.

The reaction of immigrants to America's entry into the war developed out of their earlier attitudes to the conflict. For German-Americans, the ending of neutrality was a major catastrophe, particularly since it proved to be the signal for a nativist crusade to stamp out every vestige of German culture in the United States. But though they suffered many petty persecutions and were accused by excited patriots of espionage and sabotage, not to speak of such absurdities as putting glass in Red Cross bandages, the mass of German-Americans loyally accepted the decision to go to war and gave the war effort their full support. Most Irish-Americans, too, hastened to close ranks in support of the common cause. Only a number of extremists like Jeremiah O'Leary of the American Truth Society continued to inveigh against the British and to rejoice in the news of British defeats; for continuing to express such sentiments the *Gaelic-American,* the *Irish World,* and the *Freeman's Journal* were all banned from the mails in 1918.

Among those groups whose national aspirations in Europe had been stifled by the Central Powers, the American entry into the war was greeted with enthusiasm. Wilson's announcement in January, 1918, of the Fourteen Points, with their indorsement of the doctrine of national self-determination, converted the war for these immigrants into a crusade for the liberation of their homelands. Among Americans of Polish, Czech, and South Slav origin, national liberation movements had taken root earlier, but internal squabbles had vitiated their effectiveness. But now, with the doctrine of self-determination as their guide, they put aside their earlier differences and worked unitedly for the restoration of Polish independence and for the birth of the new states of Czechoslovakia, Yugoslavia, and Albania.

Upon his return to the United States from Europe in 1919, however, Wilson discovered that practically every immigrant group in the United States had some fault to find with the treaty signed at Versailles. German-Americans, who constituted the largest single group, emerged from the war smarting from the treatment they had received and anxious for revenge on Wilson for having led America into what they considered to have been an unnecessary war. Ignoring the fact that Germany would have been still more harshly treated but for Wilson, they chose to blame him for the fact that the treaty included a German war guilt clause. Irish-Americans had been angered by Wilson's refusal to apply the principle of self-determination to Ireland, and by his scarcely concealed contempt for their more extreme leaders. In addition, they chose to interpret Article X of the League Covenant, whereby member nations undertook to help one another against external aggression, as a pledge that American soldiers, including those of Irish ancestry, might be sent to help Britain crush an Irish revolt. Hardly less bitter were Italian-Americans, who resented Wilson's efforts to deny Italy the Adriatic port of Fiume. Even immigrants of Polish and Czech origin, who might have been expected to show the President some gratitude for having presided at the rebirth of Poland and the creation of Czechoslovakia, sniped at him for failing to satisfy their national aspirations in full.

Although the various ethnic groups were among the loudest opponents of the Treaty of Versailles, it was not their influence that was responsible for its rejection; the real culprit was the mood of disillusion and isolationism which overtook the American people as a whole. Still, the intensity of immigrant reaction to the war and to the peacemaking was to have important consequences. Americans now became aware, as never before, of the persistence of Old World ties even among groups like the Germans whose assimilation they had tended hitherto to take for granted. Startled by the spectacle of ethnic disunity she appeared to present, the United States became increasingly anxious to shut the gates against further European immigration.

IX

The Demand for Restriction,
1882-1924

The dedication ceremonies for the Statue of Liberty in October, 1886, took place, ironically enough, at precisely the time that Americans were beginning seriously to doubt the wisdom of unrestricted immigration. In the prevailing atmosphere, Emma Lazarus' poetic welcome to the Old World's "huddled masses" struck an almost discordant note. Already the first barriers had been erected against the entry of undesirables. In response to public pressure Congress had suspended Chinese immigration and had taken the first tentative steps to regulate the European influx. Organized nativism, moreover, was just reviving after a lapse of a quarter of a century and would shortly be demanding restrictions of a more drastic and general nature. This renewed agitation was no passing phase. It marked, on the contrary, the opening of a prolonged debate which was not to culminate until the 1920's, when the enactment of a restrictive code brought the era of mass immigration to a close.

Of all this there was barely a hint in the twenty years that followed Appomattox. Know-Nothingism had finally expired in the atmosphere of ethnic unity produced by the Civil War, and the mood of postwar America was such as to militate against a nativist revival. An appearance of social stability precluded any tendency to think of immigrants as a threat to the status quo, and a preoccupation with material growth led Americans rather to emphasize the economic value of immigration. Thus the 1860's and 1870's produced a flood of efforts to encourage immigration rather than to restrict it. Dislike and distrust of immigrants persisted, but remained in most places beneath the surface.

There was, however, one section of which this was untrue. While nativism remained at low ebb in the nation at large, it continued to flow strongly on the Pacific Coast, especially in California, where it took the form of a virulent anti-Chinese movement. The indiscriminate anti-foreignism which had characterized California's gold-rush days soon gave way to a concentrated hostility toward the Chinese, who had become the largest and most conspicuous non-European element in the state. Antipathy stemmed largely from a mistaken belief that the Chinese were "coolies," and as such constituted a servile class whose existence degraded and threatened free labor. It was also widely believed that the Chinese were an unassimilable, even subversive group, and that their vicious customs and habits were a social menace. Throughout the 1850's and 1860's the Chinese in California were subjected to sporadic outbursts of mob violence and to discriminatory laws designed to drive out those already in the state and to discourage the immigration of others. As a result of court decisions in the 1870's, however, most of this discriminatory legislation was invalidated as an infringement either of the Fourteenth Amendment or of the Burlingame Treaty of 1868, whereby the United States had recognized the right of the Chinese to immigrate.

The California agitation against the Chinese reached new heights with the formation in 1877 or the Workingmen's Party led by Dennis Kearney, a recently naturalized Irish immigrant. Kearney's inflammatory harangues against the Chinese in a series of sand-lot demonstrations in San Francisco led first to renewed violence against them, and then to a demand, backed ultimately by nearly every section of California opinion, for a federal exclusion law. That Congress proved sympathetic was due to the rivalry of the national political parties for far western votes and to the almost complete absence of opposition to the measure. As the Burlingame Treaty was still in force President Hayes found it necessary in 1879 to veto a bill prohibiting vessels from carrying more than fifteen Chinese passengers to the United States at any one time. But in 1880 China was persuaded to make a new treaty giving the United States the right "to regulate, limit or suspend," though not to prohibit, the immigration of Chinese laborers. Accordingly, in May, 1882, the Chinese Exclusion Act suspended Chinese immigration for a period of ten years, forbade the naturalization of Chinese, and imposed other restrictions upon them.

This suspension was not intended as a repudiation of the traditional asylum concept. Chinese immigration, it was thought, was a separate issue, involving wholly different considerations from those applying to the European movement.

American Immigration

Certainly it was with no restrictive intent that Congress, three months after passing the Chinese Exclusion Act, adopted the first general federal immigration law.

The absence of federal regulation before 1882 did not, of course, mean that immigration had until then been completely uncontrolled. From the beginning of the nineteenth century, as we have seen, many states and local authorities, particularly at the main ports of arrival, had adopted laws designed to discourage pauper immigration and to provide funds for the support of sick and needy newcomers. Originally these laws had provided for head taxes on all immigrants, but after they had been declared unconstitutional in the famous Passenger Cases of 1849, amendments were adopted to allow shipmasters the option of giving bonds or paying commutation fees for healthy passengers. In 1876, however, the Supreme Court decided that these laws too were unconstitutional, on the ground that they represented a regulation of foreign commerce, which the Constitution reserved to Congress.

During the next six years the demand by immigration boards in the eastern states for a federal law to replace the invalidated measures met with no response. Steamship companies and industrial interests were opposed to a federal law which might reduce the immigrant flow, while the representatives of western states argued that since New York and Boston derived great benefits from the immigrant traffic, they should be prepared to take the evil along with the good. What finally brought matters to a head was New York's threat to close down the immigrant depot at Castle Garden unless federal aid were forthcoming. A general realization of the abuses that would follow resulted in overwhelming congressional approval for the law of August, 1882, which imposed a head tax of fifty

cents upon every alien passenger and excluded convicts, lu-
natics, idiots, and those liable to become a public charge.

Three years later Congress again responded to pressure,
this time by labor organizations, with a law prohibiting the
importation of contract labor. The demand for prohibition
originated with the window-glass workers, a small and highly
specialized group which had recently suffered from the importation on contract of skilled workers from England and
Belgium. Prohibition was also demanded by the Knights of
Labor because of a widespread but erroneous notion that the
unskilled Italians and Slavs frequently used as strikebreakers
were also being imported on contract.

As we have seen, those unskilled strikebreakers were in fact
voluntary immigrants whom the employers had obtained from
private labor agencies in the larger American cities. But according to the Knights of Labor and their congressional spokesmen, American workingmen were being subjected to the competition of a servile class whose "importation" they likened
to the Chinese coolie trade. That Congress had already legis-
lated against the Chinese was, indeed, an important reason for
its readiness to prohibit contract labor. Industrialists, for their
part, were largely indifferent to the issue, as well they might
be in view of the extremely limited use they made of contracts.
Since both the major political parties were sympathetic, the
passage of the Foran Act of February, 1885, was a foregone
conclusion. The measure made it unlawful "to assist or encourage the importation or migration of aliens . . . under
contract or agreement . . . to perform labor or service of
any kind in the United States." The prohibition was not to
apply, however, to skilled labor needed for new industries,
nor to artists, actors, lecturers, singers, and domestic servants;

and individuals in the United States were not to be prevented from assisting the immigration of their relatives and personal friends.

The immigration legislation of 1882–85 did not, it will be noticed, spring from an integrated attempt at restriction. It was devised rather to meet specific, unconnected situations, and those who supported it generally disclaimed any wider restrictive purpose. Thus in 1885 an advocate of the Foran Act could remark that "this bill in no measure seeks to restrict free immigration; such a proposition would be odious, and justly so, to the American people." This was undoubtedly true for, as yet, inherited attitudes to immigration had lost little of their potency. Even while giving their assent to the new legislative principle of qualitative exclusion, Americans were at pains to emphasize their devotion both to the asylum concept and to a cosmopolitan ideal of nationality.

The latter half of the 1880's nonetheless saw the beginning of an agitation which would recognize no such limitations. Out of a resurgence of nativism developed a demand for a more decisive change of policy. Immigration now came to be widely regarded, not as an essential condition of material progress, but rather as a problem, the solution of which required urgent and drastic action.

The eruption of nativism which characterized the decade or so after 1885 had its origin in the social tensions of the period. The recurrence of industrial strife and of economic depression, together with the revival of interest in social reform, bred an awareness of the extent to which inequality and the hardening of class lines had resulted from the growth of an urban, industrial society. The passing of the frontier served both to heighten this realization and to induce a sense of national claustrophobia. Faced with the possibility of a reversion to European conditions, and of the disappearance of their fluid, homogeneous society, Americans began to lose confidence in the process of assimilation. The result was a nationalist outburst which stressed the need for social unity and which expressed itself in a fear-ridden and sometimes hysterical hatred of foreigners. In short, the class cleavages of the 1880's produced the same xenophobic consequences that had resulted in the 1790's from political divisions and in the 1850's from sectionalism.

Nativism came to life again for the first time since the Civil War with the Haymarket bomb outrage in Chicago in May, 1886, which aroused widespread fears of immigrant radicalism. A predisposition to associate labor discontent with foreign influence had existed even earlier, especially during the Molly Maguire riots in the Pennsylvania coalfields in the early 1870's, and again at the time of the violent railroad strikes of 1877. But it was not until the Haymarket Affair, and the conviction of a group of foreign-born anarchists for their alleged part in it, that Americans became seriously alarmed at the threat of imported revolution. Now, however, came a flood of warning against wild-eyed, foreign radicals who were alleged to be undermining the foundations of American society.

Within a month of the Haymarket Affair a new nativist political party, calling itself the American Party, came into existence in California. Here, concern at the turbulent role of the Irish in the labor movement had been growing ever since the appearance of Kearney's Workingmen's Party a decade earlier; thus the Chicago incident simply catalyzed the existing anti-radicalism of California nativists. Arguing that immigrants were largely responsible for the recent nationwide wave of strikes and riots, the leaders of the American Party demanded immigration restriction, the amendment of the naturalization laws and a ban on alien ownership of real estate. But owing to the stability of the existing party structure the new organization failed to establish itself outside California, and even there its existence was short-lived.

A more broadly based phenomenon was the rapid expansion during the late eighties of patriotic, veteran, and fraternal organizations. Of these the characteristic feature was a strident nationalism which, especially in the case of fraternal orders like the Order of United American Mechanics, often took the form of attacks on immigrant radicals. Significantly enough, the membership of these organizations consisted largely of just those groups—professional men, white-collar workers, small merchants, and skilled mechanics—who were suffering most from the "status revolution" of the period and who were thus most sensitive to threats to the existing order.

In older accounts the demand for immigration restriction was represented as coming largely from organized labor; business interests, conversely, were depicted as the chief defenders of an open gates policy. But this became true only after about 1905, when employers began to make great efforts to check union growth, partly through the practice of "balancing nationalities." Up to that point, however, there was no broad or clear-cut division between capital and labor upon the immigration question. Despite their demand for the prohibition of contract labor, the unions in the eighties and nineties gave only limited support to the general restriction movement. Though the declining Knights of Labor eventually declared in favor of restriction in 1892, the American Federation of Labor, with its large foreign-born membership and international outlook, could not be prevailed upon to indorse the literacy test until 1897, and even then only after bitter debate. American employers, for their part, were at first far from unanimous or consistent in their attitude to immigration. But in the last two decades of the nineteenth century many businessmen tended to be more concerned about the supposed radical tendencies of immigrants than to be appreciative of their economic value.

The re-emergence of a second nativist theme, that of anti-Catholicism, was also due basically to the nationalist anxieties of an age of crisis. But its immediate cause was the growing strength and influence of the Catholic church. The Third Plenary Council of 1884 gave a great impetus to Catholic institutional development; twenty new dioceses were established in the next decade, and the number of parochial schools so expanded that by 1890 they claimed an enrolment of 600,000 pupils. What helped make Protestants aware of these developments were the centennial celebrations of the American hierarchy in 1889, the assertion of Catholic strength which accompanied the Chicago World's Fair four years later and the appointment, also in 1893, of Cardinal Satolli as the first Apostolic Delegate to the United States. At the same time, the growing prominence of Irish politicians in American city government focused attention upon the growth of Catholic political power. And finally, the late eighties brought a revival of controversy over the public school question. The renewal of Catholic demands for a share in public school funds and the organized Catholic resistance to efforts to place parochial schools under state supervision were interpreted by many Protestants as a foreign attack upon a basic American institution, namely, "the little red schoolhouse."

Fears of a papal conquest of the United States led to the appearance of great numbers of secret anti-Catholic societies pledged to defend the public school system and to oppose Catholic influence in politics. The largest and most powerful of these societies was the American Protective Association, founded at Clinton, Iowa, in 1887 by a lawyer named Henry F. Bowers. Though the A.P.A. soon spread throughout the upper Mississippi Valley, membership at first grew only slowly. But the onset of economic depression in 1893 brought a vast accession of strength, still mainly from the Middle West but also from the east and west coasts. Hard times created an atmosphere in which anti-Catholic hysteria could flourish, and A.P.A. allegations of a popish plot to overturn the American economy were readily believed by thousands of unemployed workingmen. Some of the most enthusiastic supporters of the A.P.A., however, were foreign-born Protestants, especially those from Ulster, Canada, and Scandinavia. Largely for this reason the movement tended to concentrate upon limiting Catholic political power rather than upon restricting immigration. In any case Protestant nativism proved short-lived. After reaching a peak in 1894, when it may have had half a million members, the A.P.A. rapidly disintegrated, partly because of factional quarrels but most of all because of its inadequacy as a vehicle of nativist expression. Not only was the religious appeal limited in an increasingly secular age; it was also irrelevant to the situation arising from the change in the sources of immigration.

Up to this point nativists had been indiscriminately anti-foreign. Henceforth they came increasingly to concentrate their fire upon immigrants from southern and eastern Europe, whose bizarre appearance offered a tempting target for nativist attack. That the cultural differences between the newcomers and native Americans was greater than in the case of older immigrants was undeniable. Yet the "new" immigrants would have not had such a hostile reception but for the accident that their coming occurred close on the heels of a nativist revival. In the event, the anti-radical and anti-Catholic traditions of nativism did not altogether disappear; but henceforth they were overshadowed by that of Anglo-Saxonism.

The tendency to distinguish between different ethnic groups first appeared during the campaign against contract labor, when spokesmen for the Knights of Labor rested their case partly upon the low living standards of Italian and Hungarian immigrants. But at this stage criticism did not go beyond a simple ethnocentricism, and for the rest of the decade most nativists not only failed to emphasize the changing sources of immigration but remained largely unaware of them. As the "new" immigrants grew more numerous and conspicuous, however, the initial repugnance excited by their appearance and habits gave way to a dread of their subversive tendencies. Already alive to the existence of a foreign menace nativists came to see a special danger in an influx of Slavs, Italians, and Jews who were associated in the prevailing ethnic stereotypes with disorder, violent crime, and avarice, respectively. In the early 1890's a wave of nativist violence directed itself against each of these groups. Slavic strikers in the Pennsylvania bituminous fields were savagely shot down by native militia; a group of Italians, accused of murdering a police superintendent in New Orleans, was lynched in 1891 by an infuriated mob; anti-Jewish riots occurred both in the rural South and in a number of northern towns. As the decade advanced, popular nativism

257

became increasingly obsessed with the threat to American institutions posed by those whom it characterized as "the murder-breeds of southern Europe."

The notion that the "new" immigrants constituted a collective entity, different from and inferior to the old, arose not from popular antipathies but from the theorizing of a handful of race-conscious New England intellectuals. The general crisis of the 1880's in American society was felt with peculiar force in New England, where a successful Irish challenge to Brahmin domination intensified class cleavages. The loss of political and educational control bred in Yankee patrician circles a mood of disillusion and skepticism, leading to doubts concerning the ultimate success of the democratic experiment and America's capacity to continue assimilating immigrants. Among old-stock New Englanders pride in their English ancestry and a tendency to stress the Teutonic origins of American institutions had been growing ever since the 1870's, when the native culture began to decline. Now, as that decline was accelerated, the New England Anglo-Saxon tradition developed nativist overtones. As early as 1888 the social scientist Richmond Mayo-Smith was querying the economic value of immigration, and the geologist Nathaniel S. Shaler was beginning to emphasize "ancestral experience" as the criterion with which to measure the desirability of immigrants. Three years later came an influential study by Francis A. Walker, president of the Massachusetts Institute of Technology, which attributed the declining birth rate of the native population to immigrant competition. The census returns, Walker claimed, proved that immigration was not adding to the American population, as had hitherto been generally assumed, but was simply replacing the older stock.

The Demand for Restriction, 1882–1924

Early in 1894 the anxieties of the New England intelligentsia for the future of their "race" and class resulted in the formation of the Immigration Restriction League. Founded by a small group of youthful Boston bluebloods, of whom Charles Warren, Robert DeCourcy Ward, and Prescott F. Hall were the guiding spirits, the League was to be the spearhead of the restrictionist movement for the next twenty-five years. From the first the League emphasized the distinction which Walker and others had already made, between "old" and "new" immigrants. This involved, of course, accepting the Irish as honorary Anglo-Saxons. But however distasteful this may have been to Brahmin susceptibilities—and there was no question of the persistence of their anti-Irish antipathies—the southern and eastern Europeans seemed to pose much graver problems for the assimilative process and for American civilization generally. Hence in the same decade that saw the formulation of Frederick Jackson Turner's celebrated frontier thesis, with its renewed emphasis on environmental influences, another group of Americans began to assert their belief in the predominance of heredity over environment. The immigration issue, as redefined by Prescott F. Hall and his associates, was whether Americans wanted their country "to be peopled by British, German and Scandinavian stock, historically free, energetic, progressive, or by Slav, Latin and Asiatic races, historically down-trodden, atavistic, and stagnant."

Unprepared, however, to commit itself to the exclusion of immigrants upon a frankly "racial" basis, the Immigration Restriction League hit upon the device of a literacy test as a more devious but equally effective method of excluding "undesirable classes" from southern and eastern Europe. This policy the League now urged in an energetic campaign directed toward civic, business, and labor organizations as well as toward congressional opinion. The agitation culminated in 1896 in the passage by both houses of Congress of a literacy bill sponsored by Senator Henry Cabot Lodge of Massachusetts and providing for the exclusion of any immigrant unable to read forty words in any language. But in his last days of office President Cleveland vetoed the measure as an unworthy repudiation of America's historic role as an asylum for the oppressed.

Though restrictionists were confident that Cleveland's veto would prove to be only a minor setback, their optimism was not borne out by events. Twenty years were in fact to elapse before the campaign for a literacy test was carried to a successful conclusion. Renewed attempts to enact literacy bills in 1898, 1902, and 1906 were all defeated in Congress, and although the measure obtained congressional majorities in 1913 and 1915, it was vetoed on both occasions, first by Taft and then by Wilson.

These repeated failures are at first sight surprising. Since the restrictionists came within an ace of success in 1897, when the "new" immigrants constituted only a bare majority of the newcomers, then surely, it might be thought, they should have been able to muster enough votes to override a presidential veto in a period which saw an astonishing rise in the proportion of southern and eastern European immigrants. That they failed to do so is proof that no correlation existed between the character of immigration and the intensity of the reaction to it. Nativism rose and fell in response not to external influences but to changes in American internal conditions.

The inability of those who advocated the literacy test to achieve their objective in the period between the Spanish-

The Demand for Restriction, 1882–1924

American War and the outbreak of World War I was due primarily to the ebbing of the nativist impulse. The return of prosperity in the last years of the nineteenth century restored confidence in national homogeneity, and the imperialistic outburst with which it was accompanied opened new xenophobic outlets. Admittedly, national optimism received another jolt from the panic of 1907 and was therefore rather less widespread during Taft's presidency than it had been during that of McKinley. But in comparison with the early 1890's this whole period was one of buoyancy. As always, dislike of the foreigner persisted, perhaps even increased. But the air of crisis, of impending social disaster, which had characterized most of the nineties, had gone, taking with it the anxieties upon which nativism had been built.

Nevertheless, since it was only by narrow margins that the literacy test failed to become law, the comparative decline of nativism would not have thwarted the restrictionists had they not been faced also with organized opposition. Part of it came from big business organizations like the National Association of Manufacturers, which lobbied continuously in Washington against proposed restrictive measures. But the most strenuous opposition came from the immigrants themselves. Although the literacy test was avowedly directed against south and east Europeans, it met with the condemnation of every immigrant group. True, it was from the newer nationalities, and especially from Russian Jews, that the most sustained and vigorous opposition came. But that the older immigrant elements were of the same mind was shown by the agreement in 1907 between the German-American Alliance and the Ancient Order of Hibernians to oppose all forms of restriction.

What gave effectiveness to this opposition was the growing

importance of foreign-born votes and the emergence of the "new" immigrants as an influential pressure group. Up to about 1900 the immigrant, and especially the Irish, associations of the Democratic party had enabled nativists to use the GOP as a vehicle for restrictionism. But as increasing numbers of Italian, Slavic, and Jewish voters became attracted to Republicanism, that party was forced to take their wishes into account. This explains, for example, why Speaker Joe Cannon made strenuous and successful efforts to defeat an attempt in 1906 to attach a literacy test to an immigration bill. Equally significant was the omission from the Republican platform between 1904 and 1912 of the restriction plank which the party had regularly included for more than a decade.

Despite its failure to enact the literacy test, the restrictionist movement was not without its legislative victories during the Progressive era. In the first place Congress steadily extended the list of excluded classes which the immigration law of 1882 had begun. An Act of 1891 denied entry to paupers, polygamists, and persons suffering from loathsome and contagious diseases, and a further law of 1903 listed epileptics, prostitutes, professional beggars, and—as a result of McKinley's assassination by Leon Czolgosz—anarchists or persons believing in the overthrow by force or violence of the government of the United States, or of any government, or in the assassination of public officials. Finally, in 1907 a consolidating statute still further extended the excluded classes to include imbeciles, sufferers from tuberculosis, and persons who had committed a crime involving moral turpitude. At the same time these laws raised the head tax by stages from fifty cents in 1882 to four dollars in 1907, and attempted also to provide more stringent enforcement machinery. The actual administration of the 1882 federal law had been left to existing state agencies, but in 1891 immigration was placed wholly under federal supervision.

The strict enforcement of these laws, as well as the contract labor laws, was a virtual impossibility. For one thing Congress' failure to vote adequate funds meant that the immigration inspectors at the main ports of arrival could not hope to examine thoroughly the arriving multitudes. For another, it was a simple matter for those who could not pass inspection at American ports to enter the United States via Canada.

While those who wished to restrict European immigration were failing to secure anything but a succession of mildly exclusive and largely ineffective statutes, the opponents of Oriental immigration were winning striking successes. The two issues continued to be separate; the agitation for Oriental exclusion remained almost wholly a concern of the Far West, while support for the restriction of the European movement still came largely from the East. Yet in an age of growing race-consciousness the attitudes evoked by each of these issues were beginning to be projected onto the other.

The Chinese Exclusion Act of 1882, which denied entry to Chinese laborers for a period of ten years, was renewed for a similar period in 1892, and in 1902 Chinese immigration was suspended for an indefinite period. As a result of these measures and of the hostility and discrimination displayed against those Chinese already in the United States, numbers of them returned home. And despite the fact that others continued to enter California illegally by way of Mexico, the anti-Chinese movement had virtually run its course by the beginning of the twentieth century.

American Immigration

It was at once succeeded, however, by a no less virulent far western campaign against the Japanese. In many respects this new agitation closely resembled the earlier anti-Chinese movement, to which in fact it owed a great deal, not least because of popular confusion of the two nationalities. This confusion was largely responsible for the transfer to the Japanese of the unfavorable stereotype of the Oriental which was the legacy of the Chinese issue. Accordingly, Japanese immigrants became widely characterized as an immoral, subversive, and servile element. As in the case of the anti-Chinese movement, the first protests against the Japanese came from the San Francisco labor unions, which complained of an influx of coolie labor and of a resulting threat to the living standards of the American workingman. From 1900 onward organized labor staged a systematic campaign against the Japanese, and in 1905 was responsible for the formation of the Japanese and Korean Exclusion League, the first of a large number of anti-Japanese societies on the west coast. But by this time support for Japanese exclusion was coming from all classes in California. The possibility of war with Japan, which was widely discussed in the United States after the Russo-Japanese War of 1905, produced in California a frenzied fear of Oriental inundation. The specter of a "Yellow Peril" resulted in an unbridled display of antipathy toward the resident Japanese population and an almost universal demand for exclusion.

What brought the issue finally to a head was the action of the San Francisco school board in October, 1906, in ordering all Oriental pupils to attend schools specially set aside for them. Ostensibly an effort to prevent overcrowding in white schools, whose numbers had been reduced by the recent earthquake, the segregation order was really an attempt to exploit the racial issue by San Francisco political leaders whose municipal graft was about to be exposed. The order provoked violent anti-American demonstrations in Japan and was a considerable diplomatic embarrassment for the Roosevelt administration. But after a conference with the President in Washington in February, 1907, the San Francisco authorities agreed to withdraw the segregation order in return for an undertaking to negotiate with Japan with a view to restricting immigration. The upshot of these negotiations was the Gentlemen's Agreement of 1907–8, whereby the Japanese government undertook to deny passports to laborers going directly from Japan to the United States. Though this gave the west coast exclusionists all they had demanded, it failed to satisfy them. After a further period of agitation the California legislature in 1913 passed an Alien Land Law, which effectively barred the Japanese—as "aliens ineligible for citizenship"—from owning agricultural land in the state, and two years later an unsuccessful attempt was made to forbid even the granting of leases to Orientals.

The anti-Japanese hysteria of the early twentieth century not only wrote a significant chapter in the history of the Pacific Coast's war on the Orientals. It marked the point at which far western concern for white supremacy broadened into an attack upon the "new" immigration. The race feelings evoked by the Japanese menace, the belief in Anglo-Saxon superiority induced by imperialism, and increasing contact with the "new" immigrants all combined to bring the Far West to a fully nativistic position. Homer Lea, California's leading publicist of the Yellow Peril, warned in 1909 that America's racial purity was being threatened no less by European than by Asiatic immigration, and the novelist Jack London preached the same doctrine to a popular audience in his fictional accounts of race war in which the Nordic element in America was swamped by the "mongrel-bloods" of southern and eastern Europe.

Similar influences were at the same time transforming another race-conscious section into a fervent supporter of immigration restriction. Hitherto the South had remained largely aloof from the restrictionist agitation, concerning itself rather with promotional campaigns to attract European immigrants. But in the early 1900's the Anglo-Saxon nationalism born of the imperialist interlude interacted with the South's long-standing racial anxieties to produce a sudden reversal of attitudes. The arrival in the South of increasing numbers of dark-skinned immigrants seemed likely, moreover, to raise new racial problems for a section which already believed it had its quota of them. In particular, the tendency of the newcomers, especially the Italians, to associate freely with Negroes threatened to blur the color line. By about 1910, therefore, southern spokesmen were overwhelmingly in favor of restricting the "new" immigration.

Meanwhile the diffuse racial thinking of the New England patricians was being transformed into a thoroughgoing ideology. This development, which forged a powerful, precise, and pseudoscientific weapon with which to attack the "new" immigration, was a result of the impact on nativist thought of European natural science. Though the practice of dividing mankind into biological types, each with its own physical and cultural characteristics, had been increasingly common ever since the appearance of the Darwinian theory of natural selection, it was not until the early twentieth century that scientists

Entering a new world, 1892. Jewish refugees from Russia passing the Statue of Liberty. (Courtesy of the Mansell Collection.)

Sicilian immigrants at Ellis Island, 1909. (From *Metropolitan Magazine*, 1909.)

began to regard racial differences as fixed and immutable. That they did so then was due to the rise of the new science of eugenics, which emphasized the biological significance of heredity and warned against the consequences of breeding from inferior stock. In the United States, where the eugenics movement enjoyed a remarkable vogue in the early years of the twentieth century, its teachings were eagerly seized upon by upper-class nativists already concerned for the survival of the Anglo-Saxon stock and haunted by fears of "race suicide." Thus about 1906 the Boston intellectuals who directed the Immigration Restriction League began to point to genetic principles as a scientific basis for their claim that immigration restriction was essential to preserve American racial purity.

A similar hereditarian determinism manifested itself in the writings of social scientists who were concerned with the immigration problem. John R. Commons, for example, asserted in 1906 that even with the help of the American environment immigrants could hardly overcome the handicaps of race and heredity, and another midwestern professor, Edward A. Ross, referred to immigrants from eastern Europe as "the beaten members of beaten breeds." Both Ross and Commons owed much to the work of the economist, William Z. Ripley, who had introduced Americans to the concept, derived from physical anthropologists, that the peoples of Europe could be classified into hereditary types or races. Ripley's *The Races of Europe*, published in 1899, divided Europeans into a northern race of Teutons, a central race of Alpines, and a southern race of Mediterraneans, each with separate, unalterable, physiological traits. It was Ripley too who, on the basis of anthropological and genetic theories, suggested in 1908 that the consequence of racial intermixture, such as America was experiencing, was a tendency to reversion and a weakening of the dominant stock.

But it was left to Madison Grant, a wealthy New York nativist who had devoted much time to the study of the natural sciences, to give the new racist philosophy its most systematic, complete, and ultimately its most influential, expression. Grant's book, *The Passing of the Great Race in America*, which appeared in 1916, was a plea, in biological, eugenicist, and anthropological terms, for racial purity and aristocracy as the twin foundations of national greatness. Castigating "the pathetic and fatuous belief in the efficacy of American institutions and environment to revise or obliterate immemorial hereditary tendencies," Grant called for the exclusion of inferior Alpine, Mediterranean, and Jewish breeds as the only means of preserving America's old Nordic stock. Unless that were done, he prophesied, the "great race," which alone possessed the qualities to make "soldiers, sailors, adventurers . . . explorers . . . rulers, organizers and aristocrats" would be replaced by "the weak, the broken and the mentally crippled of all races."

Though an immensely effective nativist force had now been born, its heyday was not to come until after World War I. Accordingly, one should beware of exaggerating the racial content of early twentieth-century nativism. As yet the new racial ideology remained the exclusive property of a handful of intellectuals, and outside the South and the Far West popular nativism was hardly touched by race thinking. Organized labor, too, though now firmly committed to restriction, opposed the "new" immigration less on racial than on economic grounds. The vigor with which the American Federation of Labor backed the literacy test from about 1906 was essentially an expression of resentment by skilled workmen at the widespread use of unskilled immigrant labor. Nor did the Dillingham Commission approach its task from as thoroughly racist a standpoint as has sometimes been claimed. The Commission certainly started from the assumption that the "new" immigration was essentially different from and inferior to the "old," and for that reason devoted its attention almost exclusively to the former. It is also true that the "Dictionary of Races" compiled by the Commission's experts, though based ostensibly upon linguistic differences, tended in fact to divide races according to physical type. Nevertheless, the Commission occupied itself largely with an examination of the economic effects of immigration, and no less than half of its forty-one-volume report was devoted to that subject. And though a majority of the Commission's members recommended in 1911 that immigration be further restricted, they did so not on racial grounds but because of their conviction that American policy governing "the admission of aliens should be based primarily upon economic and business considerations touching the prosperity and economic well-being of our people."

Convinced, for whatever reason, of the undesirability of the "new" immigration, the Commission came out strongly in favor of a literacy test as the most urgently needed form of restriction. But a further six years of agitation were to elapse before the Commission's recommendation became law. Only on the eve of America's entry into World War I did the restrictionists manage to win enough congressional support to override a second Wilsonian veto. The Immigration Law enacted in February, 1917, was a comprehensive measure which codified existing legislation, doubled the head tax to $8.00, and added chronic alcoholics, vagrants, and "persons of constitu-

American Immigration

tional psychopathic inferiority" to the list of excluded classes. The statute also established a "barred zone" in the southwest Pacific, thus excluding virtually all Asiatic immigrants not already debarred by the Chinese Exclusion Act and the Gentlemen's Agreement of 1907. Finally, the law provided for the exclusion of adult aliens unable to read a short passage in English or some other language or dialect. This requirement was not, however, to apply to aliens fleeing from religious persecution, nor was it to prevent admissible aliens from bringing in illiterate members of their immediate families.

Though the demand for the literacy test originated in prewar conditions, its enactment in 1917 was due essentially to the added strength that restrictionism derived from the anxieties provoked by the European war. World War I was a major turning point in the history of American nativism. By making Americans aware as never before of the persistence of Old World ties, and thus of their own disunity, the conflict bred a strident demand for a type of loyalty involving complete conformity to the existing national pattern. This manifestation of the nationalist spirit, which came to be generally referred to as "100 per cent Americanism," proved to be more than a mere wartime phenomenon. Persisting into the 1920's, it became an essential ingredient of the movement which carried the restrictionists to final victory.

A new insistence upon national solidarity was apparent from almost the start of the European conflict. The German-American campaign of 1914–15 for an embargo on American exports of arms to the belligerents was widely interpreted as a German-inspired attempt to overthrow American neutrality. "Germany," commented the Houston *Post* in 1915, "seems to

270

have lost all of her foreign possessions with the exception of Milwaukee, St. Louis, and Cincinnati." Complaints of the divided loyalty of the German element developed into a widespread agitation against "hyphenated Americans," with Theodore Roosevelt and Woodrow Wilson as its leading spokesmen. Though German "tools of the Kaiser" remained the main target for criticism, Irish-Americans too incurred a great deal of hostility on account of their rabid pro-Germanism. In replying to an Irish agitator, Jeremiah O'Leary, who had protested during the 1916 election campaign against Wilson's "pro-British policies," the President wrote: "I should feel deeply mortified to have you or anybody like you vote for me. Since you have access to many disloyal Americans and I have not, I will ask you to convey this message to them."

It was the Germans, however, who were the sole victims of the fresh wave of xenophobia that came in the wake of America's entry into the war. The belligerent nationalism which had earlier characterized the preparedness campaign now erupted in a wave of hysterical anti-Germanism. Despite the fact that the great mass of German-Americans loyally supported the declaration of war on Germany, wild rumors circulated of their involvement in spying and sabotage. Excited patriots, now thoroughly infected by the intolerant, coercive spirit of 100 per cent Americanism, proclaimed that loyalty demanded the complete eradication of German culture. Accordingly, the teaching of German was in many places prohibited, German music and opera were shunned, the charter of the German-American Alliance was withdrawn; towns, streets, and buildings with German names were rechristened; even sauerkraut became liberty cabbage, while hamburgers turned into Salisbury steaks.

American Immigration

The concentration of anti-foreign sentiment upon the Germans afforded the rest of the foreign-born population a welcome immunity from criticism. Non-German immigrants, indeed, found that the spirit of common purpose inspired by the war effort tended in some degree to break down the barriers which had hitherto divided them from older Americans. Moreover, the intense hatred displayed by many of the "new" immigrants for the Central Powers left no doubt of their enthusiasm for the war. No longer vilified as a threat to America's social stability, southern and eastern Europeans were warmly praised for their part in defending America against an external foe.

Yet that doubts remained concerning the loyalty of immigrants generally was demonstrated by the new direction and emphasis given by the war to the Americanization movement. The organized efforts to Americanize the immigrant which began in the first decade of the twentieth century originated in a common concern for social unity on the part of a number of divergent groups. A program of immigrant education and assimilation appealed equally to social workers anxious to alleviate the conditions of immigrant life, to employers' associations desirous of improving the economic efficiency of newcomers and of safeguarding against labor unrest, and to patriotic societies worried about the threat to American institutions posed by immigrant ignorance. In the decade before the war, therefore, widespread efforts were made, both by these voluntary groups and by state agencies, to promote immigrant welfare and education by means of pamphlets, lectures, and evening classes.

With the rise of wartime nationalism the Americanization movement underwent a rapid metamorphosis. From 1915 onward, the Americanization of the immigrant became a patriotic duty, absorbing the energies of thousands of schools, churches, fraternal orders, patriotic societies, and civic and business organizations. In their anxiety to promote national unity, zealous patriots subjected immigrant groups to a high-pressure sales campaign designed to promote naturalization and the learning of English, and to inculcate knowledge of and respect for American institutions and ideals. These had been among the aims of the prewar Americanizers, too, but it was not until American nationalists began to demand a completely conformist loyalty that the effort to teach the immigrant things like personal hygiene and industrial safety was jettisoned in favor of persuading him to forget his Old World loyalties. Having evolved from an instrument of social welfare into one of social solidarity, the Americanization movement survived briefly into the postwar era to play its part in the crusade against Bolshevism. During the course of the war the movement had become increasingly frenzied and intolerant; with the arrival of the Red Scare it fell completely under the domination of the superpatriots.

The continuing concern for national homogeneity which accounted for the peacetime survival of Americanizing programs explained also the postwar persistence of xenophobia. After the armistice, however, the anti-foreign fears and hatreds of 100 per cent Americans were transferred from the German element to alien revolutionaries and radicals. Anti-radical nativism, largely in eclipse during the previous twenty-five years, reached a new peak of intensity when 1919 brought an upsurge of radicalism, bomb outrages, and labor unrest. That the radical threat to social stability and industrial peace should have been blamed on the immigrant is not difficult to understand. Immigrant workmen were prominent both in the violent textile strikes of the spring of 1919 and in the great steel strike of the succeeding summer. The newly formed American Communist parties, too, as well as numerous other radical organizations, claimed a large foreign-born membership. The Red Scare, therefore, erupted with especial force upon the foreign-born group. In the course of the Palmer raids of 1919–20, thousands of alien radicals were seized and hundreds were deported, many of them being shipped to Russia in December, 1919, in an army transport nicknamed "The Soviet Ark."

The waning of the Red Scare early in 1920, and the decline of the Americanization movement which occurred partly in consequence, marked the point at which the new nationalism turned its attention from resident aliens to the question of immigration restriction. Since the enactment of the literacy test in 1917, questions of immigration policy had remained largely in abeyance. But the resumption of large-scale European immigration, coinciding as it did with the sharp economic depression of 1920–21, stimulated a fresh agitation for restriction that ended only with the adoption of laws which reduced immigration to a trickle.

From the very outset of the new agitation the tide flowed strongly in favor of the restrictionists. Though the Red Scare had passed, it left behind deep-seated suspicions of immigrant radicalism, as the Sacco-Vanzetti case was shortly to demonstrate. At the same time the steady withdrawal of support from the Americanization movement betokened an admission that Old World loyalties were too deep-seated to be dislodged by exhortation and education. Still more significant, perhaps, was the general revulsion against Europe that followed the collapse of Wilsonian idealism. No less than the rejection of the League of Nations, the demand for immigration restriction stemmed from the disillusioned, isolationist mood of postwar America. Underlying the whole agitation was the general anti-foreignism and the unappeased longing for unity that were the legacies of the war.

Under such circumstances organized nativism experienced a notable revival in the early 1920's. Anti-Semitism increased markedly, especially in the rural regions which had learned as long ago as the Populist era to hate and fear the "International Jew." Social discrimination against Jews increased, too, though this was less indicative of the strength of nativism than was the appearance of an anti-Semitic ideology, focusing upon an alleged world conspiracy by Jews and disseminated through such publications as Henry Ford's notorious *Dearborn Independent*. Anti-Semitism was partly responsible for the astonishing growth of the Ku Klux Klan, which after 1920 spread like wildfire in the South and Middle West and which reached a membership peak of some two and a half million by 1923. Yet the heart of Klan nativism was always to be found in its virulent anti-Catholicism, the product of that same rural fundamentalism which gave the movement as a whole its characteristic evangelistic air.

While the fiery crosses of the Klan were spreading the gospel of intolerance, American nativism generally was acquiring an increasingly racial tinge. Thanks to the writings of a group of popular authors who had absorbed Madison Grant's teachings, the racist philosophy of the intellectuals filtered down to the American masses. Especially influential in popularizing the doctrine of Nordic superiority was a series of articles in 1922 in the *Saturday Evening Post* by the novelist Kenneth Roberts, who warned that a mixture of Nordic with Alpine and Mediterranean stocks would produce only a worthless race of hybrids. About the same time, publication of the results of the United States Army's wartime psychological tests on soldiers helped still further to condition the public to race thinking. The fact that soldiers from southern and eastern Europe had markedly lower IQ scores than those from northern and western Europe and the United States was adduced as conclusive proof of Nordic intellectual superiority.

During the congressional debates on immigration restriction in 1920–21, the new racial nativism had not yet had time to develop fully. At that time the demand for restriction was based largely on the alleged need to guard against an influx of starving Europeans, whose arrival would flood an already depressed labor market. Even so, it was upon southern and eastern Europeans that criticism chiefly fell, and there was general agreement upon the need to devise some formula to exclude the "new" immigration without substantially affecting the "old." With this purpose in mind Congress enacted a provisional measure in May, 1921, which introduced the principle of numerical restriction upon the basis of nationality. The law limited the number of immigrants of each nationality during the forthcoming year to 3 per cent of the number of foreign-born persons of that nationality resident in the United States at the time of the last available census, which was that of 1910.

Extended for two more years in May, 1922, this stopgap measure was superseded in 1924 by the Johnson-Reed Act, which laid down a permanent basis for admission. By now the notion that immigration policy should be based upon racial considerations was widely accepted both by the public and by Congress. Thus the purpose of the 1924 statute was avow-

The Demand for Restriction, 1882–1924

edly to maintain the "racial preponderance [of] the basic strain on our people," and thereby to stabilize the ethnic composition of the population. The more successfully to achieve this end, the law abandoned the percentage principle for that of national origins. This involved placing an upper limit of 150,000 upon the immigration of any one year, and the assignment of quotas to each nationality in proportion to its contribution to the existing American population. But since it would take time to calculate admissions on the new basis, revised percentage quotas were to operate until 1927. These would be 2 per cent quotas based upon the 1890 census, a change designed to reduce still further the proportion of south and east European entries. Countries of the Western Hemisphere were exempted from the quota system, but a complete prohibition of Japanese immigration made the pattern of Oriental exclusion almost complete.

With the enactment of this law an epoch in American history came to an end. After three centuries of free immigration America all but completely shut her doors on newcomers. The Statue of Liberty would still stand in New York harbor, but the verses on its base would henceforth be but a tribute to a vanished ideal.

X

The Consequences of Restriction,
1924-59

Even without the restrictive immigration laws of the 1920's, the mass movement of Europeans to the United States may well have slowed down, at least for a time. In the years between the two world wars there were unmistakable signs that in Europe the era of rapid population increase was drawing to a close. Everywhere, though more especially in the countries in the north and west of the continent, the birth rate was on the decline, thus reducing Europe's emigration potential. A similar result followed from the tremendous scale upon which war losses had occurred. Thanks also to industrialization and to the spread of social legislation, there was now less incentive for Europeans to leave. Finally, with the rise of totalitarian regimes, bent on conserving manpower for the purpose of military and economic expansion, movement itself was becoming increasingly difficult.

The Consequences of Restriction, 1924–59

In the end, however, it was American policy which brought to an end the century-long mass movement from Europe. The adoption of a quota system, heavily weighted in favor of the natives of northern and western Europe, all but slammed the door on the southern and eastern Europeans who had formed the bulk of the arrivals in the prewar and immediate postwar periods. The result was that European immigration slumped from over 800,000 in 1921 to less than 150,000 by the end of the decade.

The "national origins" system, which became fully operative in 1929, promised still further to accelerate the downward trend. Under this system, as under the provisional arrangements which had come into effect in 1924, the total number of immigrants admissible annually from countries outside the Western Hemisphere remained at just over 150,000; and within this limit quotas were apportioned to northwest and southeast Europe roughly in the proportion of five to one. But in comparison with the plan which had been in operation since 1924, the national origins system doubled the British quota while drastically reducing those of Germany, Scandinavia, and the Irish Free State. Thus, despite the fact that German, Scandinavian, and Irish immigration had, during the twenties, outnumbered the British by almost three to one, Great Britain was now given a quota larger than the totals of all other countries in northwest Europe combined.

Before this change had had sufficient time to alter the pattern of immigration, however, the influx from all parts of Europe had been brought to a virtual standstill by the depression and by stricter enforcement of existing regulations. In the fall of 1930, in response to demands that immigration be further reduced during the economic crisis, the Hoover administration ordered a more rigorous enforcement of the clause of the 1917 immigration act prohibiting the admission of persons likely to become a public charge. This policy of administrative restriction, which was continued by Franklin D. Roosevelt and was not abandoned until 1937, insured the exclusion of all but the most prosperous European immigrants. Not that many Europeans wanted to come to an America crippled by economic disaster. As the depression deepened and millions remained out of work in the United States, Europe tightened its belt and decided to stay at home. During the depression decade with quotas in most cases unfilled, fewer than 350,000 Europeans entered the United States. And since, in some years, more people left the country than entered it, the net gain from immigration between 1931 and 1940 was negligible.

While American conditions thus limited the volume of immigration, events in Europe largely determined its composition. At the beginning of the decade, European immigration consisted almost entirely of relatives of those who had entered the United States earlier. But from 1933 onward it included a considerable proportion of refugees from Nazi Germany. Particularly was this so after 1938, which saw the *Anschluss* with Austria and the intensification of Hitler's anti-Semitic campaign. Owing to the refusal of Congress to consider liberalizing the immigration laws during the depression, only a fraction of the refugees were able to reach the United States. As early as 1934, it is true, Roosevelt demonstrated his sympathy with the refugees by instructing American consuls to treat their applications for admission with all the humanity and consideration possible under the law; and in 1940 the situation was further eased when the State Department unblocked German quotas by permitting consuls outside Germany to issue visas to German refugees. Yet as long as the depression lasted, there was little disposition in America to lower the barriers imposed by the quota system, and the 250,000 refugees admitted to the United States in the period 1934–41 came within the limits of existing laws.

In addition to being on a much smaller scale, the refugee influx differed in other ways from the mass movements of the nineteenth and early twentieth centuries. For one thing it was not a free flow of individuals, but a highly organized and regulated movement. For another, the refugees came from an entirely different background from the bulk of earlier immigrants. Largely though not exclusively Jewish, they were predominantly of middle-class, urban origin, most of them being white-collar workers, professional and businessmen, and manufacturers. Not a few had achieved eminence in the arts, science, and scholarship, some of the best-known being Albert Einstein, Thomas Mann, Walter Gropius, Bruno Walter, and Paul Tillich. No fewer than twelve of the refugees were Nobel Prize winners, while hundreds of others were men and women of almost equal distinction.

The class and occupational characteristics of the refugees significantly affected their American adjustment. As sophisticated, well-educated city-dwellers, they found the physical aspects of American life less strange and bewildering than had the millions of illiterate peasants uprooted earlier from European villages. But an economic foothold proved proportionately harder to secure. Jobs of any kind were difficult to get during the depression and the occupational background of the refugees was often a handicap. Unlike unskilled workers, who could resume their former occupations with relative ease, refugees found that the language difficulty was generally a bar to immediate employment of the kind for which they were fitted. Because of the depression, moreover, a great many states and professional associations had debarred aliens; the law, medicine, teaching, and a long list of occupations were in places reserved for natives. Many highly trained newcomers had thus to be content, for a time at least, with menial jobs. It was by no means uncommon in the thirties to find refugee judges working as dishwashers, businessmen as hospital orderlies, factory managers as elevator operators, and engineers as night watchmen.

In one respect the refugees were more fortunate than their predecessors; there was a great number of voluntary agencies to which they could turn for assistance in the process of re-settlement. Organizations like the National Refugee Service and the Hebrew Sheltering and Immigrant Aid Society helped many of the newcomers to locate friends and relatives, find accommodations, obtain employment, and generally find their feet in America. Thanks to this assistance the refugees escaped much of the social disorganization and physical hardship that befell the mass of their predecessors. Yet the circumstances of their expulsion insured that they would have no easy adjustment, especially in the emotional sense. The refugees arrived in the United States after a succession of harrowing, often shattering, experiences; many were for a time physically and mentally exhausted. Nor was it easy for people who had lived for years under a pall of fear to rid themselves of its atmosphere and concentrate upon building a new life. Particularly was this so in the countless instances in which relatives had remained behind, their fate a source of constant anxiety. The trauma of forced emigration, broken family life, and readjustment left its mark on those who had experienced it.

To refugees, as to Americans generally, the waning of the depression and the American entry into World War II brought new economic opportunities. With manpower increasingly in demand, and with public authorities and professional associations abandoning their earlier exclusive attitude, the newcomers were now able to move into the positions to which their qualifications entitled them. Yet many refugees, particularly those of riper years, were unable to identify themselves completely with the country of their adoption, or to repress entirely their longing for a vanished world.

Nostalgia did not, however, diminish in the least their attachment and loyalty to the United States; their anxiety to become naturalized was but the initial proof of this. Nor did it prevent the refugees from making a contribution to American life out of all proportion to their numbers. Those with capital, for instance, introduced a variety of new industries to the United States and were responsible for making New York the world center of the diamond and jewelry trades. Refugee scientists figured prominently in the development of the atomic bomb. And by their mere presence the refugees immeasurably enriched American life. Widely dispersed throughout the country, partly as a result of their occupations and partly because of the reluctance of Jewish bodies to incur nativist criticism by massing them together, this uniquely gifted and cultivated group did much to increase American appreciation of the best in European culture.

Throughout World War II European emigration remained at the low level to which it had fallen in the early thirties. Though wartime America was desperately short of manpower, the whole of Europe was conscripted for war. In any case, the disruption of transatlantic communications meant that a free flow of emigrants was out of the question.

In the immediate postwar period most of the shipping available was needed to bring the soldiers home from Europe, and emigrant transportation facilities remained extremely limited. But, as conditions improved, the continuing prosperity of the United States attracted appreciable numbers of immigrants from the countries favored by the quota system. From Britain and Germany especially came skilled artisans, small businessmen, and clerical workers who deemed the future at home too unpromising to remain. Now, too, came the European wives, fiancées, and children of American service personnel. Their path smoothed by the "War Brides" and "Fiancées" Acts of 1946, which relaxed quota requirements for their benefit, some 150,000 wives and fiancées, 25,000 children, and a few hundred husbands entered the United States from Europe in the five years after the war. Further amendment to the law in 1947 in favor of Orientals permitted the entry of nearly 5,000 Chinese and about 800 Japanese wives.

Less easily disposed of was the refugee problem which, at the end of the war, assumed unprecedentedly large proportions. By 1945 millions of people had been displaced from their homes; they included the survivors of the Nazi concentration camps, the forced laborers brought to Germany from the occupied countries, and those who had fled from the Baltic States before the Russian advance in 1944–45. After the war the number of displaced persons was further increased by anti-Semitic outbreaks in Poland and Rumania, and by the flight of Czechs, Yugoslavs, and Poles from Communist domination.

The obligations of the United States toward these unfortunate people became the subject of protracted and bitter controversy. The Truman administration, though acknowledging that this was an international rather than a purely American problem, strongly urged that the United States should set an example by admitting a generous proportion of the displaced persons. Such a course, it was argued, was dictated alike by the American tradition of asylum, by the interest of the United States in the recovery of Europe, and by the responsibilities of world leadership. But a sizable group of congressmen, drawn especially from the rural regions of the South and the Middle West, opposed a liberal displaced persons program, as did a number of veterans' organizations and hereditary patriotic societies. In their view the admission of masses of displaced persons would not only deprive returning veterans of jobs and housing but would flood the country with subversives and other undesirables.

Owing to congressional opposition, action was repeatedly postponed. A presidential directive of December, 1945, had given war refugees priority within the existing quotas. But since most of the displaced persons were from countries with low quotas, only 41,000 were able to enter the United States during the next two and a half years. Finally, however, the Displaced Persons Act of 1948, as amended in 1950, provided for the admission of some 400,000 people during a four-year period. Three-quarters of the newcomers were to be regular displaced persons, as defined by the International Refugee Organization; the remainder were to consist variously of

Volkdeutsche—people of German ethnic origin formerly resident in the Baltic States—special groups of Greek, Polish, and Italian refugees, as well as orphans and European refugees stranded in the Far East.

By the time the displaced persons program terminated in June, 1952, the great majority of those uprooted by World War II had been resettled. But a stream of refugees continued to flow westward from the Communist countries, and the recovery of both West Germany and Italy continued to be hampered by chronic overpopulation. In an attempt to solve these problems Congress passed the Refugee Relief Act in 1953; this authorized the admission of 214,000 refugees during a 41-month period.

Neither the displaced persons nor the postwar refugees were allowed to enter as non-quota immigrants. In order to preserve the quota principle the emergency relief measures of 1948–53 provided that those entering on such terms were to be charged to future quotas of their country of origin, though the mortgage was limited to 50 per cent of the quota of any one year. Despite criticism of the discriminatory features of the quota system, the American political situation was such as to make amendment difficult. Far from being liberalized, the quota system was made in some respects even more rigid and restrictive by the Immigration and Naturalization Act of 1952 (the McCarran-Walter Act), which codified existing legislation. Accordingly, when 200,000 Hungarians fled their country after the suppression of the 1956 revolution, America's ability to help was narrowly circumscribed by law. About 5,000 Hungarians were granted visas under the Refugee Relief Act, due to expire at the end of 1956, while President Eisenhower invited 30,000 more to come in on parole. Within two months these people had been air-lifted to Camp Kilmer, New Jersey, where a reception center had been prepared; and from there they dispersed throughout the country.

As had been the case with the prewar refugees, the European background of the displaced persons affected their capacity to adjust to American life. They had not only passed through demoralizing and frightening experiences during the war, but for years afterward had led a chaotic existence culminating in long, frustrating periods of waiting in displaced persons camps. Formidable tasks of reorientation thus awaited them in America; family life had to be rebuilt, old skills refurbished and adapted, and all the problems of everyday life in a free society had to be faced anew. Like the refugees of the thirties, however, they had the advantage of guidance and assistance from a variety of international, federal, state, and voluntary organizations. They were also fortunate in coming to the United States at a time of renewed economic expansion, when employment of all kinds was relatively easy to obtain. Another factor which facilitated the economic adjustment of the displaced persons was their occupational background. Though this was anything but homogeneous, the fact that the majority of the newcomers were either unskilled or semi-skilled meant that ignorance of English was usually no bar to immediate employment. Finding advantageous positions in the American economy, and meeting more friendliness and tolerance than had been the portion of the prewar refugees, the displaced persons were generally able in their new situations to make satisfactory social and emotional adjustments.

The decline of European immigration in the late 1920's led to increased arrivals from those areas exempted from the quota system. One such area was the Philippine Islands, which, for a decade after 1924, enjoyed the distinction of being the only Oriental country whose inhabitants the United States had not excluded. Because of the inducements held out by Hawaiian sugar planters, Filipino immigration to the Hawaiian Islands had been continuously in progress since 1907. But as late as 1920 there were only about 5,000 Filipinos in the continental United States. A decade later, the number was more than ten times as great. Almost wholly male, the Filipino immigrants were heavily concentrated in the Pacific Coast states, where they were chiefly employed as seasonal agricultural workers.

Though the number of arrivals had been relatively small, a demand for Filipino exclusion grew steadily after about 1928. In the forefront of this agitation were the west coast labor unions, though strong backing came from patriotic societies anxious to complete the pattern of Oriental exclusion. In 1929–30 came a rash of anti-Filipino demonstrations in California and Washington. Clashes between Filipinos and whites who were competing for employment as fruit and vegetable harvesters and packers led to some loss of life and gave the exclusion movement fresh strength. But, as had been the case in the agitations against Chinese and Japanese immigration, hostility to the Filipino was only in part economic; the chief complaint related to his alleged immorality, criminality, and unassimilability.

Since exclusion was strongly opposed by Filipino leaders, as well as by west coast and Hawaiian employers, a decision on the matter was postponed until the future of the Philippine Islands, then under discussion, was settled. Finally, in 1934 the Philippine Independence Act allotted an annual quota of fifty to the islands and provided for complete exclusion when independence was achieved. In any case Filipino immigration had now been ended by the depression, and most of the Filipino laborers in the United States were destitute and had to be assisted to return home.

The 1924 decision to exempt the Western Hemisphere from the operation of the quota system was in part a concession to southwestern ranchers and farmers who had grown to rely heavily upon Mexican labor. But a more important influence was the strength of Pan-Americanism. The restrictive immigration laws, as we have seen, were essentially an expression of American revulsion from the Old World; and since, as a consequence of her isolationism, the United States tended to draw closer to other American countries, it was natural for her to place immigration from them upon a special footing. For more than a decade after 1924 restrictionists continued to press for the abolition of the Western Hemisphere exemption. But although Mexican immigration was checked by administrative action during the depression, every demand that immigration from the Americas should be placed on a quota basis was rejected in the interests of what eventually became known as the "Good Neighbor" policy.

After 1924, therefore, newcomers from the Western Hemisphere formed a much larger proportion of the total immigration than before. Most of them came from countries nearest to the United States, with Canada, Mexico, and the West Indies heading the list. Immigration from these areas conformed to a common pattern; it was wholly economic in origin, it was largely impermanent, at least in its earlier stages, and each group was concentrated in a particular region of the United States.

For a time the most fruitful source of immigration was

American Immigration

Canada. Ever since the Revolution, Canada and the United States had been regularly exchanging populations, the tide at one time setting in a southerly direction, at another toward the north. And while the balance had swung in Canada's favor during the settlement of her prairie provinces just before World War I, the 1920's belonged to the United States. In the course of the decade nearly a million Canadians crossed the forty-ninth parallel to share in American prosperity. Some were French-Canadians, who moved southward to join the tightly knit communities their compatriots had established in the mill towns of New England. But the core of the influx consisted of Canadians of British ancestry, who flowed steadily throughout the decade from Ontario into the great industrial centers of the Middle West. By 1930, however, immigration from Canada had largely run its course. As a result of the depression, only about 100,000 Canadians entered the United States during the 1930's; and during and after World War II the rapid industrialization of Canada prevented the southward movement from recovering its former momentum.

More persistent, and at the same time more conspicuous, was the immigrant influx from across the southwestern border of the United States. Immigration from Mexico began on a large scale about 1900, when railroad-building and phenomenally rapid agricultural expansion in the Southwest created a pressing demand for cheap, unskilled, migratory labor. During the next thirty years, as the citrus fruit and vegetable industries boomed and the center of cotton cultivation marched steadily westward, Mexican immigration increased in proportion. The number of Mexicans officially recorded as entering the United States rose from 49,000 in the decade 1901–10 to 219,000 in 1911–20 and then to 459,000 in 1921–30. But the actual arrivals, especially in the 1920's, were well in excess of the official figures. Partly because many Mexicans were unable to fulfil literacy test requirements, but more because of the expense and delay involved in obtaining American visas as stipulated by the 1924 Immigration Act, great numbers entered the United States illegally, a large proportion of these "wetbacks" being smuggled in by American labor contractors.

However they came, legally or otherwise, Mexican immigrants remained heavily concentrated, both geographically and occupationally. While in 1930 there were considerable numbers in Colorado and Kansas, the great majority were to be found in the three states of Texas, Arizona, and California. Although some found work on the railroads, on the stock ranches, or in the mines, Mexican laborers were employed chiefly in the cultivation, harvesting, and packing of fruit, vegetables, cotton, and sugar cane. In the production of all these commodities they formed, indeed, the backbone of the Southwest's labor force.

Although during the depression Mexican immigration was greatly reduced, it never ceased entirely. Then, after 1940, an acute shortage of manpower prompted a reversal of policy and gave the movement fresh impetus. From 1942 onward, after agreement had been reached with Mexico, the United States government undertook the organized recruitment of Mexicans for seasonal agricultural work and railroad maintenance. While, under these arrangements, scores of thousands of Mexicans entered the United States temporarily during World War II, even greater numbers came independently. By 1945 the number of the Mexican-born in the United States exceeded two and a half million, and in the postwar era the persistence of both legal and "wetback" immigration swelled

the total still further. In the forties, too, the traditional pattern
of settlement showed the first signs of crumbling. Most Mexicans were still to be found in the Southwest, where they formed
a vast migratory army following the "big swing" through the
cotton, fruit, and vegetable regions. But as the increasing mech-
anization of agriculture steadily narrowed their opportunities
in the Southwest, they began to fan out, first to the Rocky
Mountain states and then to the Middle West. In these areas
some continued to be seasonal agricultural workers, as in the
sugar-beet fields of Michigan and Minnesota. But increasing
numbers began to enter industry, especially in Chicago, Toledo,
and Detroit, where small Mexican colonies had remained in
existence ever since World War I.

The Mexican immigrant's adjustment to the United States
was determined by his background, the circumstances of his
migration, and the nature of his employment. Poverty-stricken,
illiterate, and coming in the main from a self-sufficient, homogeneous, isolated folk culture, Mexicans were ill-prepared for
a rapid transition to a complex, highly industrialized, urban
society. The product of several centuries of ethnic intermixture, particularly between Spaniard and Indian, they were
fated, wherever they happened to settle in the United States,
to suffer the penalties attached to color. Their concentration
in the Southwest, an acutely race-conscious section, condemned
them to a distinct status as a lower caste, nearly always suffering discrimination in employment and social life, and segregation in housing and education. Their religion, too, Roman
Catholic in ritual but strongly tinged with native folk practices, set Mexicans apart from other groups, especially in regions as fundamentalist in belief as Texas. Ignorant both of
the English language and of American working conditions,

they were ripe objects for exploitation by labor contractors and employers, especially when they had entered the United States illegally. The fact, moreover, that they worked in isolated groups, often deliberately insulated from outside influences by their employers, was a major obstacle to their acculturation. At the same time, the migratory nature of their work delayed the growth of fixed settlements and hindered the development of a stable group life.

As others had done before them, immigrants from Mexico leaned on each other for mutual support. As early as the 1920's they had begun to form agricultural labor unions and to strike against exploitation. From about 1940, as Mexicans began to move up the occupational ladder and their settlements took on a greater appearance of permanence, their group life became at once more firmly based and more highly organized.

About the turn of the century, just as the first sizable groups of immigrants were making their way to the United States from Mexico, a comparable movement set in from the West Indies. During each of the next three decades well over 100,-000 immigrants entered the United States from that area, and although the influx fell off during the depression and World War II, it soared to new, if indeterminate, heights after 1945. The sources of West Indian immigration did not remain the same throughout the period. Up to about 1945 the movement consisted largely of Negroes from the British West Indies, with smaller contingents from the French West Indies, Cuba, and Haiti; thereafter it was overwhelmingly and increasingly Puerto Rican.

Because of the nature of the economic opportunities they sought, West Indian Negro immigrants settled largely in urban centers along the Atlantic seaboard, particularly in New York and Boston. An unusually diverse group both in background and in training, they entered a greater variety of occupations than was the case with most immigrant groups. Though a majority of the West Indians were probably unskilled, some, like the Jamaican and Cuban cigar-makers, were highly trained workers who were able in America to take up familiar and profitable employment. West Indian women, too, were sometimes able to make use of old country skills, as in the case of those who entered the New York needle and garment trades. In addition, not a few of the newcomers possessed professional qualifications which, allied to a knowledge of English, generally opened the door to prosperity. Thus it was that, by the 1930's, a high proportion of New York's Negro physicians, dentists, and lawyers were immigrants from the British West Indies.

While most Negro newcomers succeeded in obtaining for themselves favorable positions in the American economy, they found other aspects of the process of adjustment more difficult. In the West Indies status had been determined only in part by color and many West Indians, unaccustomed to broad discrimination on a racial basis, found it galling to have to adjust to America's biracial pattern. Nor was adjustment made any easier by the differing cultural backgrounds of American and West Indian Negroes. The bulk of the latter were generally better educated than American Negroes, their religious affiliation was Episcopal rather than Baptist or Methodist, and, as a result of their contact with British culture, they had a predominantly European attitude toward the role of the family. Looking down upon American Negroes for their alleged ignorance and supineness, the newcomers were cordially disliked in return for their supposed aloofness and aggressiveness.

The Consequences of Restriction, 1924–59

Rejected, therefore, by native whites and Negroes alike, yet lacking any bond save that of a common loyalty to the British crown, West Indian immigrants sought nevertheless to construct a self-sufficient associational life of their own. Their ability to do so was increased by the persistence of ties with the West Indies, not the least significant of which was the steady influx of newcomers of similar background. But the McCarran-Walter Act of 1952 entirely changed the situation. Allowed hitherto to make use of the unfilled portion of the large British quota, the West Indians were now allocated a tiny quota of their own. This effectually brought the movement to the United States to an end; henceforth West Indians migrated to London, Birmingham, and other British industrial cities.

By this time the typical West Indian immigrant was not from the British colonies of Jamaica or Trinidad but from the American territory of Puerto Rico. Ever since 1900, when Puerto Rico became an unincorporated territory, its inhabitants have enjoyed the right of free entry into the continental United States. The number of Puerto Rican immigrants was insignificant until the 1920's, but with the ending of mass immigration from Europe, American employment opportunities began to attract increasing numbers from an island incapable of supporting its rapidly swelling population. The depression, of course, halted the flow, and even in 1940 there were still fewer than 70,000 Puerto Ricans on the American mainland. But in 1945 the restlessness induced by the war, the lure of American prosperity, and the inauguration of low-cost air transportation services, which brought New York within eight hours of San Juan, combined to set in motion a veritable flood of immigration. Exactly how many Puerto Ricans subsequently moved to the mainland is difficult to say, since no official records are kept of the movement of American citizens from one part of the United States to another. Much of the Puerto Rican movement was tentative in character, and there was a good deal of shuttling back and forth between the island and New York. Yet by 1957 there were more than 550,000 Puerto Ricans living in New York City, and perhaps 175,000 more were scattered between Chicago, Philadelphia, and a number of smaller industrial centers in the Northeast.

The Puerto Rican concentration in New York originated in the fact that the city has long been the main outlet for the island's trade. Then, as distinctive Puerto Rican communities took root in East Harlem, South Bronx, and Brooklyn, other Puerto Ricans gravitated there, especially if they intended, as many did, to return eventually to their old homes. But within the last decade or so, as Puerto Ricans have become more deeply committed to the mainland, a significant trend toward dispersion has developed.

The economic role of the Puerto Rican immigrant has been to fill in part the vacuum in unskilled and semiskilled labor left by the virtual ending of European immigration. Restricted at first by their color, their ignorance of English, and the economic depression of the thirties to the most menial jobs, they infiltrated in time into light industry and the garment trade, retaining also a firm foothold in hotel and restaurant work. But only a few entered domestic service because of the language barrier, the persistence of island prejudices against that form of employment, and the fact that the women usually had large families to care for.

As a result of half a century of American suzerainty over Puerto Rico, immigrants from the island came to the United

States with a better knowledge of the world they were entering than had been possible for any other group. In most cases
Puerto Ricans had been exposed since birth to American ideals,
institutions, and products. They were thus familiar with the
electoral process, public education, and the media of mass communication, as well as with a variety of American foods, clothes,
and appliances. Semi-Americanized as they already were, major
problems of adjustment nevertheless confronted them on the
mainland. As it was to other West Indians, the rigidity of the
color line was both a shock and an ever present source of restriction and confusion. Color prejudice not only limited still
further the economic opportunities of a group already handicapped by its lack of usable skills, but forced the newcomers
to crowd together in slum tenements. And while their Catholicism and the fact that they were Spanish-speaking kept
them apart from native Negroes, their color barred their acceptance by white American Catholics. Then again, the rapid
turnover of the Puerto Rican immigrant population delayed
the development of a stable group life. To the Puerto Rican,
therefore, as to millions of his predecessors, the American
world was essentially alien, his adjustment to it painfully slow.

By drastically limiting the volume of European immigration,
the restrictive policy adopted in the 1920's accelerated the
Americanization of those groups which had come earlier. With
reinforcements no longer arriving from across the ocean, ties
with Europe were gradually weakened and memories of the
old life grew dimmer with each year that passed. The gradual
disintegration of the ethnic ghettos helped produce a similar
result. As immigrants grew more familiar with American conditions, they burst out of their occupational and residential

confines and moved nearer the mainstream of American life.

During the prosperous decade of the 1920's, more than 90,-000 of New York's Italians moved out of the congested districts of East Harlem and the Lower East Side into the suburbs and into Westchester and Long Island, and a similar movement was discernible among the Italians of Chicago, Boston, and Philadelphia. The depression slowed down the exodus, but by 1940 less than half of New York's Italian-born lived in the so-called Italian areas. The same tendency toward dispersion was to be found among the Poles of Buffalo, the Czechs of Chicago, and the Boston Irish. Although each of these groups tended to recongregate in the suburbs, they were no longer so restricted in their contacts with America. For the immigrant, escape from the ghetto was the first great stride toward the anonymity of American middle-class life.

To the second generation, which had never known the old country, the ethnic tie became increasingly meaningless. Culturally estranged from their parents by their American education, and wanting nothing so much as to become and to be accepted as Americans, many second-generation immigrants made deliberate efforts to rid themselves of their heritage. The adoption of American clothes, speech, and interests, often accompanied by the shedding of an exotic surname, were all part of a process whereby antecedents were repudiated as a means of improving status.

As a result of these developments immigrant organizations lost steadily in membership, vitality, and purpose. The extent to which this occurred was due not only to the ending of mass immigration and the passage of time, but to changing American conditions. The growth of the means of mass communication tended to undermine those institutions which had been most effective in giving substance and expression to group life. The immigrant press, for instance, was hopelessly handicapped by lack of resources in its efforts to withstand competition from the picture tabloids which made their appearance in the 1920's. Though a number of foreign-language newspapers switched to English in an attempt to hold the second generation, the decline in circulation could not be halted. The depression further reduced subscription lists and deprived many journals of much of their advertising revenue. Still another blow was the outbreak of World War II, which cut off the supply of news and of advertising income hitherto supplied by European government agencies like the Italian Stefani Agency and the German Transocean News Service. Accordingly, during the single decade 1940–49 more than one-third of the total number of foreign-language publications passed out of existence. At the same time, the rise of the movies and of the radio brought about the almost complete disappearance of the immigrant theater. Finally, the phenomenal spread of television greatly accentuated the trend whereby all Americans, irrespective of origin, were exposed to a common set of influences.

The depression, World War II, and the postwar boom each played a vital part in dissolving the ethnic tie. The depression greatly sharpened the sense of class division in American society and tended to override the cultural differences which had hitherto kept apart the various ethnic elements in the American working population. Perhaps the most striking proof of this was the formation of the CIO, which brought together immigrant and native workers in those very mass-production industries in which ethnic discord had been most marked. The depression did much also to weaken immigrant social and cultural organizations, many of which were simply unable to carry on because of lack of funds. Then, too, the coming of the New Deal taught immigrants to look for help to governmental agencies rather than to their own mutual aid and benevolent societies.

Concern with the American present, however, did not entirely blot out recollection of the European past. That immigrants retained a sense of solidarity with their country of origin was apparent from their reaction to events in Europe in the 1930's. Particularly sensitive to European happenings were immigrants from countries whose totalitarian regimes incurred increasing American criticism as World War II loomed nearer. Italian-Americans, for example, whose approval of Mussolini had grown steadily since his 1929 Concordat with the Vatican, strongly opposed the attitude of the Roosevelt administration toward the Ethiopian war. Virtually the whole of the Italian-American press and hundreds of Italian-American societies protested against the President's administration of the Neutrality Act and against his efforts to discourage the export of oil and other war materials to Italy. Yet that this agitation implied widespread sympathy with Fascism is open to question. Certainly many Italian-American newspapers echoed Fascist propaganda, but the mass of Italian-Americans seem to have been more or less indifferent to Fascism, whilst retaining a sentimental attachment to Italy and resenting criticism of and discrimination against her. Nor, among German-Americans, could the substratum of sympathy that remained for the Fatherland be equated with pro-Nazi tendencies. Admittedly, Fritz Kuhn's German-American Bund, complete with storm troopers and parades on the Nazi model, attracted a certain amount of support for a time, though not exclusively from German-Americans. But as the implications of Nazism became clearer, the Bund's strength dwindled. By 1938 the German ambassador to the United States was forced to report to Hitler that not more than one-third of the Americans of German origin or descent maintained any interest in German traditions or in any organized form of German-American life. And of that number many were hostile to Nazism, a majority were indifferent to politics, and only an infinitesimal fraction were Nazis.

The sensitiveness of German-Americans to European affairs was in fact demonstrated less clearly by their attitude to Nazism than by the persistence of their isolationism. It has recently been suggested that the isolationism of the Middle West has been due less to the region's physical insularity than to the views of its German-descended inhabitants. While this may be an exaggerated claim, there is no question that from 1920 onward the German-settled areas, both in the Middle West and in other parts of the Union, remained a hard isolationist core. Even so, this isolationism was not a measure of the concern German-Americans felt for the welfare of the Fatherland; it reflected, rather, the extent to which World War I had taught them to associate American involvement in war with attacks upon themselves.

German-American attachment to isolationism became still stronger after the European war broke out in September, 1939. Italian-American and Irish-American groups, too, persistently agitated during the next two years against America's involvement in the conflict. Among other groups, however, the spread of Axis domination aroused other emotions. Americans of British, Polish, Dutch, Norwegian, Yugoslav, and Greek descent were generally agreed in opposing United States intervention; but they were united in demanding that all aid short of war should be afforded the Allies.

The continuing importance of the ethnic tie was demonstrated in the 1940 presidential election. With foreign policy a major issue, Roosevelt suffered striking losses as compared with 1936 in German-settled areas; many Italian-Americans, too, who had been affronted by the President's reference to the "stab in the back" dealt to France by Mussolini, withdrew their support from the Democrats. Yet to offset these losses was the strength Roosevelt drew from voters of Polish, Norwegian, and Jewish extraction, all of whom were anxious to see the defeat of Hitler. More significant still, perhaps, were Roosevelt's gains in regions dominated by descendants of the original English settlers. It was a remarkable tribute to the persistence of ethnic sentiment that the South and the Yankee strongholds in New England were more favorable than the country generally to aid and intervention.

Whatever differences of opinion had existed during the period of American neutrality were quickly swept away by the Japanese attack on Pearl Harbor. The debate about intervention now became academic, and all elements in the population united in support of the war effort. Though there were almost one million enemy aliens in the United States in 1941, in addition to millions of naturalized citizens who had been born in enemy territory, all but a handful were unwavering in their American allegiance. In the case of those of German or Italian origin this fact was widely appreciated, and neither group was subjected to the kind of treatment suffered by German-Americans during World War I. Thus out of nearly 700,000 Italian enemy aliens, only 4,000 were apprehended by the FBI and of these only about 200 were interned. An initial reluctance to employ unnaturalized Italians in war industries, because of possible sabotage, was soon dispelled, and in the fall of 1942 they were relieved of the disabilities of their enemy status. Nor were the mass of German-Americans molested. Despite the fact that this was the second time within twenty-five years that the United States had been at war with Germany, and that most Americans regarded Germany as the major enemy, there was little disposition to question the loyalty of those of German origin. Of the 300,000 enemy aliens from Germany only a few hundred were interned; the rest suffered no serious discrimination and were freely accepted both in war industries and in the armed services.

Less fortunate were Japanese aliens and Americans of Japanese ancestry. Highly concentrated on the Pacific Coast, and particularly in California, where they had remained the object of deep-seated suspicion and animosity, the Japanese now became the victims of an episode unquestionably tragic and acknowledged subsequently by many Americans to have been "a great and evil blotch on our national history." A little more than two months after Pearl Harbor the commanding general of the Western Defense Command, John L. DeWitt, concluded that military necessity demanded the immediate evacuation of all Japanese from the Pacific Coast area. Official approval having been obtained, more than 110,000 people of Japanese ancestry, two-thirds of them American citizens, were transferred under the supervision of the United States Army to ten relocation centers situated in isolated parts of the western, mountain, and plains states. There, behind barbed wire and under armed guard, the majority of the evacuees sat out the war, cut off from their homes, deprived of their occupations and much of their property, and denied their constitutional and legal rights.

Responsibility for the evacuation is still a matter of controversy. Liberals, and some constitutionalists, have attributed it to the influence of selfishly motivated pressure groups anxious to eliminate Japanese competition or to secure the lands held by the Japanese, as well as to the noisy clamor of Pacific Coast politicians desirous of popular approval. But the activity of such organizations and individuals seems to have been "greatly exaggerated both as to extent and influence." Nor, again, does it seem just to make General DeWitt the scapegoat for what happened. Though DeWitt's plea of military necessity cannot, in retrospect, be upheld, his was but a subordinate role. The evacuation program he initiated was, after all, sanctioned by the President, indorsed by both houses of Congress, and sustained by the Supreme Court.

It is difficult, indeed, not to agree with the conclusion of a recent study that responsibility for the evacuation rests primarily with the American people. For half a century and more, the people of the nation at large, though especially those on the west coast, had built up a stereotyped picture of the Oriental immigrant as a sly, unscrupulous, and above all things subversive element. The attack on Pearl Harbor completely activated the stereotype and predisposed Americans to believe wild rumors—later found to be unsubstantiated—of espionage and sabotage by Japanese-Americans. Thus in the early months of 1942, when a series of smashing Japanese victories in the southwest Pacific had bred an atmosphere of anger, fear, and frustration in the United States, few voices were raised to prevent the commission of a great wrong.

The Consequences of Restriction, 1924–59

Not surprisingly, the evacuees were severely shaken, sometimes demoralized, by the treatment they received. More than 5,000 Japanese-Americans renounced their American citizenship during the course of the war, though a number subsequently reclaimed it, and a slightly larger number took the first opportunity of returning to Japan. Yet the great majority remained staunchly loyal to the United States, and more than 12,000 Nisei—people born in America of Japanese parentage —served with honor and distinction in American combat units during World War II.

Having thus proved their loyalty, Japanese-Americans were enabled in the postwar era to adjust to America more satisfactorily than ever before. Though a majority returned to the Pacific Coast, others spread out throughout the nation and developed flourishing communities in places like Chicago, Minneapolis, Denver, Philadelphia, and Cleveland. At the same time, their occupational concentration was significantly reduced. Before 1941 most Japanese-Americans had been truck farmers, gardeners, fishermen, and domestic servants. Because of the wartime manpower shortage, however, considerable numbers were allowed to leave the relocation camps to take up industrial and other employment in the Middle West and the East. After 1945, with discrimination against them everywhere on the wane—even in the Far West—Japanese-Americans increasingly became factory workers, small businessmen, even doctors, teachers, and lawyers.

Despite the mass evacuation of the Japanese-Americans, and despite, too, the Los Angeles "zoot-suit" riots of 1943, in which mob violence found a victim in Mexican-Americans, the war years were a period of increasing ethnic unity. With Hitler's gas chambers providing horrifying evidence of the lengths to which racism could lead, Americans became more tolerant of difference. The same result was produced by increasing contact, both in the armed services and in the factories, between people of different ethnic origin. The appearance of an external threat to American security had the effect, moreover, of suppressing ethnic and other internal antagonisms. Furthermore the prosperity of wartime, persisting into the postwar era, lessened the competition for places which might otherwise have brought a renewal of group divisions.

It was prosperity, too, which now paved the way for the rise to political power of the "new" immigrant groups from south and east Europe. In the 1920's American politics began to feel the delayed impact of the "new" immigration. As the children of Italian, Polish, Czech, Jewish, Greek, and South Slav immigrants reached voting age they broke the Republican hold on the cities that had persisted since the Civil War and helped transform the United States from a country with a normally Republican to one with a normally Democratic majority.

None of the newer ethnic minorities could achieve political recognition in its own right, however, until the growth of its voting power was accompanied by the rise of a middle class to provide leadership and financial backing. In the case of the Czechs, who had been the earliest of the "new" immigrants, these conditions had been met by 1930, when Anton J. Cermak was elected mayor of Chicago. Other ethnic groups had to wait until World War II had solidified their economic power. Then, in the decade after 1945 Joseph Mruc became the first Polish-American mayor of Buffalo, Abraham A. Ribicoff the first Jewish governor of Connecticut, and John Pastore of Rhode Island the first United States senator of Italian origin.

Italian-Americans, indeed, carried all before them wherever they were concentrated. Besides capturing the highest offices in Rhode Island, they elected mayors in a number of New Jersey cities and in 1947 displaced the Irish as the masters of Tammany Hall.

After a generation of restricted immigration, the ethnic tie remained but the foundations of group loyalty were being steadily, if slowly, eroded, not only by the influences we have been considering but by the changing structure of American society. As differences between sects diminished, as church membership increased, and as religion became the major focus of social activity, religious affiliation rather than ethnic origin became the primary method of self-identification and social grouping. Indeed, with religion now tending to set the bounds within which intermarriage might occur, a tripartite division of the American population into Protestant, Catholic, and Jew, was often the only meaningful one.

In the middle of the twentieth century ethnic distinctions might still persist. But they were less sharp, less conspicuous than before and they were fading rapidly from view.

Conclusion

The significance of immigration in American history is at once apparent and difficult to define. At each stage of national development from the colonial period to the present the immigrant has left his impress upon American life; hardly an aspect of the total culture has remained untouched by his presence. Yet it must never be forgotten that immigrants were an integral part of an organic whole. Nothing they did in America had any meaning save in the larger context of the life of the nation. For this reason the immigrant impact upon American society and culture cannot be isolated, identified, and labeled as though it were a chemical element. All that can be done in a summary of this kind is to suggest in general terms the scope and nature of the "contribution" of immigrants in various fields.

The most obvious consequences of immigration have been demographic and economic. The continuous flow of great numbers of immigrants into the United States has been, in the first place, an important factor in the steady increase in

Conclusion

her population. The point would hardly need stressing but for widespread acceptance of the theory, put forward in 1891 by Francis A. Walker, a former Superintendent of the Census, that the foreign-born were not reinforcing but replacing the native stock. It was true, as Walker claimed, that the birth rate of the native population had been dwindling ever since 1830, about the time when large-scale immigration began. But the same period had seen a comparable fall in the birth rate in certain European countries which had experienced no immigration. For this and other reasons it is now generally believed that the fall in the native American birth rate was a consequence not of immigration but of such factors as urbanization and industrialization, and that without the heavy influx of the nineteenth century, the rate of American population growth would have declined even more sharply than it did. As it was, immigration made an even greater contribution to the total population than the number of arrivals would indicate, since immigrants consisted preponderantly of comparatively young people: among late-nineteenth-century immigrants, for example, over 80 per cent were under forty-five years of age.

The realization of America's vast economic potential has likewise been due in significant measure to the efforts of immigrants. They supplied much of the labor and technical skill needed to tap the undeveloped resources of a virgin continent. This was most obviously true during the colonial period, when not only the pace of economic expansion but the very survival of the colonies was largely dependent upon a constant supply of new blood, whether in the shape of free immigrants, indentured servants, or Negro slaves. But immigrants were just as indispensable in the nineteenth century, when they contributed to the rapid settlement of the West and the transformation of the United States into a leading industrial power.

The role of the immigrant in the westward movement has been far from constant. The first arrivals in the colonies were, by definition, the cutting edge of the frontier, and throughout the colonial period there was a steady movement of newly arrived land-seekers to the western margins of settlement. Sometimes, indeed, colonial authorities took a hand in planting immigrants on the frontier in the hope of creating a buffer against Indian attack. But during the first half of the nineteenth century, while the frontier advanced from the Appalachians to the Mississippi and beyond, immigrants were to be found less frequently in the van of settlement. In an age of mass immigration only a small minority of the newcomers had the capital necessary to embark on American agriculture. Moreover the cultivation of thickly wooded prairie called for specialized techniques which newly arrived Europeans did not possess. For these reasons the immigrant's role in the westward movement was then to follow in the wake of the first settlers, from whom they bought partially cleared lands.

When the frontier began to advance into the Great Plains in the years following the Civil War, the picture changed once more. Lack of resources, as well as of inclination, still kept the bulk of new arrivals away from the West. But although the arid, treeless plains presented the immigrant farmer with problems as formidable and as unfamiliar as any he had encountered on the prairies, they were not of the kind that needed special training. Accordingly, appreciable numbers of German, British, Scandinavian, Czech, and Russian-German pioneers settled in Kansas, Nebraska, and the Dakotas, thus helping to swell the area under cultivation. In the East meantime, farms abandoned by their native owners in the face of

Conclusion

western competition were brought back into cultivation by Polish, Italian, Portuguese, and other immigrants. When one takes into account also the prominent, though by no means uniform, role of Japanese, Italian, Filipino, and Mexican farmers and agricultural workers in the growth of farming on the Pacific Coast, the level and character of American agricultural production clearly owe much to immigrant effort.

Much better known is the part immigrants played at various times in the construction of transportation and public utilities systems. In the early decades of the nineteenth century it was immigrant labor, especially that of the Irish, which performed the heavy and hazardous work of road- and canal-building. In railroad construction the bulk of the labor force at all times consisted of immigrants—in the East usually Irish, German, Scandinavian, and Italian, in the Far West Chinese and Mexican. Nor did the situation differ materially in the construction of public works, and particularly in gas, electricity, and water projects, in all of which the Italians ultimately predominated. Bearing in mind the unwillingness of nearly all native Americans to undertake the back-breaking work involved in these enterprises it is evident that, without immigrant labor, they must all have been seriously delayed.

In the rise of American industry a key factor was the transit of technical skills and methods as a result of immigration. This was apparent to some extent even in the colonial period, which witnessed a steady influx of European craftsmen and artisans, especially to the seaboard towns. But it was not until the early nineteenth century that immigrants began to carry to the United States the new technology which was to be the basis of industrialization. Each of the formative industries—textiles, mining, and iron and steel—leaned heavily upon immigration of European, especially British, artisans, operatives, superintendents, and entrepreneurs; in some cases, as in the pottery industry, progress was the result of direct transplantation from Europe. The influx of skilled immigrant labor was, however, confined to the initial phases of industrial development. As American industry expanded and adapted itself to new conditions, it lost its dependence upon immigrant technicians. After the Civil War, thanks to improved machinery and to new production methods, it was able—indeed, was required—to replace skilled workers with cheap, unskilled labor. Once again it was to immigration that manufacturers and mine operators turned to supply their needs, and it was in the "new" immigration from southern and eastern Europe that they found what they sought. By 1900 the bulk of the employees in each of the leading American industries was of foreign origin, most of them being Italians, Slavs, Russian Jews, Greeks, Portuguese, or French-Canadians. Without the "new" immigration, as the Dillingham Commission pointed out in 1911, the enormous industrial expansion of the previous twenty years could not have taken place.

It has sometimes been asserted that, while immigration may have supplied industry with the labor it needed for expansion, it has nevertheless had deleterious economic consequences for the country as a whole. This was the view, for instance, of the Dillingham Commission, which charged, among other things, that immigrants had lowered wages, intensified unemployment, and displaced native workers from jobs. These allegations—which, far from being novel, were almost as old as immigration itself—have now been shown by economists to have been based upon fallacies and misconceptions. There seems to be no evidence, for example, that the long-range ef-

Conclusion

fect of immigration has been to lower the wage scale and thus depress the American standard of living. To be sure, the wage levels of immigrants were generally below those of native workers; but that was simply a reflection of the fact that immigrants tended to enter the poorer-paid occupations. It is likewise incorrect to believe that immigration has, over any prolonged period, added appreciably to the number of the unemployed. Nineteenth-century immigration declined rapidly with the onset of every depression and remained low until business conditions improved. Irrespective of conditions in Europe the United States could attract immigrants only when specific job opportunities existed; immigration was thus not an important factor in unemployment, the real cause of which was the fluctuation of the business cycle. It was erroneous, too, to suppose that immigration deprived any appreciable numbers of native workers of employment. To assert the contrary was to ignore the fluidity of modern industrial economies, in which the number of jobs tends to expand with increases in population. In any case, the usual kind of displacement resulting from immigration has been displacement in an upward direction. Since immigrants tended to gravitate to the lowest rungs of the economic ladder, their coming enabled both the native population and earlier immigrants either to rise to supervisory or managerial positions or to take advantage of the increased opportunities for skilled, professional, and white-collar workers which economic expansion made possible.

The fact that fresh groups of immigrants were continually arriving to occupy the base of the economic pyramid has had profound social consequences. Immigration has first of all endowed American society with a fluidity and a mobility which have counteracted any tendency to reproduce the stratified social pattern of Europe. It may even have been responsible in part for that unique characteristic of the American social order, namely, the absence of rigid class divisions. At the same time, however, immigration has produced contrary tendencies. The lack of a feudal past and the mobility of her inhabitants did not prevent the hardening of class lines which was such a feature of late-nineteenth-century America.

Immigrant influence upon American politics was felt both directly and indirectly. As voters and officeholders, immigrants significantly affected the political structure and did as much as anything to determine long-range political alignments. Their mere presence, moreover, has from time to time become a hotly debated political issue, again with striking effects upon alignments.

The immigrant's unfamiliarity with political processes, his lack of acquaintance with American issues, and the necessity he faced of concentrating upon the physical aspects of adjustment insured that politics were not his primary focus of interest. These circumstances led to the rise of the immigrant bosses and of the political machines, whose understanding of the needs of the newcomers enabled them to control votes and thus to seize control of governments for their own, often corrupt, purposes. While corruption in American politics did not originate with immigration, it was nonetheless the presence of the immigrant and the conditions which shaped his reaction to politics that enabled the evil to grow.

That the mass of immigrants were extremely conservative in politics was attributable to their fundamental patterns of thought. It was not so much perhaps that their preponderantly peasant origins had bred an attitude of acceptance which remained with them even in the New World; had that been the

Conclusion

case, the majority would never have crossed the Atlantic. Nor was submission to clerical leadership a universal factor. It was rather that their political inexperience, and the need for immediate practical help imposed upon them by circumstance, combined to prevent their accepting, or even grasping, the strange new assumption that politics was a sphere wherein the general good might be realized through common action. Reform thus remained to them a remote and fanciful panacea, irrelevant to their needs.

Immigration subtly affected the theory of American democracy no less than its practice. The gradual expansion of the frontiers of immigration forced upon Americans the necessity of broadening the concept of equality to which the nation had been dedicated at birth. When the Founding Fathers subscribed to the doctrine that "all men are created equal," they could not have envisaged that the infant republic would be invaded by men from every corner of the earth anxious to test the truth of what they proclaimed. Even in the 1850's Emerson, one of the most enthusiastic supporters of immigration, could rejoice that, for the most part, it was the "fair-haired, the blue-eyed" who came, and that "the Europe of Europe," remained behind. As the history of nativism shows, Americans were at times reluctant to accept a definition of democracy that involved the granting of equal rights to all men of whatever origin. Yet step by step Americans have brought their practices in this respect nearer to the professions of the Founders, thus giving to democratic thought an ever widening content.

It has sometimes been asserted that the existence of large groups of voters of foreign origin has seriously hampered the formulation and execution of American foreign policy. It is beyond question that the State Department has from time to time responded to the agitation of ethnic pressure-groups; the dismissal of Sackville-West in 1888 and the rapidity with which Truman recognized the independence of Israel in 1948 afford two examples among many. Nor, from the time that ethnic votes first became sufficiently numerous to matter, has any national politician been able to ignore the susceptibilities of groups whose attitudes were affected by their European origin. At Yalta in 1944, for example, Roosevelt informed Stalin that, in order not to lose the Polish vote, he preferred not to publish until after the election the agreement whereby the eastern third of Poland went to Russia.

This incident, however, illustrates perfectly the limits of ethnic influence upon foreign policy. Concern for the Polish vote might lead Roosevelt to delay the announcement of a policy decision; but it did not affect the decision itself. Whenever ethnic aspirations have conflicted with the national interests of the United States, as interpreted by the State Department and the Senate, the former have always had to give way. For this reason the Irish were unable to prevent the closer American relationship with Britain at the turn of the century; nor did the Germans, despite their being at the time the largest ethnic group, succeed in keeping the United States out of World War I.

Most difficult of all to assess is the cultural impact of immigration. The commonest way of tackling the problem has been to compile lists of distinguished people of foreign birth or parentage as evidence of the "contribution" of various ethnic groups. Quite apart from the fact that this approach has led to exaggerated and absurd claims, any attempt to define cultural influences in this way is misconceived. For one thing,

Conclusion

American culture is more than the sum of its parts; essentially a unit, it cannot be broken up into component parts, each of them attributable to particular groups or individuals. For another, such attempts to analyze "contributions" inevitably concentrate upon a comparatively small group of exceptional immigrants to the neglect of the great majority.

A more rewarding approach is one which attempts to examine the organized life of immigrants against the background of American culture as a whole. Each immigrant group, anxious to preserve traditional ways, at first endeavored to create a subculture of its own. In order to do so it was obliged to develop separate religious, educational, and benevolent institutions. But this step alone showed how strong was the pressure toward conformity with the existing American pattern, for these voluntary organizations, none of which had existed in Europe, adopted a common American form.

This tendency became increasingly evident with the passage of time. Even among first-generation immigrants only a proportion participated fully in the life of the group, and most of the second generation abandoned it altogether. Hence the only means whereby the old ways could survive was by being grafted onto the existing body of culture, a process necessarily involving the further modification of immigrant institutions. The immigrant press, for example, became in style and content indistinguishable from American newspapers generally, and immigrant schools and colleges likewise adapted themselves to a common mold.

It was in the immigrant churches, however, that the tendency toward accommodation was most clearly evident. It is true, of course, that many American religious denominations have retained their ethnic character; to this, indeed, the multiplicity of American sects is to be mainly attributed. In some cases the ethnic association is apparent from the name of the sect itself; the 1958 census of American religious bodies lists, among others, the Lithuanian and Polish National Catholic churches, the Finnish Evangelical Lutheran Church, the Free Magyar Reformed Church, and the Albanian, Carpatho-Russian, Assyrian, Greek, Romanian, Russian, Serbian, Syrian, and Ukrainian Orthodox churches. No less ethnic in character are a number of churches whose names no longer indicate the fact; thus the Augustana Evangelical Lutheran Church is largely Swedish in membership, the Lutheran Free Church is Norwegian, and both the Evangelical Lutheran Church and the United Lutheran Church are German. Even churches founded in colonial days have not entirely lost their ethnic coloring: the Presbyterian Church is to some extent Scotch-Irish and Scottish, the Protestant Episcopal Church mainly English, and the Reformed Churches are either Dutch or German.

Even so, these churches resemble each other, not only in having adopted the English language but in having taken on an American form of church life. Transplanted from Europe, where they had usually been part of the political structure, into the competitive American environment produced by the separation of church and state, the immigrant churches were forced to reorganize. Obliged to compete actively for members, they have become evangelical in tone and have tended to stress personal religious experience at the expense of dogma. Freed from a hierarchical control no less political than religious, they have embraced democratic forms of church government, usually involving lay representation. Shorn of their connection with the state, they have discarded their old polit-

Conclusion

ical loyalties and have become avowedly non-political. In a word, they have been metamorphosed into characteristically American institutions.

This subtle yet profound type of alchemy provides the key not only to the immigrant contribution to American culture but also to the paradox of immigrant loyalties. To some observers there has been an element of contradiction in the fact that immigrants assert their American patriotism as members of separate groups. But the contradiction is only superficial. When Polish-Americans observe Pulaski Day, when Irish-Americans parade in honor of St. Patrick, when Italian-Americans gather to fete San Rocco or San Genaro, and even when Americans of Greek, Mexican, or Armenian origin celebrate the old country's independence day, they are merely asserting their cultural distinctiveness, merely seeking to make clear their own identity in the larger American community. And even while doing so, they rededicate themselves to the common national ideals that bind them together.

In this way immigrants have infused new meaning into the national motto. To the Founding Fathers *e pluribus unum* meant the fusion of thirteen separate states into a single political unit; to the mid-twentieth-century American it also denotes the unity that has developed from the mingling of peoples diverse in origin but sharing a common devotion to liberty, democracy, and tolerance.

Important Dates

1607	Founding of Virginia
1619	First American legislative assembly meets at Jamestown
	First shipload of Negroes to reach America landed at Jamestown
1620	Voyage of the *Mayflower*
1623	Settlement of New Netherland by Dutch West India Company begins
1630–40	Puritan migration to New England
1634	Founding of Maryland
1642	Outbreak of English Civil War
1649	Maryland Toleration Act
1654	First Jewish immigrants to reach America arrive at New Amsterdam
1660	Emigration from England officially discouraged
1664	New Netherland passes to English crown
1670	Settlement of the Carolinas begins
1681	Founding of Pennsylvania
1683	First German settlers to reach New World arrive in Pennsylvania
1685	Revocation of Edict of Nantes by Louis XIV
1697	Royal African Company's monopoly ended; slave trade expands
1707	Act of Union between England and Scotland

Important Dates

1709   Exodus from German Palatinate begins
1717   Transportation of felons to American colonies authorized
        by Parliament
1718   Parliament prohibits emigration of skilled artisans
        Large-scale Scotch-Irish immigration begins
1720   Redemptioner trade becomes systematized
1727   Pennsylvania requires alien immigrants on arrival to
        swear allegiance to crown
1730   Colonization of the southern back-country by Germans
        and Scotch-Irish from Pennsylvania begins
1732   Founding of Georgia
        Appearance of the *Philadelphische Zeitung*, the first
        German-language newspaper published in America
1740   Parliament enacts Naturalization Act conferring British
        citizenship upon alien immigrants to colonies
1745   Jacobite rebellion in Scotland
1755   Expulsion of Acadians from Nova Scotia
1764   Paxton Boys revolt
1768–71 Regulator movement in North Carolina
1771–73 Depression in Ulster linen trade
1775   British government suspends emigration upon outbreak
        of hostilities in America
1789   Outbreak of French Revolution
1791   Negro revolt in Santo Domingo
1793   Beginning of the Wars of the French Revolution
1798   Unsuccessful Irish rebellion
        Alien and Sedition Acts
1802   Resumption of war between England and France
1803   British Passenger Act limits numbers to be carried by
        emigrant ships
1807   Congress prohibits importation of Negro slaves into
        United States
        Jeffersonian embargo
1814   Treaty of Ghent
1818   Black Ball Line of sailing packets begins regular Liver-
        pool–New York service
1825   Great Britain repeals laws prohibiting emigration
        Arrival in United States of first group of Norwegian
        immigrants in sloop *Restaurationen*

American Immigration

1830	Polish revolution
1834	Burning of the Ursuline Convent at Charlestown, Mass.
	Samuel F. B. Morse's *A Foreign Conspiracy against the Liberties of the United States*
1836	Maria Monk's *Awful Disclosures of the Hôtel Dieu Nunnery of Montreal*
1837	Financial panic in United States
	Abortive Canadian rebellion
1838	Irish Poor Law Act
1840	Cunard Line founded
	First Mormon overseas mission begins in England
1840–44	New York Bible-reading controversy
1844	Anti-Catholic riots in Philadelphia
1845	Native American Party founded
1845–49	Irish potato famine
1846	Crop failures in Germany and Holland
1848	Revolution in Germany
	Emancipation of the peasants completed in Germany and Austria-Hungary
	Collapse of Young Ireland movement
	Taiping rebellion in southeast China
1849	Passenger Cases passed on by United States Supreme Court
1853	Demonstrations in Cincinnati against papal legate Mgr. Bedini
1854–56	Know-Nothing Movement at its height
1855	Opening of Castle Garden immigrant depot
1856	Irish Catholic Colonization Convention at Buffalo, N.Y.
1857	American financial panic
1861–65	American Civil War
1863	New York draft riots
1864	Congress legalizes contract labor
1866	Fenian invasions of Canada
1871–75	Molly Maguire outrages in Pennsylvania coalfields
1879	Renewed famine in Ireland
1882	First federal immigration law
	Chinese Exclusion Act
	Outbreak of anti-Semitism in Russia
1885	Foran Act prohibits importation of contract labor

Important Dates

1886	Statue of Liberty dedicated
	Haymarket Affair
1888	Murchison Letter
1890	Superintendent of the Census announces disappearance of the frontier
	Cahensly controversy in Catholic church
1892	Ellis Island opened
1893	Financial panic in United States
1894	Immigration Restriction League organized
1894–95	American Protective Association at its height
1894–96	Armenian massacres
1897	Literacy test defeated in Congress
1905	Japanese and Korean Exclusion League organized
1907	Depression in United States
1907–8	Gentlemen's Agreement
1911	Dillingham Commission Report
1914–18	World War I
1916–19	Americanization movement at its height
1916	Madison Grant's *The Passing of the Great Race in America*
1917	Literacy test for immigrants adopted
1919	Big Red Scare
1921	Emergency immigration restriction law introduces quota system
1923	Ku Klux Klan reaches its peak
1924	National Origins Act adopted
1927	Execution of Sacco and Vanzetti
1929	National Origins Act becomes operative
	Stock market crash
1933	Hitler becomes German chancellor; anti-Semitic campaign begins
1934	Philippine Independence Act restricts Filipino immigration
1939	World War II begins
1941	Pearl Harbor
1942	Evacuation of Japanese-Americans from Pacific Coast
1943	Los Angeles "zoot-suit" riots
1946	War Brides Act provides for admission of foreign-born wives of servicemen

323

1948	Displaced Persons Act
1952	Immigration and Naturalization Act
1953	Refugee Relief Act
1954	Ellis Island closed
1956	Hungarian Revolution

Suggested Reading

This selective bibliography of American Immigration mentions
only a small fraction of the vast body of writing on the subject. I
have listed merely the works which I have found most useful and
to whose authors I wish to acknowledge my indebtedness. The
listing of a book or article under a particular chapter does not, of
course, imply that that is the only chapter for which it is relevant.

GENERAL WORKS

There is no satisfactory general account of American immigration. George M. Stephenson's *A History of American Immigration,
1820–1924* (1926) is an early attempt at synthesis which concentrates
upon political aspects. Carl Wittke's *We Who Built America: The
Saga of the Immigrant* (1939) is a vast storehouse of information
with little attempt at interpretation or generalization. Maurice R.
Davie's *World Immigration, with Special Reference to the United
States* (1936) is a useful survey, as is Donald R. Taft's *Human Migration* (1936).

Two invaluable source books, both compiled by Edith Abbott,
are *Immigration: Select Documents and Case Records* (1924) and
Historical Aspects of the Immigration Problem (1926). *Immigration as a Factor in American History*, edited by Oscar Handlin, is

a well-chosen collection of documents interspersed with the editor's shrewd comments.

Most historians of immigration have been reluctant to consider its wider implications, but valuable insights may be obtained from the following collections of interpretative essays: Marcus L. Hansen, *The Immigrant in American History* (1940); David F. Bowers (ed.), *Foreign Influences in American Life* (1944); and Oscar Handlin, *Race and Nationality in American Life* (1957). A stimulating discussion of "The Role of the Immigrant" is to be found in Arthur M. Schlesinger's *Paths to the Present* (1949). See also the introductory essays in *A Report on World Population Migrations As Related to the United States* (1956), which contains the fullest bibliography on the subject. The international aspects of immigration may be studied in *The Positive Contribution of Immigrants* (1955), edited by Oscar Handlin.

CHAPTER I

The settlement of the colonies is covered in such general works on the colonial period as Charles M. Andrews, *The Colonial Period of American History* (1934–38); Edward Channing, *History of the United States* (1905–25), Vols. I–III; H. L. Osgood, *The American Colonies in the Seventeenth Century* (1904–7) and *The American Colonies in the Eighteenth Century* (1924–25). T. J. Wertenbaker's three volumes, *The Founding of American Civilization* (1938–47), are valuable for the space they devote to non-English elements.

The underlying purposes of the first colonists are learnedly discussed in Perry Miller's *Errand into the Wilderness* (1956). What later generations thought those purposes to be is the subject of Wesley F. Craven's stimulating book, *The Legend of the Founding Fathers* (1956). For differing views of the origins of the Puritan migration see A. P. Newton, *The Colonizing Activities of English Puritans* (1914); Nellis M. Crouse, "Causes of the Great Migration," *New England Quarterly*, V (1932), 3–36; and C. E. Banks and S. E. Morison, "Persecution as a Factor in Emigration," *Massachusetts Historical Society Proceedings*, LXIII (1930), 136–54.

A comprehensive account of indentured servitude may be found in Abbot Emerson Smith's *Colonists in Bondage: White Servitude and Convict Labor in America, 1607–1776* (1947). The legal basis

Suggested Reading

of the institution is more fully considered in Richard B. Morris'
Government and Labor in Early America (1946), which makes
skilful use of colonial court records. Marcus W. Jernegan's *Laboring and Dependent Classes in Colonial America, 1607–1783* (1931)
remains a useful guide. Of a large number of studies dealing with
individual colonies the best are perhaps C. A. Herrick, *White
Servitude in Pennsylvania* (1926); E. I. McCormac, *White Servitude in Maryland, 1634–1820* (1904); and Samuel McKee, Jr.,
Labor in Colonial New York, 1664–1776 (1935).

The impact of the American environment upon the various
groups of colonists is provocatively discussed in Daniel J. Boorstin's
The Americans: The Colonial Experience (1958). On this subject
see also Louis B. Wright, *The Cultural Life of the American
Colonies* (1957); Thomas J. Wertenbaker, *The First Americans,
1607–1690* (1927); James Truslow Adams, *Provincial Society,
1690–1763* (1928); and Carl Bridenbaugh, *Myths and Realities:
Societies of the Colonial South* (1952).

The national origins of the American white population in 1790
are authoritatively discussed in the American Council of Learned
Societies Report of the Committee on Linguistic and National
Stocks in the Population of the United States published in the
*Annual Report of the American Historical Association for the
Year 1931* (1932).

Of a large number of works dealing with the colonial Germans
the most useful are Albert B. Faust, *The German Element in the
United States* (1927), and Dieter Cunz, *The Maryland Germans*
(1948), both of which continue into later periods. More specialized
are W. A. Knittle, *Early Eighteenth Century Palatine Emigration*
(1936); Ralph Wood (ed.), *The Pennsylvania Germans* (1942);
C. H. Smith, *Mennonite Immigration to Pennsylvania* (1929); and
Adelaide L. Fries, *Records of the Moravians in North Carolina*
(7 vols., 1922–47). The best general work on the Scotch-Irish is
Henry J. Ford's *The Scotch-Irish in America* (1915), but it should
be supplemented by Wayland F. Dunaway's *The Scotch-Irish of
Colonial Pennsylvania* (1944). Ian C. C. Graham's *Colonists from
Scotland: Emigration to North America, 1707–1783* (1956) super-
sedes all previous accounts. A. C. Myers' *Immigration of the Irish
Quakers into Pennsylvania, 1682–1750* (1902) and Charles H.
Browning's *Welsh Settlement of Pennsylvania* (1912) are based

upon painstaking research. Among numerous studies of Huguenot immigration the best in English are Charles W. Baird, *History of the Huguenot Emigration* (1885); Lucian J. Fosdick, *French Blood in America* (1906); and Arthur H. Hirsch, *The Huguenots of Colonial South Carolina* (1928). Jacob R. Marcus' *Early American Jewry* (1951–52) is the most detailed account of the Jews in the colonial period, but it may be supplemented by Abram V. Goodman's *American Overture* (1947). For the Dutch and the Swedes see, respectively, Maud W. Goodwin, *Dutch and English on the Hudson* (1919), and Amandus Johnson, *The Swedish Settlements on the Delaware . . . 1638–1664* (1911).

CHAPTER II

The study of immigration regulation during the colonial period may be approached through Emberson E. Proper, *Colonial Immigration Laws* (1900), and Erna Risch, "Encouragement of Immigration as Revealed in Colonial Legislation," *Virginia Magazine of History and Biography*, LXV (1937), 1–10. Additional material on this subject, as well as on other aspects of immigration may be found in Carl Bridenbaugh's discerning studies, *Cities in the Wilderness: The First Century of Urban Life in America, 1625–1742* (1938) and *Cities in Revolt: Urban Life in America, 1743–1776* (1955).

Ethnic rivalries are described in a number of scattered articles, of which the most helpful are William T. Johnson, "Some Aspects of the Relations of the Government and German Settlers in Colonial Pennsylvania, 1683–1754," Parts I and II, *Pennsylvania History*, XI (1944), 81–102, 200–207; T. P. Meyer, "The Germans of Pennsylvania: Their Coming and Conflicts with the Irish," *Pennsylvania German*, XI (1910), 38–47; S. E. Weber, "The Germans and the Charity School Movement," *Pennsylvania German*, VIII (1907), 305–12; Whitfield J. Bell, Jr., "Benjamin Franklin and the German Charity Schools," *Proceedings of the American Philosophical Society*, XCIX (1955), 381–87; and Glenn Weaver, "Benjamin Franklin and the Pennsylvania Germans," *William and Mary Quarterly*, 3d ser., XIV (1957), 536–59.

The influence of the American environment upon the Germans is discussed in Glenn Weaver, "The Lutheran Church during the

Suggested Reading

French and Indian War," *Lutheran Quarterly*, VI (1954), 248–56, and in two articles by Andreas Dorpalen, "The Political Influence of the German Element in Colonial America," Parts I and II, *Pennsylvania History*, VI (1939), 147–58, 221–39.

Theodore G. Tappert corrects some long-standing misconceptions about the German role in the Revolution in "Henry Melchior Muhlenberg and the Revolution," *Church History*, IX (1942), 284–301, which is based upon a study of Muhlenberg's journals. Of similar interest is A. Gertrude Ward's "John Ettwein and the Moravians in the Revolution," *Pennsylvania History*, I (1934), 191–201. The myth of unanimous Jewish support for the Revolution is refuted in Cecil Roth, "Some Jewish Loyalists in the War of American Independence," *Publications of the American Jewish Historical Society*, XXXVIII (1948), 81–107.

CHAPTER III

The period 1783–1815 has received little attention from historians of immigration. A number of special aspects have, however, been intensively studied. Of the many works on French émigré groups Howard Mumford Jones's *America and French Culture, 1750–1848* (1927) is the most polished, and Frances S. Childs's *French Refugee Life in the United States, 1790–1800* (1940) the most detailed. There are a number of biographies of individual immigrants. Dumas Malone's *The Public Life of Thomas Cooper, 1783–1831* (1926) is the most distinguished while E. F. Smith's *Priestley in America, 1794–1804* (1920) and Mary Elizabeth Clark's *Peter Porcupine in America: The Career of William Cobbett, 1792–1800* (1939) are adequate. Still valuable is G. S. White's *Memoirs of Samuel Slater, the Father of American Manufactures* (1836).

The Americanizing effect of the lull in immigration is analyzed in Andreas Dorpalen's "The German Element in Early Pennsylvania Politics, 1789–1800," *Pennsylvania History*, IX (1942), 176–90, and in William H. Gehrke's "The Transition from the German to the English Language in North Carolina," *North Carolina Historical Review*, XII (1935), 1–19. The legend that, during the Revolution, the Pennsylvania Assembly considered the substitution of German for English as the official language of the state is demolished in Robert A. Feer's "Official Use of the German Language in Pennsyl-

American Immigration

vania," *Pennsylvania Magazine of History and Biography*, LXXVI (1952), 394–405.

William Miller's "The Effects of the American Revolution on Indentured Servitude," *Pennsylvania History*, VII (1940), 131–41, is a brief treatment of a subject that still remains partly shrouded in mystery.

The Alien and Sedition Acts have been the subject of two recent studies. John C. Miller's *Crisis in Freedom* (1951) is slight, and has now been superseded by James Morton Smith's exhaustive *Freedom's Fetters* (1956).

CHAPTER IV

Pre-eminent in its field is Marcus Lee Hansen's *The Atlantic Migration, 1607–1860* (1940) which focuses chiefly upon the European background of the movement. William F. Adams' *Ireland and Irish Emigration to the New World from 1815 to the Famine* (1932) is a conscientious and valuable study which, however, leans too heavily upon official sources. A well-informed and sympathetic essay by Oliver MacDonagh, "Irish Overseas Emigration during the Famine," is to be found in R. D. Edwards and T. D. Williams (eds.), *The Great Famine* (1957).

Among studies of British immigration Rowland T. Berthoff's *British Immigrants in Industrial America, 1789–1950* (1953) is an outstanding study based upon wide research. Nineteenth-century emigration from Great Britain and Ireland is examined against the background of developments in the Atlantic economy in Brinley Thomas' *Migration and Economic Growth* (1954). Less satisfactory are Stanley C. Johnson's *A History of Emigration from the United Kingdom to North America, 1763–1912* (1913), and W. A. Carrothers' *Emigration from the British Isles* (1929), both of which rely excessively upon official records. Wilbur S. Shepperson's *British Emigration to North America* (1957) is a rambling account of early Victorian emigration projects, most of which failed to materialize.

Scholarly material upon the German background is patchy. The economic origins of the mid-century movement are brought into focus in Marcus Lee Hansen's "The Revolutions of 1848 and German Emigration," *Journal of Economic and Business History*, II

Suggested Reading

(1930), 630–58. Carl Wittke, *Refugees of Revolution: The German Forty-eighters in America* (1952), and A. E. Zucker (ed.), *The Forty-eighters* (1950), deal exhaustively with a small but important group.

Theodore C. Blegen's *Norwegian Migration to America, 1825–1860* (1931) is detailed and scholarly, while Florence E. Janson's *The Background of Swedish Immigration, 1840–1930* (1931) is a model of its kind. Henry S. Lucas' *Netherlanders in America: Dutch Immigration to the United States and Canada, 1789–1950* (1955) deals exhaustively with the movement from Holland.

Marcus L. Hansen's *The Mingling of the Canadian and American Peoples* (1940) is a pioneering study spanning the seventeenth through the twentieth centuries. It should be supplemented by Gustave Lanctot's *Les Canadiens français et leurs voisins du sud* (1941) and E. Hamon's *Les Canadiens-français de la Nouvelle-Angleterre* (1891).

The process of immigration has been little studied and no adequate account of the immigrant trade has yet appeared. Edwin C. Guillet's *The Great Migration: The Atlantic Crossing by Sailing Ship since 1770* (1937) is sketchy but has some interesting material.

CHAPTER V

The most perceptive account of immigrant adjustment to America is Oscar Handlin's classic work, *Boston's Immigrants: A Study in Acculturation* (1941; rev. ed., 1959), which is concerned chiefly with the Irish. Another area study covering the same period is Robert Ernst's *Immigrant Life in New York City, 1825–1863* (1949).

Carl F. Wittke's *The Irish in America* (1951) is a somewhat sketchy survey. John A. Hawgood's *The Tragedy of German-America* (1940) has a good account of the efforts to establish new Germanies on American soil and deals also with other aspects of German immigrant life. Emmet H. Rothan's *The German Catholic Immigrant in the United States, 1830–1860* (1946) is a mere outline of the subject. Carl Wittke's *The German-Language Press in America* (1957), which is concerned mainly with the nineteenth century, contains valuable material. German-Jewish immigration is stimulatingly discussed in Eric F. Hirshler (ed.), *Jews from Germany in the United States* (1955) and in Rudolph Glanz, *Jews in Relation*

American Immigration

to the Cultural Milieu of the Germans in America (1947). Theodore C. Blegen's Norwegian Migration to America: The American Transition (1940) is based upon solid research, as is George M. Stephenson's The Religious Aspects of Swedish Immigration (1932).

H. Richard Niebuhr's The Social Sources of Denominationalism (1929) discusses the reorganization which transplantation to the New World forced upon immigrant churches. On this subject see also Vergilius Ferm's The Crisis in American Lutheran Theology (1927) and Carl Mauelshagen's American Lutheranism Surrenders to the Forces of Conservatism (1936).

Two valuable collections of "America letters" are Theodore C. Blegen (ed.), Land of Their Choice: The Immigrants Write Home (1955), and Henry S. Lucas, Dutch Immigrant Memoirs and Related Writings (2 vols., 1955).

Mark Holloway's Heavens on Earth: Utopian Communities in America, 1680–1880 (1951) is a popular account. The same topic, at least in its sectarian and Owenite phases, is dealt with in masterly fashion by Arthur E. Bestor, Jr., in Backwoods Utopias (1950). Other organized migration schemes are examined in Sister Mary G. Kelly, Catholic Immigrant Colonization Projects in the United States, 1815–1860 (1939), and Jerzy J. Lerski, A Polish Chapter in Jacksonian America: The United States and the Polish Exiles of 1831 (1958).

The most substantial work on Mormon immigration is William Mulder, Homeward to Zion: The Mormon Migration from Scandinavia (1957). The movement from the British Isles has been the subject of a number of articles, of which the most revealing is Philip A. M. Taylor, "Why Did British Mormons Emigrate?," Utah Historical Quarterly, XXII (1954), 249–70. Further aspects are treated in M. Hamlin Cannon, "Migration of English Mormons to America," American Historical Review, LII (1947), 436–55, and "The English Mormons in America," ibid., LVII (1952), 893–908, and in Gustive O. Larsen, "The Perpetual Emigrating Fund," Mississippi Valley Historical Review, XVIII (1931), 184–94.

CHAPTER VI

Although Ray Allen Billington's The Protestant Crusade, 1800–1860: A Study of the Origins of American Nativism overstresses

Suggested Reading

the anti-Catholic factor in Pre-Civil War nativism, it remains the most substantial work on the subject. The inconsistency and incongruity which characterized Know-Nothingism are ably demonstrated in Harry J. Carman and Reinhard H. Luthin, "Some Aspects of the Know-Nothing Movement Reconsidered," *South Atlantic Quarterly*, XXXIX (1940), 213–34, which also stresses the close relationship between nativism and the slavery agitation. The reform and antislavery origins of New England nativism are analyzed in William G. Bean, "An Aspect of Know-Nothingism—the Immigrant and Slavery," *South Atlantic Quarterly*, XXIII (1924), 319–34, and in "Puritan versus Celt, 1850–1860," *New England Quarterly*, VII (1934), 70–89, while W. Darrell Overdyke's *The Know-Nothing Party in the South* (1950), and M. Evangeline Thomas' *Nativism in the Old Northwest, 1850–1860* (1936) deal with the growth of anti-alien sentiment in other sections. Of the many studies of nativist politics in individual states, the most valuable are Louis D. Scisco, *Political Nativism in New York State* (1901); L. F. Schmeckebier, *History of the Know-Nothing Party in Maryland* (1899); and Joseph Schafer, "Know-Nothingism in Wisconsin," *Wisconsin Magazine of History*, VIII (1924), 3–21. A minor but significant aspect is treated in Robert Ernst, "Economic Nativism in New York City during the 1840's," *New York History*, XXIX (1948), 170–86.

The role of the foreign-born in the slavery controversy and the Civil War has been widely, though not always critically, discussed. The claim that foreign-born Republican votes were the decisive factor in Lincoln's election is advanced in Donnal V. Smith, "The Influence of the Foreign-Born of the Northwest in the Election of 1860," *Mississippi Valley Historical Review*, XIX (1932), 192–204, and, more cautiously, in Jay Monaghan, "Did Abraham Lincoln Receive the Illinois German Vote?" *Illinois State Historical Society Journal*, XXXV (1942), 133–39. The contrary view is argued by Joseph Schafer in "Who Elected Lincoln?" *American Historical Review*, XLVII (1941), 51–63, which subjects the vote in Wisconsin to close analysis. That the German vote was very much divided is apparent from Andreas Dorpalen, "The German Element and the Issues of the Civil War," *Mississippi Valley Historical Review*, XXIX (1942), 55–76. Other useful studies are Virgil C. Blum, "The Political and Military Activities of the German Element in St. Louis, 1859–61," *Missouri Historical Review*, XLII (1947–1948), 103–29, and Charles W. Emery, "The Iowa Germans in the Election of 1860," *Annals of Iowa,* XXII (1940), 421–53.

The role of the Irish may be studied in Albon P. Man, Jr., "The Irish in New York in the Early Eighteen-sixties," *Irish Historical Studies,* VII (1950), 81–108 and in Florence E. Gibson, *The Attitudes of the New York Irish toward State and National Affairs, 1848–1892* (1951), which is based upon newspaper opinion. A similar study is Arlow W. Andersen, *The Immigrant Takes His Stand: The Norwegian-American Press and Public Affairs, 1847–1872* (1953). Bertram W. Korn's *American Jewry and the Civil War* (1951) is a scholarly piece of work which tends to exaggerate the strength of contemporary anti-Semitism.

The military contribution of the foreign-born is amply covered in two books by Ella Lonn, *Foreigners in the Confederacy* (1940) and *Foreigners in the Union Army and Navy* (1951).

CHAPTER VII

A vast amount of data upon every aspect of the "new" immigration is to be found in the 41-volume *Report of the United States Immigration Commission* (1911)—the Dillingham Commission. While much of the material is invaluable, it needs to be used with great care owing to the restrictionist bias of the compilers. The same is true of Jeremiah W. Jenks and W. Jett Lauck (eds.), *The Immigration Problem* (6th ed., 1926), which summarizes the Commission's findings. Oscar Handlin's essay, "Old Immigrants and New," in his *Race and Nationality in American Life* (1957) is a devastating exposé of the Commission's methods of interpreting its data. Also helpful is Paul H. Douglas, "Is the New Immigration more Unskilled than the Old?" *Publications of the American Statistical Association,* XVI (1918–19), 393–403.

In the absence of a comprehensive account of the forces underlying the post–Civil War Atlantic migration reference may be made to works dealing with particular ethnic groups. Emily G. Balch's *Our Slavic Fellow Citizens* (1910) is a sympathetic account, based upon personal observation, of Slavic immigration from the Austro-Hungarian Empire. Robert F. Foerster's *The Italian Emigration of Our Times* (1919) throws light upon the economic background of the various population movements from Italy. There is

Suggested Reading

no adequate treatment in English of Jewish immigration from eastern Europe, but its main outlines are described in Samuel Joseph's *Jewish Immigration to the United States from 1881 to 1910* (1914), which may be supplemented by Oscar Handlin's *Adventure in Freedom* (1954), dealing with Jewish life in America from the seventeenth through the twentieth centuries. Other useful studies are Henry P. Fairchild's *Greek Immigration to the United States* (1911), J. P. Xenides' *The Greeks in America* (1922), Wasyl Halich's *Ukrainians in the United States* (1937), Jerome Davis' *The Russian Immigrant* (1922), Thomas Čapek's *The Czechs (Bohemians) in America* (1920), Paul Fox's *The Poles in America* (1922), Philip K. Hitti's *The Syrians in America* (1924), and Malcolm H. Vartan's *The Armenians in America* (1919).

Among works on Oriental immigration Mary R. Coolidge's *Chinese Immigration* (1909) has never been superseded. The best book on the coming of the Japanese is Yamato Ichihashi, *Japanese in the United States* (1932).

Charlotte Erickson's *American Industry and the European Immigrant, 1860–1885* (1957) demonstrates how rarely contract labor was used by American industrialists. Harry V. Jerome's *Migration and Business Cycles* (1926) illustrates how American economic conditions affected immigration.

The encouragement of immigration by individual states is treated in Theodore C. Blegen, "The Competition of the Northwestern States for Immigrants," *Wisconsin Magazine of History*, III (1919), 3–29; Marcus L. Hansen, "Official Encouragement of Immigration in Iowa," *Iowa Journal of History and Politics*, XIX (1921), 159–95; Maurice G. Baxter, "Encouragement of Immigration to the Middle West during the Era of the Civil War," *Indiana Magazine of History*, XLVI (1950), 25–38; and Livia Appel and Theodore C. Blegen, "Official Encouragement of Immigration to Minnesota during the Territorial Period," *Minnesota History Bulletin*, V (1923), 167–203.

On railroad colonization there are two full-length studies: Paul W. Gates, *The Illinois Central Railroad and Its Colonization Work* (1934), and Richard C. Overton, *Burlington West: A Colonization History of the Burlington Railroad* (1941). Additional material is to be found in Glenn D. Bradley, *The Story of the Santa Fe* (1920), and in the following articles: James B. Hedges, "The Colonization Work of the Northern Pacific Railroad," *Mississippi Valley His-*

American Immigration

torical Review, XIII (1926), 311–42; Harold F. Petersen, "Some Colonization Projects of the Northern Pacific Railroad," *Minnesota History*, X (1929), 127–44; and Edna M. Parker, "The Southern Pacific Railroad and Settlement in Southern California," *Pacific Historical Review*, VI (1937), 103–19.

CHAPTER VIII

The difficulties of immigrant adjustment in this period are imaginatively suggested in Oscar Handlin's *The Uprooted* (1951), a work of real insight which I have found invaluable. Peter Roberts' *The New Immigration* (1912) is a general account of the social and economic life of the "new" immigrants; see also the same author's *Anthracite Coal Communities* (1904). Other helpful studies of immigrant community life are Robert E. Park and Herbert A. Miller, *Old World Traits Transplanted* (1921); Robert A. Woods, *The City Wilderness* (1899) and *Americans in Process* (1902).

Similar questions are discussed in a number of studies relating to particular ethnic groups. William I. Thomas' and Florian Znaniecki's *The Polish Peasant in Europe and America* (1918, reprinted 1958) is a sociological study which has become a classic. See also Donald R. Taft, *Two Portuguese Communities in New England* (1923); Iris S. Podea, "Quebec to 'Little Canada': the Coming of the French Canadians to New England in the Nineteenth Century," *New England Quarterly*, XXIII (1950), 365–80; and Phyllis H. Williams, *South Italian Folkways in Europe and America* (1938).

Economic aspects of the "new" immigration are examined in Isaac A. Hourwich, *Immigration and Labor* (1912), which sets out to challenge the conclusions of the Dillingham Commission. Further studies of this subject include Herman Feldman, *Racial Factors in American Industry* (1931); Frank J. Warne, *The Slav Invasion and the Mine Workers* (1904); and William M. Leiserson, *Adjusting Immigrant and Industry* (1924).

Jack Barbash discusses "Ethnic Factors in the Development of the American Labor Movement," in Industrial Relations Research Association, *Interpreting the Labor Movement* (1952), while the emphasis is reversed in Carroll D. Wright, "The Influence of Trade Unions on Immigrants," *Bulletin of the Bureau of Labor*, No. 56

Suggested Reading

(1905), 1–8. Clifton K. Yearley, Jr., *Britons in American Labor* (1957) is a detailed study of the influence of British immigrants upon the American labor movement.

The extent of Catholic growth from immigration is estimated in Gerald Shaughnessy, *Has the Immigrant Kept the Faith?* (1925). Colman J. Barry's *The Catholic Church and German-Americans* (1953) is a reassessment of the Cahenslyite controversy. See also such biographies as John Tracy Ellis' *The Life of James Cardinal Gibbons, Archbishop of Baltimore, 1834–1921* (1952) and James H. Moynihan's *The Life of Archbishop John Ireland* (1953).

Robert E. Park, *The Immigrant Press and Its Control* (1922) is an excellent study of an important immigrant institution.

James P. Shannon's *Catholic Colonization on the Western Frontier* (1957) provides an account of the colonization work of Bishop Ireland of St. Paul. See also Sister Mary Evangela Henthorne, *The Career of the Right Reverend John Lancaster Spalding, Bishop of Peoria, as President of the Irish Catholic Colonization Association of the United States, 1879–1892* (1932). Leo Shpall, "Jewish Agricultural Colonies in the United States," *Agricultural History*, XXIV (1950), 120–45 is a convenient summary.

There are some stimulating comments upon the political role of immigrants in Richard Hofstadter's *The Age of Reform* (1954). For the rise of the Irish in machine politics see M. R. Werner, *Tammany Hall* (1928); Lothrop Stoddard, *Master of Manhattan: The Life of Richard Croker* (1931); and J. P. Bocock, "Irish Conquest of Our Cities," *Forum*, XVII (1894), 186–95.

Evidence of the persistence of Old World loyalties is presented in William D'Arcy, *The Fenian Movement in the United States, 1858–1886* (1947) and, still more strikingly, in Charles C. Tansill's intemperate and biased book, *America and the Fight for Irish Freedom, 1866–1922* (1957). See also James J. Green, "American Catholics and the Land League, 1879–1882," *Catholic Historical Review*, XXXV (1949), 19–42. Clifton J. Child's *The German-Americans in Politics, 1914–1917* (1939) and Carl Wittke's *German-Americans and the World War* (1936) are valuable studies. L. L. Gerson's *Woodrow Wilson and the Rebirth of Poland, 1914–1920* (1953) is a not very successful attempt to assess the influence on American foreign policy of a minority group of foreign origin.

American Immigration

The standard work on post–Civil War nativism is John Higham's *Strangers in the Land: Patterns of American Nativism, 1860–1925* (1955). This book, to which this chapter is heavily indebted, analyzes the shifting sources of hostility to European newcomers. Higham, however, has qualified some of his own conclusions in an important article, "Another Look at Nativism," *Catholic Historical Review*, XLIV (1958), 147–58. Another suggestive study is Barbara M. Solomon's *Ancestors and Immigrants: A Changing New England Tradition* (1956), which examines the intellectual background of the restrictionist movement.

Humphrey J. Desmond's *The A.P.A. Movement* (1912), though extremely brief, contains material not available elsewhere. John Higham's "The Mind of a Nativist: Henry F. Bowers and the A.P.A.," *American Quarterly*, IV (1952), 16–24, is a psychological study of the movement's founder. Daniel F. Reilly's *The School Controversy, 1891–1893* (1943) provides a detailed account of an issue that contributed largely to anti-Catholic sentiment. Morrell Heald, "Business Attitudes toward European Immigration, 1880–1900," *Journal of Economic History*, XIII (1953), 291–304, shatters some widely held illusions, and the attitude of organized labor may be discerned from Arthur Mann's provocative essay, "Gompers and the Irony of Racism," *Antioch Review*, XIII (1953), 203–14. Rowland T. Berthoff has written a careful account of "Southern Attitudes toward Immigration, 1865–1914," *Journal of Southern History*, XVII (1951), 328–60.

The best short history of immigration legislation is to be found in Charles P. Howland (ed.), *Survey of American Foreign Relations, 1929* (1929), which may be supplemented by J. P. Shalloo, "United States Immigration Policy, 1882–1948," in D. E. Lee and G. E. McReynolds (eds.), *Essays in History and International Relations in Honor of George Hubbard Blakeslee* (1949). A more extended work by an avowed nativist is Roy L. Garis' *Immigration Restriction: A Study of the Opposition to and Regulation of Immigration to the United States* (1927).

Henry David's *The History of the Haymarket Affair* (1936) and Robert K. Murray's *Red Scare: A Study in National Hysteria, 1919–*

Suggested Reading

1920 (1955) are standard works which deal capably with episodes important to the growth of nativism.

Edward G. Hartmann's *The Movement To Americanize the Immigrant* (1948) is a detailed but prosaic account of a subject treated with great insight by Horace Kallen in *Culture and Democracy in the United States* (1924).

Practically none of the works cited above has more than a passing mention of the question of Oriental exclusion. Elmer C. Sandmeyer's *The Anti-Chinese Movement in California* (1939) supersedes all previous accounts in the area it covers but may be supplemented by two articles by Jules Karlin, "The Anti-Chinese Outbreak in Tacoma, 1885," *Pacific Historical Review*, XXIII (1954), 271–83 and "The Anti-Chinese Outbreaks in Seattle, 1885–1886," *Pacific Northwest Quarterly*, XXXIX (1948), 103–30. A neglected aspect is treated in Robert Seager II, "Some Denominational Reactions to Chinese Immigration to California, 1856–1892," *Pacific Historical Review*, XXVIII (1959), 49–66. For nativist hostility to Japanese immigrants see Eleanor Tupper and G. E. McReynolds, *Japan in American Public Opinion* (1937); Thomas A. Bailey, *Theodore Roosevelt and the Japanese-American Crises* (1934); and R. L. Buell, "The Development of the Anti-Japanese Agitation in the United States," *Political Science Quarterly*, XXXVII (1922), 605–38.

CHAPTER X

Robert A. Divine's *American Immigration Policy, 1924–1952* (1957), as yet the only detailed work on this subject, is disappointingly slight. The origin and effects of the quota system are analyzed in William S. Bernard (ed.), *American Immigration Policy* (1950). David Brody, in "American Jewry, the Refugees and Immigration Restriction, 1932–1942," *Publications of the American Jewish Historical Society*, XLV (1956), 219–47, comments upon the virtual absence of Jewish pressure for reform of the immigration laws. The forces underlying the repeal of the Chinese Exclusion Act during World War II are the subject of Fred W. Riggs's *Pressures on Congress* (1950).

Maurice R. Davie and others, *Refugees in America* (1947), which relates to the period 1933–45, is the most comprehensive survey of the subject. Donald P. Kent's *The Refugee Intellectual: The Amer-*

icanization of the Immigrant of 1933–41 (1953) is a valuable study of an important group. Little serious work has yet been done upon post–World War II refugees, but an exception is Rudolph Heberle and Dudley S. Hall, *New Americans: A Study of Displaced Persons in Louisiana and Mississippi* (1951).

Bruno Lasker's *Filipino Immigration to Continental United States and Hawaii* (1931) is a well-informed account commissioned by the American Council of the Institute of Pacific Relations. Ira de A. Reid's *The Negro Immigrant, His Background Characteristics and Social Adjustment, 1899–1937* (1939) is a pioneering study of foreign-born Negroes, chiefly from the British West Indies. Of the numerous studies of Mexican immigration Manuel Gamio's *Mexican Immigration to the United States* (1930) is an early attempt to analyze problems of assimilation, while Paul S. Taylor's *Mexican Labor in the United States* (3 vols., 1930–33) discusses the economic role of the newcomers. Among area studies of Mexican immigrants Pauline S. Kibbe's *Latin Americans in Texas* (1946) is competent, while Ruth D. Tuck's *Not with the Fist* (1946) is a penetrating analysis of group relations in the California town of San Bernardino. On Puerto Rican immigration there is a rapidly growing body of literature. C. Wright Mills and others, *The Puerto Rican Journey* (1950), though in some respects outdated, is a conscientious and well-informed study. Elena Padilla's *Up from Puerto Rico* (1958) is an intensive study of a New York immigrant community by an anthropologist. Christopher Rand's *The Puerto Ricans* (1958) is a sharply observed piece of reporting originally published in the form of magazine articles; a similar work is Dan Wakefield's *Island in the City* (1959).

The changing patterns of group life are provocatively discussed in Oscar Handlin's *The American People in the Twentieth Century* (1954). There are also a number of valuable sociological studies of specific ethnic communities. W. Lloyd Warner and Leo Srole, *The Social Systems of American Ethnic Groups* (1945) is one of the Yankee City series dealing with Newburyport, Massachusetts. Elin W. Anderson's *We Americans: A Study of Cleavage in an American City* (1937) examines ethnic relations in Burlington, Vermont. Bessie B. Wessel's *An Ethnic Survey of Woonsocket, Rhode Island* (1931) focuses upon the French-Canadians, while Ar-

Suggested Reading

thur Evans Wood, *Hamtramck, Then and Now* (1955) examines a distinctive Polish-American community.

The continuing political importance of the ethnic tie is convincingly argued in Samuel Lubell's *The Future of American Politics* (1952), which is based upon a close analysis of immigrant voting behavior. Edmund A. Moore's *A Catholic Runs for President* (1956) discusses the influence of religious prejudice in the presidential election of 1928. Oscar Handlin's *Al Smith and His America* (1958) is a sympathetic study which possibly errs in ascribing Smith's 1928 defeat largely to discrimination against the representative of a minority group.

The attitudes of Italian and German immigrants to the rise of dictatorships in their homelands are considered, respectively, by John Norman, "Influence of Pro-Fascist Propaganda on American Neutrality, 1935–36," in D. E. Lee and G. E. McReynolds (eds.), *Essays in History and International Relations* (1949), and by Joachim Remak, "Friends of the New Germany: The Bund and German-American Relations," *Journal of Modern History*, XXIX (1957), 38–41. The problem of immigrant loyalties in World War II is discussed in Jeremiah Shalloo and Donald Young, "Minority Peoples in a Nation at War," *Annals of the American Academy of Political and Social Sciences*, CCXXIII (1942), 1–276.

The removal of Japanese-Americans from the Pacific Coast in 1942 has been the subject of some excellent work. The sociological aspects of the episode are ably treated in Dorothy S. Thomas and Richard S. Nishimoto, *The Spoilage* (1946), and Dorothy S. Thomas, *The Salvage* (1952). The conclusions of Morton Grodzins in *Americans Betrayed: Politics and the Japanese Evacuation* (1949) are modified, and in some cases contradicted, by Jacobus tenBroek, Edward N. Barnhart, and Floyd W. Matson in *Prejudice, War, and the Constitution* (1954).

Index

Abbelen, Rev. Peter M., 226
Abolitionism, 168
Acadians, 31
Act of Union (1707), 26
Adams, Abigail, 87
Adams, John, 7, 8, 16, 86, 87, 88
Adams, Stephen, 158, 159
Adelsverein, 124
Adjustment, problems of, 127–30, 132–46, chap. VIII *passim*, 281–83, 287, 292–93, 296–97
Afgescheidenen, 114
African slave trade, 31
Agriculture, immigrants in, 120, 210–16, 290, 291–92, 310–11
Agricultural conditions: general relation of to migration, 96, 192–93; in Austria-Hungary, 198–99; in Bulgaria, 203; in Canada, 115; in Finland, 203; in Germany, 110–12, 193–94; in Great Britain, 193–94; in Greece, 202; in Holland, 114; in Ireland, 107–10; in Italy, 199–201; in Rumania, 203; in Scandinavia, 113–14, 193–94
"Alabama," 184
Alexander II, tsar of Russia, 201

Alien and Sedition Acts, 72, 83, 86–87, 88
Allentown (Pa.), 77
Allgemeine Auswanderungs-Zeitung, 99
Alliance Israélite Universelle, 213
Alliance (N.J.), 213
Alsace and Lorraine, 94
Altgeld, John P., 234
Amalgamated Clothing Workers of America, 223
Amana (Iowa), 125
"America letters," 100, 134
American Catholicism, 72, 148, 225–28
American Celt, 122
American culture, immigration and, 316–19
American Federation of Labor, 222, 254–55, 268
American Laboring Confederacy, 155
American nationalism, 65, 147–48
American Party (1886–91), 253–54
American Protective Association (A.P.A.), 256

Index

American religion, immigration and, 317–19
American Revolution, 8, 37–38, 39–40, 76, 79; immigrants in, 53–63
American society, immigration and, 313–14
American Truth Society, 245
Americanism, 100 per cent, 270, 271, 272, 273
Americanization, factors affecting, 48–53, 65, 75 ff., 175, 297–300
Americanization movement, 272–74
Amsterdam, 29
Anchor Line, 186
Ancient Order of Hibernians, 261
Anglicans, 37
Anglo-German commercial rivalry, 186
Anglo-Saxon tradition, 257, 258, 265, 266, 267
Anti-Catholicism, 43, 148–52, 255–56, 275
Anti-Chinese agitation, 248–49, 263
Anti-Japanese agitation, 264–65
Anti-Semitism, 201–2, 257, 275, 284
Argentina, 2, 200
Arizona, 291
"Ark," 13
Arkansas, 122
Armenia, emigration from, 203
Armenian-Americans, 319
Armenian massacres, 203
Armenians, 205
Artisans, 67–68, 69, 111, 112, 194–95, 311–12
Assisted emigration, 109, 111, 112, 115–16
Astor, John Jacob, 65
Asylum, concept of America as, 79 ff., 84, 143, 157, 161, 249–50, 252, 260, 285
Asylum (Pa.), 71
Atchison, Topeka, and Santa Fe Railroad, 189
Atlantic crossing, 3, 103, 106–7, 183–84
Augsburg Confession, 138

Augustana Evangelical Lutheran Church, 318
Aurora (Ore.), 126
Australia, immigration to, 2, 101, 115, 196
Austria-Hungary: emigration from, 179, 197–99; emigration policy of, 197; steamship agents in, 182
Azores, 203

Baden, 110
Baltimore, 71, 77, 117, 152, 165, 215, 217
Baltimore, Lord, 13, 14
Barbados, 18
Barlow, Joel, 70
Baron de Hirsch Fund, 213
"Barred zone," 270
Baumeler, Joseph, 125
Bavaria, 110, 194
Bayard-Chamberlain agreement, 24
Bedini, Monsignor, 151
Beecher, Rev. Lyman, *A Plea for the West*, 149
Belfast, 24, 45, 75
Bell, John, 165
Benedicta (Me.), 122
Benét, Stephen Vincent, 10–11, 12
Benjamin, Judah P., 165
Bennett Law, 236
Bennington, Battle of (1777), 55
Bergen, 184
Berger, Victor, 229
Bethel (Mo.), 126
Bethlehem (Pa.), 27
Beverley, Robert, 11
Bible-reading controversy, 150, 175
Big business, attitude of to immigration, 254–55, 261
Birkbeck, Morris, 99, 112–13
Birmingham (England), 295
Bishop Hill (Ill.), 126
Blaine, James G., 235
Blenker, Ludwig, 176
Bohemians (Czechs), 180, 181, 198, 214, 215, 227, 306, 310

343

Index

Bond, Phineas, 66
Boston (Mass.), 20, 45, 46, 47, 50, 117, 118, 119, 133, 152, 186, 224, 244, 250, 259, 267, 294, 298
Boston *Pilot*, 140, 167, 241
Boudinot, Elias, 62
Boulter, Hugh, archbishop of Armagh, 24
Bowdoin, James, 51
Bowers, Henry F., 256
Brazil, immigration to, 101, 200, 202
Breckinridge, John C., 165, 169
Bremen, 102, 104, 105
Bridenbaugh, Carl, 49
Bristol, 73
British immigrants, 69, 70, 72–73, 74, 126, 208–9, 310
British Isles, emigration from, 94, 193, 194–95
British North America, immigration to, 101
Brooklyn, 223, 296
Brown, John, 169
Bryan, George, 53, 56
Buchanan, James, 143
Büchel, August, 171
Buffalo (N.Y.), 122, 125, 151, 224, 298, 306
Bulgarians, 220
Burchard, Rev. Samuel D., 235–36
Burgoyne, General John, 54
Burk, John Daly, 87, 88
Burlingame Treaty, 249
Burlington and Missouri Railroad, 189
Burns, Anthony, 159
Business cycles, migration and, 100, 313
Butler, Pierce, 81
Butler's Rangers, 60
Byrne, Andrew, bishop of Little Rock, 122

Cabet, Étienne, 126
Cahensly, Peter Paul, 226
Cahenslyism, 225–27

California, 200, 204, 209, 215, 248, 249, 254, 263, 264, 265, 288, 291, 303
Callender, James Thompson, 87, 88
Cambria County (Pa.), 73
Camden, Battle of (1780), 54
Camp Kilmer (N.J.), 287
Campbell, Lachlan, 26
Canada: emigration from, 114–15, 203–4, 289, 290; immigration to, 61–62, 70, 196, 290
Canadians, 115, 209, 290. *See also* French-Canadians
Canal-building, immigrants in, 131
Cannon, Joseph, 262
Cape Fear (N.C.), 27, 60
Cape Verde Islands, 203
Carey, Mathew, 65, 68
Carmel (N.J.), 213
Castle Garden, 128–29, 173, 250
Catherine the Great, 201
Catholic church, 72, 139–40, 148–51, 225–28, 230; "leakage" from, 227
Catholic emancipation, 144
Catholics, 13, 54, 72, 139–40, 148–51, 225–30. *See also* Anti-Catholicism
Cermak, Anton, 306
Champion of American Labor, 155
Charles II, 18
Charleston (S.C.), 18, 20, 25, 31, 71
Charlestown (Mass.), 149
Chartists, 97
Cheetham, James, 73
Cherry Valley massacre, 60
Chesney, Alexander, 55
Chicago, 117, 118, 162, 217, 223, 241, 244, 253, 292, 298, 306
Chicago World's Fair, 255
China, emigration from, 204
Chinese, 204, 239, 247, 248–49, 251, 263, 284, 311
Chinese Exclusion Acts, 204, 249, 250, 251, 263, 270
Cholera, 106–7, 185
Church and state, separation of, 37, 318

Index

Cincinnati, 117, 119, 151, 162, 226, 271

Cincinnati *Volksblatt*, 140

CIO, 299

Cities: immigrants in, 117, 134–35, 178, 180, 207, 209–10; "Irish conquest of," 233–34

Civil War: Americanizing effect of, 175–76; attitude of immigrants to, 169–71; foreign-born soldiers in, 171–73

Clan-na-Gael movement, 241, 242

Clark, Aaron, 152

Clark, Champ, 239

Clay, Henry, 143

Cleveland (Ohio), 305

Cleveland, Grover, 235, 236, 260

Clinton (Iowa), 256

Clinton, De Witt, 76

Clinton, Sir Henry, 54

Coal-mining, immigrants in, 216–17

Cobbett, William, 65, 113

Cobden's Treaty, 195

Cohen, Moses, 212

Colfax, Schuyler, 235

Colonists, chap. i, *passim*

Colorado, 291

Commerce, emigration and, 103 ff., 119

Committee on Immigration and Naturalization (1890), 186

Common Sense, 79

Commons, John R., 267

Communist Labor Party, 230, 274

Communist Party, 230, 274

Communitarian societies, 125–26

Compagnie Générale Transatlantique, 184

Confederacy, foreign-born soldiers in army of, 170–71

Congregationalists, 37

Congress, 81, 123, 249, 250, 251, 280, 286

Connecticut, 158, 215, 306

Conscription Act (1863), 173–74

Constitution of United States, 81, 250

Constitutional Convention of 1787, 80–81

Constitutional Union Party, 165

Continental Army, 54

Continental Congress, 8, 57, 62, 66, 67

Contract labor, 190, 251; prohibition of, 251–52, 254

Convicts, 21, 43–44, 67, 251

Cooper, Thomas, 73, 87, 88

Copperheadism, 175

Corn Laws, repeal of, 113

Cornish immigrants, 119–20

Cornwallis, Charles, Lord, 54

Cosby, William, governor of New York, 26

Cotopaxi (Colo.), 213

Cotton trade, 103–4, 119

Coughlin, "Bathhouse" John, 233

Coxe, Tench, 68

Crèvecœur, Michel-Guillaume Jean de, 10, 48, 63

Criminals, foreign-born, 133, 152–53

Croats, 198

Croker, Richard, 233

Cromwell, Oliver, 13

Cuba, 293

Cumberland County (N.C.), 60

Cumberland Valley, 29, 35, 47, 49

Cunard Line, 184

Czolgosz, Leon, 262

Dakotas, 189, 201, 214, 310

Dalmatians, 180, 198

Danes, 209

Dearborn Independent, 275

Debs, Eugene V., 239

Declaration of Independence, 10, 160

DeLancey family, 62

Democracy, immigrants and, 160, 230 ff., 315

Democratic party, 142–44, 162, 163, 166, 169, 235, 236, 244, 262, 302

Index

Democratic-Republican clubs, 84
Democratic Review, 92
Denver, 305
Department of the Tennessee, expulsion of Jews from, 174
Depression (of the 1930's), 280, 297, 299–300
Detroit, 117, 216, 292
Deutsche Gesellschaft (New York), 128
Deutsches Haus Convention, 162
Devoy, John, 235
DeWitt, General John L., 303, 304
Dictionary of Races, 269
Dielli, 229
Dillingham Commission, 177–83, 209, 214, 217, 218, 222, 224, 269, 312
Displaced Persons, 284–86
Displaced Persons Act (1948), 285
District of Columbia, 67
Dominion Line, 184
Domschke, Bernhard, 155
Donegal (Pa.), 25
Donne, John, 9
Douai, Adolf, 164
Douglas, Stephen A., 162, 165, 169
"Dove," 13
Duane, William, 87, 88
Duden Gottfried, 99
Dulany, Daniel, 30
Dunkers, 19
Dunmore, Lord, governor of Virginia, 61
Dutch, 16–17, 50, 51, 114, 118, 138, 166–67
Dutch language, 50, 76
Dutch Reformed Church, 76, 98, 114, 138
Dutch West India Company, 17

East Liverpool (Ohio), 120
East New Jersey, 26
Easter Rebellion, 242
Economic growth, effect of immigration on, 309–10
Einhorn, David, 166

Einstein, Albert, 281
Eisenhower, Dwight D., 286
Ellis Island, 129
Emancipation Proclamation, 174
Emerson, Ralph Waldo, 93, 160, 315
Emigrant guidebooks, 99
Emigration, forces underlying nineteenth-century, 94–95, 192; economic, 95–97, 192–95; political, 97–98; religious, 98–99
Emigration, restrictions on, 18, 64, 67, 68, 196, removal of, 101–3, 197, 204
Emigration societies, 116
England: emigration from, 11–16, 18, 20, 21, 69, 72–74, 94, 112–13, 194–95; Mormon missions in, 126
English Civil War, 16
English immigrants, chap. i *passim,* 69, 180, 217
English language, 36, 76
Ethiopian War, 300
Eugenics, 267
Europe, emigration from, 100–101. *See also separate countries by name*
Evangelical Lutheran Church, 318
Excluded classes, 251, 252, 262, 269–70

Fall River (Mass.), 216, 217
Fares, 105
Fascism, 300
FBI, 302
Federal Bureau of Immigration, 220
Federal immigration laws: of 1882, 262, 263; of 1891, 262; of 1903, 262; of 1907, 262; of 1917, 269–70, 280; of 1921, 276; of 1924, 276–77, 291; of 1952, 286, 295
Federalists, 74, 83, 85, 86, 87, 88, 89, 90, 148
Felsenthal, Bernhard, 166
Fenian movement, 241
Fenwick, Benedict J., bishop of Boston, 122
"Fiancées" Act, 284

Index

Filipinos, 288–89
Fillmore, Millard, 157, 160
Finnish Evangelical Lutheran Church, 318
Finns, 180, 202, 209, 220
Fiume, 186, 246
Five Points, 134
Florida, 200
Foran Act, 190, 251, 252
Ford, Henry, 275
Ford, Patrick, 235
Foreign-born, numbers of: (1860), 117; (1910), 208–9; (1914), 240
Foreign Conspiracy against the Liberties of the United States, 149
Foreign policy, immigrant groups and, 238, 240, 315–16
Forty-eighters, 97, 110, 129, 145, 151, 154, 155, 162, 163, 164, 240
Founding Fathers, 315, 319
Fourteen Points, 245
Franco-Prussian War, 240
Franklin, Benjamin, 29, 43, 48
Franks, David, 62
Fredericksburg, Battle of (1862), 170
Free Magyar Reformed Church, 318
"Freedom dues," 33
French-Canadians, 115, 118, 139, 219, 225, 226, 237, 290, 312
French immigrants, 70, 71, 72, 83, 84, 87, 88–89. *See also* Huguenots
French language, 76
French Revolution, 70, 74
Frenchtown (R.I.), 44
Freneau, Philip, 79
Friends of Ireland, 144
Frontier, immigrants and the, 69–70, 120, 210–14, 310–11
Froude, James Anthony, 53
Fugitive Slave Act (1850), 159

Gaelic-American, 245
Gales, Joseph, 73
Galicia: emigration from, 198; steamship agents in, 182
Gallatin, Albert, 65
Gallipolis (Ohio), 70

Garibaldi, Giuseppe, 145
Garment industry, 217, 219–20, 294
Genoa, 186
Gentlemen's Agreement, 204–5, 265, 270
George III, 58, 60, 74
Georgia, 21, 26, 35, 36, 42, 57, 170
German-American Alliance, 261, 271
German-American Bund, 300–301
German-Americans, 240; and Nazism, 300–301; and Treaty of Versailles, 245–46; and World War I, 243–45, 270–71; and World War II, 302–3
German-born congressmen, 234
German Catholics, 139, 163, 236; rivalry of with Irish, 225–26
German language, 76, 124, 137
German Lutherans, 58, 137–38, 139, 163
German Reformed Church, 28, 58, 137
Germanna (Va.), 30
Germans, 66, 68, 70, 74, 118, 119, 123–25, 137–38, 139, 144, 154, 156, 180, 185, 208, 209, 210, 217, 225–26, 310; and American Revolution, 57–60; and Civil War, 169–71, 176; and slavery controversy, 161–65; in the colonies, 27–30, 34, 35, 41; in New York City, 130, 131–32, 135, 223; in post–Civil War politics, 234; in the South, 164–65
Germantauner Zeitung, 58
Germantown (Pa.), 19, 124
Germany: emigration from, 19, 27–29, 70, 94, 110–12, 125, 193, 194, 195; industrialization of, 196; Mormon missions in, 126
Gerry, Elbridge, 81
Ghettos, ethnic, 50, 134–35, 156, 223–24, 297–98
Giessener Gesellschaft, 124
Girondists, 71
Glas Narodna, 229
Glasgow, 26

Index

Goebel, William, 234
Göttingen, Royal University of, 60
Gompers, Samuel, 222
Good Neighbor policy, 289
Grace, William P., 234
Graffenried, Christoph de, 30
Granger movement, 230
Grant, Madison, 268, 275
Grant, Ulysses S., 174, 235
Great Britain: emigration policy of, 17–18, 67–68, 101–2, 196; Irish immigration to, 101, 102; Mormon mission in, 126; West Indian immigration to, 295
Great Migration (of Puritans), 15–16
Great Northern Railroad, 189
Great Plains, 189, 215
Great Salt Lake Valley, 99, 116, 127
Greece: emigration from, 179, 192, 202; steamship agents in, 182
Greek-Americans, 301, 306, 319
Greeks, 181, 192, 216, 217, 220, 312
Greeley, Horace, 172, 235
Gropius, Walter, 281
Group life, 135, 136, 225, 295, 298–99, 317–18
Group migration, 125–27
Guion Line, 184
Gunton, George, 221

Haiti, 293
Hale, Edward Everett, 131
Hall, Prescott F., 259
Hambach, 97
Hamburg, 105
Hamburg-Amerika Line, 184, 185, 186
Hamilton, Alexander, 69, 81, 89
Hammerling, Louis, 238
Hansen, Marcus Lee, 44, 110, 115
Harmony (Pa.), 125
Harper, Robert Goodloe, 86
Hart family, 63
Hartford Convention, 89
Hassaurek, Friedrich, 162
Hasselquist, Rev. Tuve N., 167
Haugeanism, 113

Hawaii, 204, 288
Hayes, Rutherford B., 234, 249
Haymarket Affair, 253
Head Taxes, 47, 128, 250, 262, 269
Headright system, 13, 14, 42
Hearst, William Randolph, 238, 239
Hebrew Emigrant Aid Society, 213
Hebrew Sheltering and Immigrant Aid Society, 282
Hecker, Friedrich, 162
Heidelberg Confession, 138
Heilprin, Michael, 212
Heinzen, Karl, 155, 163
Hemlandet, 167
Hessians, 59, 66
Hillquit, Morris, 229
Hinchcliffe, John, 221
Hitler, Adolf, 280, 301, 302, 305
Hobkirk's Hill, Battle of (1781), 54
Holland-America Line, 184
Homestead Act, 166, 173
Hong Kong, 204
Houston Post, 270
Howard, Robert, 221
Howe, General Sir William, 59
Hudson Valley: Dutch in, 50; Palatines in, 28; Scottish Highlanders in, 27
Hughes, Charles Evans, 243, 244
Hughes, John Joseph, bishop (later archbishop) of New York, 123, 140, 150, 151, 168
Huguenots, 17, 18, 19–20, 30, 34, 41, 44, 45, 51–52
Hungarian Revolution (1956), 286
Hungarians. See Magyars
Hungry Hollow (Ill.), 220
"Hyphenated Americans," 243, 271

Icarian settlement, 126
Illinois, 112, 117, 118, 120, 123, 162, 208, 209, 224, 244
Illinois Bureau of Labor, 221
Illinois Central Railroad, 188–89
Immigrant "banks," 191
Immigrant churches, 37, 52, 76, 136–39, 225–28, 317–19
Immigrant control stations, 185–86

Index

Immigrant press, 58, 72, 77, 78–79, 140–41, 228–29, 299

Immigrant societies, 135, 136, 225, 298–99, 317

Immigrant trade, 23–24, 67–68, 75, 103–7, 183–84, 250

Immigrants: American patriotism of, 171, 319; clannishness of, 156, 178, 180; conservatism of, 230–32, 314–15; distribution of 117 ff., 209 ff.; economic adjustment of, 129–31, 210–20, 281–82, 287, 290–92, 293–94, 296; health of, 133; housing conditions of, 132–34, 224–25; illiteracy among, 180; motives of, 4–5, 9, 11, 13, 14, 15, 19, chap. iv *passim*, chap. vii *passim*; political rights of, 80–81; religious life of, 76–77, 136–40, 225–28, 292, 317–19; sex of, 180; unskilled, 180. *See also* Adjustment, problems of; Group life; Politics, immigrants in; *and nationalities by name*

Immigration: and foreign policy, 315–16; cultural effects of, 316–19; demographic effects of, 308–9; economic effects of, 132, 309–13; federal regulation of, 250–51; restriction of, chapter ix *passim*, 279–80, 285–86, 289; social effects of, 132, 313–14. *See also* Promotion of Immigration; Volume of **Immigration**

Immigration policy, 41–44, 91, 173, 247, chap. ix *passim*, 278–81, 284–86. *See also* Federal immigration laws

Immigration restriction: consequences of, chap. x *passim;* demand for, chap. ix *passim*, 278–81, 285–86, 289

Immigration Restriction League, 259, 267

Impressment, 75, 90

Indentured servants, 9, 12–13, 20–21, 24, 32–34, 42, 66, 67, 309

Indiana, 126, 212

Industrial Revolution, 96

Industrial workers, emigration of, 21, 68–69, 96, 112, 119–20, 194–95

Industry, immigrants in, 69, 119–20, 131, 216–21, 311–13

Inman Line, 184

Inspirationists, 125

Intermarriage, 49, 307

International Ladies Garment Workers' Union, 223

International Refugee Organization, 285

Iowa, 114, 118, 122, 127, 167, 188, 189, 214

Ireland, emigration from, 74, 75, 78, 107–10, 193

Ireland, John, bishop of St. Paul, 211, 212

Irish, 67, 84–85, 89–90, 131, 133, 139, 150, 180, 181, 208, 217; American patriotism of, 171; and abolitionism, 167–68; and Democratic party, 143–44, 169, 235, 236, 244, 262; and government of cities, 233; and Irish causes, 144, 156, 211, 240–46; and Negro competition, 168–69, 173–74; and New York draft riots, 173–74; and Republican party, 235–36; and slavery, 159; aversion of, to agriculture, 121–23, 210–12; distribution of, 118, 119, 209; in Canada, 101; in Great Britain, 101, 102; in New England, 119, 259; in New York City, 89, 130, 133, 134, 223; in politics, 154, 233–34; in railroad-building, 311; in the Civil War, 170, 171, 172, 173–74; in the colonies, 22; refugees of 1798 rebellion, 74; rural colonization of, 122, 211–12; urban concentration of, 121–22, 210–11

Irish-Americans, 307, 319; and Treaty of Versailles, 246; and World War I, 242–45, 271; and World War II, 301; Anglophobia of, 240–42

Irish Catholic Benevolent Union, 211

Index

Irish Catholic Colonization Association (1879), 211
Irish Catholic Colonization Convention (1856), 122
Irish Emigrant Society of New York, 105, 123, 128
Irish famine, 101, 109–10
Irish Land League, 211, 241
Irish militia companies, 90, 135, 159
Irish Nation, 235
Irish nationalism, 78
Irish Poor Law Act (1838), 108–9
Irish Race Convention, 242
Irish rebellion of 1798, 74, 88
Irish vote, 85, 89, 143, 167
Irish World, 235, 245
Isaacs, Samuel M., 166
Isolationism, 301
Israel, recognition of, 316
Italian-Americans: and Ethiopian War, 300; and Treaty of Versailles, 246; and World War II, 301, 302–3; political gains of, 306–7, 319
Italians, 180, 181, 257, 312; and *padrone* system, 191–92; and Republican party, 262; as strikebreakers, 190, 222, 251; become Protestants, 227; distribution of, 209; in agriculture, 214, 215; in construction work, 220, 311; in industry, 217, 219; in New York City, 224; in the South, 266; religious life of, 225, 226
Italy: emigration from, 179, 191, 199–201; emigration policy of, 197

Jackson, Andrew, 142, 143
Jackson, James, 82
Jacobins, 71, 83
Jacobite rebellions, 26, 61
Jamaica, 295
James, Henry, 207
Jamestown (Va.), 9, 11
Janson, Eric, 126
Japan, emigration from, 204–5
Japanese, 204–5, 264, 265, 277, 284, 303–5, 311

Japanese-Americans, evacuation of from Pacific Coast, 303–5; and World War II, 304–5
Japanese and Korean Exclusion League, 264
Jarrett, John, 221
Jay, John, 39, 40, 62, 90
Jay's Treaty, 85
Jefferson, Thomas, 16, 75, 80, 88, 89, 90, 142
Jersey City, 224
Jewish-Americans, 302, 306
Jewish Messenger, 166
Jews, 120, 129, 139, 180, 185, 201–2, 205, 214, 261, 281, 312; and American Revolution, 62–63; and Republican party, 262; and slavery controversy, 165–66; in the colonies, 17, 31, 34; in the garment industry, 219–20; in New York City, 223, 257; rural colonization of, 212–13
Johnson, Edward, *Wonder-working Providence*, 20
Johnson, Sir John, 60
Johnson-Reed Act, 276
Johnson, Robert, governor of South Carolina, 41
Jones, John Paul, 60

Kalm, Peter, 51
Kansas, 169, 189, 201, 211, 214, 291
Kansas City, 224
Kansas-Nebraska Act, 158, 162, 169
Kearney, Dennis, 249, 253
Keil, Wilhelm, 125–26
Kelly, "Honest John," 233
Kenna, "Hinky Dink," 233
King, Rufus, 87, 88
King's Mountain, Battle of (1780), 60
Kishineff massacres, 240
Knights of Labor, 222, 251, 254, 257
Körner, Gustav, 124, 162
Kossuth, Louis, 145
Know-Nothing Party, 157–61, 248
Kuhn, Fritz, 300
Ku Klux Klan, 275

Index

Labadists, 125
Labor: skilled, 68–69, 96, 112, 119–20, 181–82, 190, 194–95, 251, 311–12; unskilled, 129–30, 180, 181–82
Labor agencies, 182–83, 220–21, 251
Labor organizations: and immigration, 251, 254–55, 264, 288; role of immigrants in, 221–23, 299. *See also* American Federation of Labor; CIO; Knights of Labor; National Labor Union
Lafayette, Marquis de, 54
Lancaster (Pa.), 77
Lancaster County (Pa.), 29, 47, 124
Land speculation, 70
L'Association Canada-Américaine, 225
Laurens, Henry, 62
Lazarus, Emma, 247
Lea, Homer, 265
League of Nations, 246, 275
Lecky, William E. H., 53
Lee, General "Light-Horse" Harry, 54
Le Havre, 104, 105, 119, 121, 184
Leopold Association, 149
Lewiston (Me.), 237
Libau (Lepaya), 186
Liberty Party, 143
Lincoln, Abraham, 160, 161, 162, 165, 169, 173, 174
Literacy test, 244, 259, 260–61, 262, 269–70, 274, 291
Lithuanian National Catholic Church, 318
Lithuanians, 202, 218, 226
Lititz (Pa.), 27
Liverpool, 32, 103, 104, 105, 126, 184, 186
Livingston, Philip, 89
Lodge, Henry Cabot, 260
Logan, James, 25, 46, 47
London, 295
London, Jack, 266
Londonderry (Ireland), 24, 25, 45, 75
Londonderry (N.H.), 24

Long Island, 298
Long Island, Battle of (1776), 55
Lopez, Aaron, 62
Loras, Mathias, bishop of Dubuque, 122
Los Angeles, 305
Louis Philippe, 71
Louisiana, 31, 215
Louisville Platform, 154
Lowell (Mass.), 216, 217, 224
Loyal Irish Volunteers, 54
Loyalists, 54–63
Loyalsock Creek (Pa.), 73
Lucerne Memorial, 226
Lutheran Free Church, 318
Lynch, Patrick, 140
Lyon, Matthew, 87

McCarran-Walter Act (1952), 286, 295
McClenachan, Blair, 85
McGee, Thomas D'Arcy, 122, 171
McKean, Thomas, 53
McKinley Tariff, 199
McKinley, William, 261, 262
McLaughlin, Daniel, 221
Madison, James, 81, 90
Magyars (Hungarians), 198, 222, 224, 257
Maine, 43, 219
Manakin Town (Va.), 20
Manchester (N.H.), 237
Manitoba, 203
Mann, Thomas, 281
Maritime Provinces, 115, 119, 203
Maryland, 13–14, 20, 21, 29, 30, 34, 35, 77, 117, 124
Mason, George, 81
Mason and Dixon's Line, 35, 117
Massachusetts, 117, 128, 152, 158, 159, 163–64, 208, 209, 215, 219
Massachusetts Bay, colony of, 8, 15, 20, 36, 43
Mather, Cotton, 45
May Laws (1882), 201
"Mayflower," 14
Mayo-Smith, Richmond, 258

Index

Meagher, General Thomas Francis, 170, 172
Mennonites: German, 19; Russo-German, 201
Metz, Christian, 125
Mexican-Americans, 319
Mexicans, 290–93, 311
Mexico, emigration from, 290–92
Michigan, 114, 115, 118, 120, 187, 209, 216, 218, 292
Military service, hostility to, 194
Militia units, foreign-born, 90, 135, 156, 159; disbandment of, 158
Miller, Heinrich, 59
Milwaukee, 117, 163, 216, 226, 236, 244, 271
Minneapolis, 305
Minnesota, 118, 122, 188, 189, 209, 211, 212, 214, 218, 243, 292
Mississippi River, 119, 126
Missouri, 117, 118, 170
Missouri Synod, 138, 163, 167
Mitchel, John, 168
Mohawk Valley, 27, 28, 57, 60
Molly Maguire riots, 253
Monk, Maria, *Awful Disclosures of the Hôtel Dieu Nunnery of Montreal,* 149
Montefiore Agricultural Society, 213
Moore's Creek Bridge, Battle of (1776), 60
Moravians, 27–28, 58, 125
Mormons, 98–99, 116, 126–27
Morris, Gouverneur, 81
Morrisey, John, 233
Morristown (N.J.), 54
Morse, Samuel F. B., 149, 175
Mount Vernon, 67
Mruc, Joseph, 306
Muhlenberg, Frederick A., 59
Muhlenberg, Rev. Henry Melchior, 59–60
Muhlenberg, Peter, 58
Munch, Friedrich, 162
Murchison Letter, 241
Murphy, Charles F., 233

Murray, William Vans, 82
Mussolini, Benito, 300, 302

Naples, 186
Napoleonic Wars, 65, 68, 74, 93, 103
National Labor Union, 222
National Line, 184, 185
National origins system, 276–77, 279
National Refugee Service, 282
National Repeal Convention, 144
National Association of Manufacturers, 261
Native American Party, 156
Native labor, effect of immigration on, 131–32, 155–56, 217–18
Nativism, 40, 44–48, 82–83, 85–88, 89, 93, 147–61, 252–61, 265–76, 315
Natural selection, Darwin's theory of, 266
Naturalization frauds, 154
Naturalization laws, 42; of 1790, 82; of 1795, 82–83; of 1798, 86, 88, 89; of 1802, 89, 90
Nauvoo (Ill.), 127
Nazareth (Pa.), 27
Nazism, 300–301
Nebraska, 122, 189, 201, 211, 214, 310
Negro slavery, 13, 18, 31–33, 120
Negroes, 13, 17, 18, 31–33, 34, 35, 42, 164, 173–74, 293–94, 295, 297
Nelson, Knute, 234
Netherlands (Holland), emigration from, 16–17, 94, 98, 114
Neutrality Act, 300
New Bedford (Mass.), 216, 217
New Bern (N.C.), 30
New Bordeaux (S.C.), 30
New Braunfels (Tex.), 165, 171
New Brunswick, 119
New Deal, 300
New England, 33, 34, 35, 37, 41, 43, 46, 54, 69, 85, 87, 89, 115, 118, 171, 218, 219, 258, 266, 290, 302
New Germany, concept of, 123–25
New Hampshire, 219
New Harmony, 126

Index

"New" immigration, 4, 178–82, 210, 216 ff., 237–39, 256–57, 265, 276, 306–7

New Jersey, 118, 209, 213, 215, 218, 307

New Netherland, 16–17, 50, 76

New Odessa (Ore.), 213

New Orleans, 105, 117, 118, 119, 126, 154, 156, 165, 168, 186, 257

New Orleans Emerald Guards, 170

New Rochelle (N.Y.), 20

New Sweden, 16–17, 50–51

New York (city), 66, 88, 89, 105, 128, 131, 133, 144, 150, 152, 154, 184, 186, 217, 244, 250; draft riots in, 173–74; Dutch language in, 50; French in, 71; Germans in, 130, 134, 135, 223; Huguenots in, 20; Irish in, 84, 90, 130, 134, 168, 223; Italians in, 223, 224, 298; Jews in, 31, 223; nativism in, 156; Negroes in, 168; Puerto Ricans in, 295–96; slums in, 224; West Indians in, 293, 294

New York (colony), 17, 26, 28, 44

New York (state), 62, 66, 67, 70, 76, 115, 117, 118, 120, 128, 143, 208, 209, 215, 218

New York Bureau of Labor, 222

New York *Citizen*, 168

New York *Freeman's Journal*, 140, 167, 245

New York *Irish-American*, 140, 171

New York *Nation*, 122

New York *Observer*, 149

New York *Staats-Zeitung und Herold*, 140

New York State Commissioners of Immigration, 128, 184

New York *Time Piece*, 87

"Newlanders," 29

Newport (R.I.), 31, 62–63

Ninety Six (S.C.), 55

Nisei, 305

Noailles, Vicomte de, 71

Nobel Prize winners, 281

Non-importation agreement, 61

Nonęs, Benjamin, 62

Nordic superiority, 275–76

Norfolk (Va.), 61

North Carolina, 27, 30, 35, 56–57, 58, 60, 77

North German Lloyd Line, 184, 186

Northern Pacific Railroad, 189

Northumberland (Pa.), 73

Norway, emigration from, 94, 98, 103, 114

Norwegian Lutherans, 138–39

Norwegians, 118, 141, 209; and slavery controversy, 166–67; political role of, 234

Notes on Virginia, 80

Nova Scotia, 21, 31

O'Brien, Hugh, 234

O'Connell, Daniel, 144, 168

O'Connor, Charles, 175

O'Connor, James P., bishop of Omaha, 211

Odessa, 184

O'Gorman, Richard, 175

Ohio, 117, 118, 209, 212, 224

"Old" immigration, 4, 177–81

Old Lutherans, 98, 138

Old World loyalties, 53, 58, 59–60, 61–63, 144–45, 156, 240–46, 270, 274

O'Leary, Jeremiah, 245, 271

Olmsted, Frederick Law, 169

Olney-Pauncefote Treaty, 241

Oneida County (N.Y.), 74

Order of Sons of Italy, 225

Order of the Star-Spangled Banner, 157

Order of United American Mechanics, 254

Order of United Americans, 156

Oregon, 188, 243

Oriental Exclusion, 248–49, 263–65, 277, 288

Orthodox churches, 318

Otis, Harrison Gray, 85, 86

Owen, Robert, 126

Oxford (Mass.), 20, 41

Index

Paddy's Run (Ohio), 74
Padrone system, 191–92
Page, John, 82
Paine, Thomas, 79
Palatines, 28, 30, 48
Palermo, 184, 186
Palmer raids, 274
Pan-Americanism, 289
Pan-Hellenic Union, 225
Pan-Slav nationalism, 201
Parker, Theodore, 161
Parnell, Charles Stewart, 211, 241
Passenger Acts, 67, 68, 75, 106
Passenger agents, 104, 105, 186
Passenger Cases, 250
Passing of the Great Race in America, 268
Pastor, Joseph, 227
Pastore, John, 306
Pastorius, Francis Daniel, 19
Paterson (N.J.), 69, 223
Patriotic societies, 254, 273, 285, 288
Paupers, 43, 47, 82, 111, 128, 133, 152–53, 250
Pawtucket (R.I.), 69
Paxton Boys, 56
Pearl Harbor, 302, 303, 304
Penn, William, 18, 42, 98
Pennsylvania, 18, 19, 20, 24, 27, 28, 30, 33, 34, 35, 41, 42, 44, 53–54, 55, 56, 57, 58, 66, 67, 84, 117, 118, 119, 120, 124, 143, 208, 209, 212, 217, 218, 222, 224, 253, 257
Pennsylvania Assembly, 47, 54
Pennsylvania Germans, 29, 47–48, 49, 88
Pennsylvania Line, 54
Pennsylvanische Staats Courier, 59
Penrose, Boies, 238
Perpetual Emigrating Fund, 116
Perth Amboy (N.J.), 26
Philadelphia, 19, 24, 25, 28, 42, 50, 54, 56, 58, 59, 66, 67, 71, 74, 77, 78, 84, 85, 124, 151, 152, 154, 215, 296, 298
Philadelphia *Aurora*, 87
Philadelphia Riots (1844), 150, 151

Philadelphische Staatsbote, 59
Philippine Independence Act, 288
Philippine Islands, 288
Pierce, Franklin, 143
Pilgrims, 14
Pittsburgh, 224
Pokrok, 227
Poles, 123, 198, 202, 215, 216, 217, 218, 223, 225, 227–28
Polish-Americans, 244, 245, 302, 306, 319
Polish National Alliance, 225
Polish National Catholic Church, 226, 318
Political machines, 141–42, 154, 232, 314
Politics, immigrants and, 85, 88–89, 141–46, 153–55, 161, 229 ff., 306–7, 314–15
Pollock family, 63
Poor Law Amendment Act, 113
Poor relief, problem of, 43, 46, 152–53
Population growth: effect of immigration on American, 258, 308–9; European, 95, 192–93; Japanese, 204
Populism, 230
Portugal, emigration from, 202
Portuguese, 180, 202–3, 215, 216, 217, 220, 312
Pothier, Aram J., 237
Prepaid passages, 105, 186–87
Presbyterian church, 78, 318
Presidential election, of 1800, 88–89; of 1828, 143; of 1844, 143; of 1852, 143; of 1856, 143, 160; of 1860, 161–69; of 1912, 238–39; of 1916, 243–44; of 1940, 302
Priestley, Joseph, 73
Progressivism, 230–31
Promotion of immigration: by colonial governments, 41–43; by English parishes, 113, 115; by German municipalities, 111; by industrialists 69, 116; by land companies, 70; by Mormons, 116;

Index

Promotion of immigration (*cont.*)
by northwestern states, 187–88;
by railroads, 188–90; by southern
states, 188; by steamship com-
panies, 182–83; by the federal
government, 173; by trade un-
ions, 116
Protestant Episcopal Church, 318
Providence (R.I.), 119
Prussia, emigration from, 98
Puerto Ricans, 295–97
Pulaski Day, 319
Pulteney estate (N.Y.), 70
Puritans, 6, 8, 14, 15–16, 45, 79, 98
Pury, Jean Peter, 30
Purysburg (S.C.), 30

Quakers, 19, 98, 113
Quasi-war with France (1798), 72
Quay, Matthew S., 238
Quebec (city), 105
Quebec (province), 115, 203
Quebec Act, 54
Queen's Own Loyal Virginians, 61
Queenstown, 184
Quota system, 276–77, 279, 281, 284,
285, 286, 287

Raalte, Rev. Albertus C. Van, 167
Racism, 258–59, 265, 266–68, 275–
76, 277
Radicalism, immigrants and, 72–73,
82, 83, 85–87, 89, 154–55, 229–30,
253
Railroad-building, immigrants in,
131, 220, 311
Railroad colonization, 178, 179,
188–90
Raleigh Register, 73
Randolph, Edmund, 81
Raphall, Morris J., 165
Rapp, George, 125
Rawdon, Lord, 55
Reading (Pa.), 77
Red Scare, 273–74
Red Star Line, 184, 186
Redemptioners, 28–29, 66, 68

Redmond, John, 242
Reed, Joseph, 53
Reform, immigrants and, 230–32,
315
Refugee Relief Act, 286
Refugees, 71, 72–75, 97, 110, 115,
123, 201–2, 203, 280–83, 284–87.
See also Forty-eighters
Regulator movement, 56–57
Religious freedom, 37
Report on Manufactures, 69
Republican party (Jeffersonian),
83, 84, 85, 88, 90
Republican party, 161–64, 235–36,
237–39, 262
Revere, Paul, 51
Revolutions of 1830, 97, 123
Revolutions of 1848, 97, 102, 110,
151
Reynolds, James, 74, 85
Rhine River, 29
Rhode Island, 215, 219, 306, 307
Rhys, Morgan John, 73, 74
Ribicoff, Abraham A., 306
Ripley, William Z., *The Races of
Europe*, 267
Roberts, Kenneth, 275
Rochefoucauld-Liancourt, Duc de,
71
Roosevelt, Franklin D., 280, 300,
302, 316
Roosevelt, Theodore, 238, 239, 240,
243, 244, 265, 271
Rosenhayn (N.J.), 213
Ross, Edward A., 267
Rotterdam, 29, 68, 185
Rowan, Archibald Hamilton, 74,
85
Royal African Company, 30
Rudolstadt, 99
Rumania, emigration from, 179
Rumanians, 198
Rural colonization schemes, 122–
24, 211–13
Russia: emigration from, 179,
201–2; emigration policy of, 197;
immigration to, 101; steamship
agents in, 182

Index

Russo-Germans, 189, 201, 202, 214, 215
Russo-Japanese War, 264
Russo-Turkish War, 197
Ruthenians, 198
Rynning, Ole, 99

Sacco-Vanzetti case, 274
Sackville-West, Sir Lionel, 241, 316
St. Andrew's (New Brunswick), 119
St. Clair, Arthur, 60
St. John (New Brunswick), 119
St. Louis (Mo.), 117, 119, 124, 226, 244, 271
St. Louis *Anzeiger des Westens*, 140
St. Paul (Minn.), 212
San Antonio (Tex.), 164
San Antonio *Zeitung*, 164
San Francisco, 117, 118, 204, 249, 264; school segregation order in, 264–65
San Juan (Puerto Rico), 295
Santo Domingo, 71, 83, 87
Saskatchewan, 203
Satolli, Cardinal, 255
Saturday Evening Post, 275
Saur, Christopher II, 58
Savannah River, 35
Saxony, 138, 194
Scandinavia: emigration from, 113–14, 194; Mormon missionaries in, 126
Scandinavians, 180, 310, 311
Schiff, Jacob, 212
Scholte, Rev. Hendrik P., 167
School controversy, 139–40, 255
Schurz, Carl, 124, 162–63, 176, 234, 236
Schwenckfelders, 19
Scioto venture, 70
Scotch-Irish, 22–25, 34, 35, 41, 47, 49–50, 62, 65, 74, 84, 151; in American Revolution, 53–57; in New England, 45, 46; in Pennsylvania, 24–25, 34, 46–47
Scotland, emigration from, 25–27, 69, 94, 112

Scots, 25–27, 34, 69, 116, 181, 217; in American Revolution, 60–62
Scranton (Pa.), 226
Seasonal migration, 184, 187
Sectionalism, immigration and, 2, 35, 55–57, 65, 158–60
Sedgwick, Theodore, 82
Separatists, 125
Serbs, 198
Seward, William H., 150, 172–73
Shakers, 125
Shaler, Nathaniel S., 258
Shalom (N.Y.), 212
Shamrock, 78
Shenandoah Valley, 29
Shields, James, 172
Ship fever, 106–7
Ships, emigrant, 43, 64, 65, 75, 103–4, 106–7
Siberia, immigration to, 202
Sicily, 200
Sicily Island (La.), 213
Sigel, Franz, 176
Silesia, 194
Siney, John, 221
"Sisters," 73
Slater, Samuel, 69
Slave states, 117, 120–21
Slavery controversy, 142, 143, 155, 158–60, 161 ff.
Slavs, 180, 190, 198, 214, 216, 220, 222, 224, 251, 257, 262, 312
Slovaks, 198, 217, 218
Slovenes, 198
Slums, 132–34, 224–25
Smith, Rev. William, 48
Socialist Labor Party, 229
Socialist Party of America, 229
Society for Useful Manufactures, 69
Solomon, Haym, 62
South, 120–21, 158, 302; and immigration restriction, 266; Germans in, 164–65; promotion of immigration by, 188
South Africa, immigration to, 2, 196
South Carolina, 18, 20, 25, 30, 35, 41, 42, 55

Index

Southern Pacific Railroad, 189
Spalding, John Lancaster, bishop of Peoria, 211
Spotswood, Alexander, governor of Virginia, 30
Stalin, Joseph, 316
Stamp Act controversy, 7, 10, 59
Stark, John, 54
Stark, William, 55
Staten Island, 128
Statue of Liberty, 247, 277
Stavanger, 98, 113
Steerage conditions, 3, 106–7, 184–85
Steamship companies: opposition of, to federal regulation of immigration, 250; promotion of immigration by, 178, 179, 182–83, 184
Steamship conferences, 186
Steamships, entry of into emigrant trade, 184–87
Stefani Agency, 299
Straus, Oscar, 238
Strikebreakers, immigrants as, 191, 222, 251
Stuart's Town (S.C.), 26
Supreme Court, 250
Svornost, 227
Sweden, emigration from, 94, 102–3, 194, 196
Swedes, 16–17, 34, 50, 51, 209; and slavery controversy, 166–67; antipathy of to Irish, 166
Swedish language, 50–51
Swedish Lutherans, 138–39
Sweetman colony (Minn.), 212
Swiss, 30, 41
Switzerland: emigration from, 94; Mormon missionaries in, 126
Syrians, 192, 203, 205, 216, 217, 220
Szabadszag, 229

Taft, William H., 238, 239, 260, 261
Taiping rebellion, 204
Talleyrand, 72
Tammany Hall, 144, 233, 307
Tammany Society of Philadelphia, 90

Tandy, James Napper, 74, 85
Taylor, General Richard, 171
Test Act (1704), 22
Texas, 117, 124, 126, 170–71, 214, 215, 291, 292
Textile industry, 217, 218, 219
Third Plenary Council, 255
Thirty Years' War, 227
Tillich, Paul, 281
Timber trade, 103, 119
Tobacco trade, 103–4
Tocqueville, Alexis de, *Democracy in America*, 6–7
Toledo (Ohio), 292
Tone, Theobald Wolfe, 74, 85
Tracy, Uriah, 85
Transient immigration, 180–81, 187
Transocean News Service, 299
Treaty of Versailles (1919), 245–46
Trenton (N.J.), 120
Trevellick, Richard, 221
Trieste, 186
Trinidad, 295
True Dutch Reformed Church, 138
Truman, Harry S., 284, 316
Trusteeism controversy, 150–51
Turkey: emigration from, 179; emigration policy of, 197
Turner, Frederick Jackson, 259
Turnvereine, 136
Tweed, William Marcy, 233

Ulster, emigration from, 22–25, 78, 108
Unemployment, 312–13
Union Pacific Railroad, 127
United Evangelical Church, 98
United Irishmen, 74, 83, 85
United Lutheran Church, 318
United Mine Workers, 223
United States, popular knowledge of, 99
United States Industrial Commission, 186

Vermont, 120
Virginia, 11–13, 14, 20, 21, 26, 35, 37, 44, 49, 56, 60, 66, 77, 87, 211

Index

Virginia Assembly, 42
Virginia Company, 12
Volume of immigration: (1783–1815), 64–65, 74; (1815–1914), 93; (1816–60), 93–94; (1860–1914), 178–79; (1920–30), 279; (1930–40), 280
Volunteers of Ireland, 54

"Wachovia" (N.C.), 27
Wage-rates, immigration and, 312–13
Wales, emigration from, 94, 112
Walker, Francis A., 221, 258, 259, 309
Walsh, Mike, 233
Walter, Bruno, 281
Walther, C. F. W., 138
"War Brides" Act, 284
War of 1812, 65, 75, 90
Ward, Robert DeCourcy, 259
Ward's Island, 128
Warren, Charles, 259
Wartburg, 97
Washington, George, 64, 67, 68, 79
Washington (state), 209, 288
Washington Constitutional Society, 89
Waxhaws (S.C.), 55
Weitling, Wilhelm, 155
Wells, H. G., 207
Welsh immigrants, 19, 73–74, 119, 120, 141, 217
Welsh language, 76
Welsh Tract, 19
West Indians, 293–95, 297
West Indies, 31, 32, 67, 293, 294
Westchester (N.Y.), 298
Western Hemisphere, immigration from, 277, 279, 289
Western Star, 78
Westward movement, immigrants and, 69–70, 120, 122, 210–14, 310–11
"Wetbacks," 291

Whig party, 143
White, Rev. John, *The Planter's Plea*, 15
White Star Line, 184
Whittier, John Greenleaf, 51
Williamsburg (S.C.), 25
Wilson, Henry, 235
Wilson, James, 60
Wilson, Woodrow, 239, 240, 242, 243, 244, 245, 246, 260, 269, 271
Winthrop, John, 15
Wisconsin, 114, 115, 118, 120, 124, 162, 163, 187, 188, 209, 216
Wisconsin Synod, 163
Wise, Isaac Meyer, 165–66
Witherspoon, John, 60
Wittke, Carl, 77
Wolcott, Oliver, 82
Wood, Fernando, 152, 233
Woodbine (N.J.), 213
Woonsocket (R.I.), 237
Worcester (Mass.), 24, 45
Workingmen's Party (Calif.), 249, 253
World War I, 93, 240, 242–45, 270–73, 316
World War II, 283–84, 290, 291, 299, 302–6
Württemberg, 110
Wyoming, 127

XYZ dispatches, 83

Yalta, 316
Yamasee War, 41
"Yellow Peril," 264, 265
York County (Pa.), 47, 124
Young, Brigham, 127
Young Ireland movement, 97, 122, 144
Yulee, David, 165

Zdrubek, F. B., 227
Zoar (Ohio), 125
"Zoot-suit" riots, 305

Index

Virginia Assembly, 42

Virginia Company, 12

Volume of immigration: (1783–1815), 64–65, 74; (1815–1914), 93; (1816–60), 93–94; (1860–1914), 178–79; (1920–30), 279; (1930–40), 280

Volunteers of Ireland, 54

"Wachovia" (N.C.), 27

Wage-rates, immigration and, 312–13

Wales, emigration from, 94, 112

Walker, Francis A., 221, 258, 259, 309

Walsh, Mike, 233

Walter, Bruno, 281

Walther, C. F. W., 138

"War Brides" Act, 284

War of 1812, 65, 75, 90

Ward, Robert DeCourcy, 259

Ward's Island, 128

Warren, Charles, 259

Wartburg, 97

Washington, George, 64, 67, 68, 79

Washington (state), 209, 288

Washington Constitutional Society, 89

Waxhaws (S.C.), 55

Weitling, Wilhelm, 155

Wells, H. G., 207

Welsh immigrants, 19, 73–74, 119, 120, 141, 217

Welsh language, 76

Welsh Tract, 19

West Indians, 293–95, 297

West Indies, 31, 32, 67, 293, 294

Westchester (N.Y.), 298

Western Hemisphere, immigration from, 277, 279, 289

Western Star, 78

Westward movement, immigrants and, 69–70, 120, 122, 210–14, 310–11

"Wetbacks," 291

Whig party, 143

White, Rev. John, *The Planter's Plea*, 15

White Star Line, 184

Whittier, John Greenleaf, 51

Williamsburg (S.C.), 25

Wilson, Henry, 235

Wilson, James, 60

Wilson, Woodrow, 239, 240, 242, 243, 244, 245, 246, 260, 269, 271

Winthrop, John, 15

Wisconsin, 114, 115, 118, 120, 124, 162, 163, 187, 188, 209, 216

Wisconsin Synod, 163

Wise, Isaac Meyer, 165–66

Witherspoon, John, 60

Wittke, Carl, 77

Wolcott, Oliver, 82

Wood, Fernando, 152, 233

Woodbine (N.J.), 213

Woonsocket (R.I.), 237

Worcester (Mass.), 24, 45

Workingmen's Party (Calif.), 249, 253

World War I, 93, 240, 242–45, 270–73, 316

World War II, 283–84, 290, 291, 299, 302–6

Württemberg, 110

Wyoming, 127

XYZ dispatches, 83

Yalta, 316

Yamasee War, 41

"Yellow Peril," 264, 265

York County (Pa.), 47, 124

Young, Brigham, 127

Young Ireland movement, 97, 122, 144

Yulee, David, 165

Zdrubek, F. B., 227

Zoar (Ohio), 125

"Zoot-suit" riots, 305

THE CHICAGO HISTORY OF AMERICAN CIVILIZATION

DANIEL J. BOORSTIN, EDITOR

Edmund S. Morgan, *The Birth of the Republic: 1763–89*

Marcus Cunliffe, *The Nation Takes Shape: 1789–1837*

John Hope Franklin, *Reconstruction: After the Civil War*

Samuel P. Hays, *The Response to Industrialism: 1885–1914*

William E. Leuchtenburg, *The Perils of Prosperity: 1914–32*

Dexter Perkins, *The New Age of Franklin Roosevelt: 1932–45*

Herbert Agar, *The Price of Power: America since 1945*

* * *

Robert H. Bremner, *American Philanthropy*

Richard M. Dorson, *American Folklore*

John Tracy Ellis, *American Catholicism*

Nathan Glazer, *American Judaism*

William T. Hagan, *American Indians*

Winthrop S. Hudson, *American Protestantism*

Maldwyn Allen Jones, *American Immigration*

Robert G. McCloskey, *The American Supreme Court*

Howard H. Peckham, *The War for Independence: A Military History*

*Howard H. Peckham, *The Colonial Wars: 1689–1762*

Henry Pelling, *American Labor*

Charles P. Roland, *The Confederacy*

Otis A. Singletary, *The Mexican War*

John F. Stover, *American Railroads*

*Bernard A. Weisberger, *The American Newspaperman*

* Available in cloth only. All other books published in both cloth and paperback editions.

Date Due